Call No One Father

What happened to the reforms of Vatican II? Here one of the 'People in the Pews', not a professional theologian but deeply committed to her beloved and battered Church, shows how the laity see the clericalism repudiated by Pope Francis. For her, the laity are not simply the not-clergy but exercise the *sensus fidelium*, the tacit but steadily evolving consensus that gives the whole Church its identity and sense of purpose. The conduct of many of the clergy and the hierarchy belies their belief in a loving God, resembling the defensiveness of banks and corporations rather than the humility of God's people. Heasly's response is to draw on her decades as a teacher and educational researcher to set out a program of critical thinking, the formation of conscience and personal responsibility which would ensure that ordinands become disciples. A prophetic book, the harbinger of a long-awaited paradigm shift.

John D'Arcy May,
Trinity College Dublin, Australian Catholic University

The findings of the Australian Royal Commission into Institutional Responses to Child Sexual Abuse provide ample evidence of the need for substantive structural changes in the Roman Catholic institution. Eliminating clericalism is one major overhaul necessary if not sufficient to the task. The Roman Catholic Church's current dilemmas will not be solved by mindless repetition of Catholic theology. Rather, Berise Heasly demonstrates the usefulness of educational theory, principles of architecture and physics, as well as common sense born of outrage, to move the whole church in a healthy, safer direction.

Mary E. Hunt, Ph.D,
Women's Alliance for Theology, Ethics and Ritual (USA)

Pope Francis calls clericalism "the ugliest perversion of the Church", "a danger most threatening the Church" and "one of the worst evils".

After 5 years of inquiry the Australian Royal Commission into the Institutional Responses to Child Sexual Abuse concluded that "clericalism has been a highly significant contributing factor to the occurrence of child sexual abuse in the Catholic Church and the inadequate or non-existent response by Catholic Church personnel". The culture of clericalism, it found, sits at the centre of a tightly intertwined cluster of factors - individual psychosexual, structural and cultural – which helped establish a 'horizon of abuse'. It is the single most important factor, because it combines with, and in some instances is the root or foundation of all the others.

The Catholic Church in Australia is currently preparing for its first plenary council in over 80 years, and clericalism has to be a priority issue on its agenda. Berise Heasly has done a huge service to all Catholics with this book - shining a light and her clear understanding on this perverse culture which continues to operate and has to be eradicated.

Dr Peter Wilkinson,
President, Catholics for Renewal

Call No One Father

Countering Clericalism in the Catholic Tradition

BERISE HEASLY

COVENTRY
PRESS

Published in Australia by
Coventry Press
33 Scoresby Road
Bayswater Vic. 3153
Australia

ISBN 9780648497752

Copyright © Berise T. Heasly 2019

All rights reserved. Other than for the purposes and subject to the conditions prescribed under the *Copyright Act*, no part of this publication may be reproduced, stored in a retrieval system, or transmitted in any form or by any means, electronic, mechanical, photocopying, recording or otherwise, without the prior permission of the publisher.

Scripture quotations are from the *New Revised Standard Version Bible*, copyright 1989, Division of Christian Education of the National Council of the Churches of Christ in the United States of America. Used by permission. All rights reserved.

Cataloguing-in-Publication entry is available from the National Library of Australia http:/catalogue.nla.gov.au/.

Design by Megan Low (Filmshot Graphics - FSG)
Cover by Ian James - www.jgd.com.au
Cover photograph: Michael Coyne©
Printed in Australia

Contents

Acknowledgments 9

Reflection on Matthew 23:9
Michael Elligate 11

Clericalism and catholicity
Constant J. Mews 13

Introduction 17

Chapter 1 : What is clericalism in the Catholic tradition?.. 43

Chapter 2 : Voices of People in the Pews 71

Chapter 3 : Theological sign-posts of clericalism 97

Chapter 4 : Three vexed areas of complexity in
clericalism today 115

Chapter 5 : Change Processes already familiar in
Education: theory, practice and praxis. 145

Chapter 6 : The 'how' of developing Conscience 175

Chapter 7 : Applying *Theo-tensegrity*: the concept of a
church of accountability, inclusivity,
diversity and transparency 211

Chapter 8 : Reductionism, Restorationism,
Regenerationism, Reform in the Catholic
tradition. 235

Reference List 259

Acknowledgments

The urgency with which this project came to fruition has generated excitement, energy and some scandalised astonishment as I shaped the research content, and developed a balanced approach to the topic. Clericalism has been with us for so long, and careful thinking and consultation was needed. It is therefore important that I advise readers that my career was in Education over close to four decades. I am a student of theology, but not a theologian.

I would like to thank academic colleague, Professor John McDowell, University of Divinity, who first encouraged me to pursue this topic and supported my effort to attain clarity and cohesion in the finished product – a friend indeed!

I would like to thank Professor Constant Mews, Monash University, whose patience, academic listening and careful questions, directions and discussions clarified much as I strode through the mountain of social media and current literature to shape the final outcome. His historical contribution to the text gives depth and focus to the whole project.

I would like to thank Professor John D'Arcy May, Australian Catholic University, for his erudite and balanced knowledge and patient listening as I sought to identify the kernel of the topic and connect the side issues authentically.

I would like to thank most sincerely my Parish Priest and valued friend, Michael Elligate AM, who has supported me pastorally, liturgically, academically and theologically at every step of the way. His reflection on the Matthew 23:9 is a valuable setting from which the whole project has developed.

I would thank also the several women's groups in our Parish, who have nourished me and offered women's wisdom in so many ways. Their consultations and discussions have been a highlight on this journey.

I would thank most sincerely my son, Denis Heasly, for patience and careful leadership with technological support and direction.

I must thank Professor William Johnston for his particular efforts clarifying for me some of the content and the crucial thinking when beginning this project.

I thank sincerely Dr Claire Renkin, Yarra Theological Union, for generous support but also for helping with clarifying resources at significant points on this journey.

I thank Dr Adrian Hubbard, osteopath, for introducing me to the concept of tensegrity and for ongoing discussions clarifying subtle and significant details for the concept of theo-tensegrity.

I thank publisher Hugh McGinlay of Coventry Press, Melbourne, for his timely interventions and advice as I journeyed through the writing of this project: much appreciated.

I thank also Michael Coyne, photographer extraordinaire, for his photo of the Ceremony of Light at the Vigil Mass for Easter Sunday. Our parish is blessed to have many of his photographic records of liturgical celebrations.

There may be occasions that present in this work that the reader considers problematic. Ideas and concepts presented are put forward with careful consideration but if something does not appear justified, the author takes responsibility for the content, for process theology and for modelling the development of the central concept of theo-tensegrity. It is important for people of more academic bent to recognise that I have given enough details in the Reference list to allow research and critique to take place, if study of the text is undertaken.

Berise Heasly, Ph.D.

Reflection on Matthew 23:9

Call no one father

The Gospel stories reflect many moods, many emotions during Jesus' journey to Jerusalem. In each of the Gospels, Jesus sometimes has a sharp tongue, often following observations and reactions that he has had to the religious establishment, particularly towards the Temple community in Jerusalem. He often sounded off about duplicity and hypocrisy in the religious ranks.

Moreover, discomfort with the Jewish establishment had exploded into a deep intensity in the decades after Jesus' death. This is the time when followers gradually went their separate ways from Temple worship and from its long established rituals. It was during this time that the expulsions from the synagogues also took place.

Scholars suggest that when Matthew's Gospel was being written, the rhythm of established Jewish life had been thrown into chaos. The Holy City was a war zone and, with the total destruction of the place, there was ruin and trauma everywhere.

Matthew's Gospel records the struggle to establish a new Jewish faith community centred on the person and teachings of Jesus of Nazareth. The genius of Matthew is that he gathers the treasures of the synagogue and the temple and takes them to the new House Communities. The treasures were the Torah, the writings of the Prophets and the prayerful psalms.

There was a deep conviction that the enduring covenant between God and his people would continue. So Matthew, the wise discerning scribe, is shocked to see the presence again of arrogance, triumphalism and even a tendency towards pharisaism within the followers of the Nazarene.

So a strong twist in the Gospel is where Matthew's Jesus condemns these pitfalls in the sharpest possible way. Matthew's Jesus spits out condemnation and angrily challenges the people who remain with the corrupt ways of both the synagogue and the temple. Jesus here resists titles of honour and leaders glorying in the exercise of power and privilege.

Hence: 'Call no one your father on earth' (Matthew 23:9).

It is more likely that these injunctions were uttered during the struggle of the Pharisees to gather the broken remnants of the old Jewish order so that their religious lives could continue. Matthew embraces the Jewish traditions as he presents the teaching of Jesus the crucified and risen one.

The true followers of the Way are called to humble care and service amongst one another. Beyond genuine prayer, substantial energy was to be used in correcting injustice and the abuse of power.

So we come to the contemporary issue of clericalism. Leadership is to do with care and service, and not seeking entitlement and comfortable privilege. To set oneself apart in a self-sufficient world is so contrary to the teaching of Jesus.

What Matthew names as wrong in his early communities, we must dare to name in ministry today. Our church must work towards transparency and inclusive measures that renew and reform the age old temptations to bully, dominate and exclude.

One clear shortfall is the use of exclusive titles conferred upon leaders in privileged positions with authority.

As Luke has Jesus say: 'This must not happen with you' (Luke 22:26).

Michael Elligate
Feast of St Andrew, 30th November 2018

Clericalism and catholicity

Catholicity, meaning universality, has long been a treasured ideal among the followers of Jesus. Unfortunately, the word catholic came to have a different meaning – namely of being aligned with the Roman papacy – as a result of the religious wars of the sixteenth century. Yet, if we look back over two millennia of Christian history, the notion of catholicity has always implied acknowledgment of a wide range of liturgical practices and theological traditions. The New Testament itself celebrates a range of ways in which the message of Jesus has been presented, offering a common foundation for a range of perspectives. The fact that it includes letters attributed to Peter, James and Jude, alongside those of Paul, reflects recognition of the diverse backgrounds of the followers of Jesus, some shaped by Jewish tradition, others influenced more by the Hellenistic culture that shaped so much of the ancient world. It did not take long, however, for the ideal of catholicity to be challenged by clericalism, a legacy of the ecclesiastical bureaucracy that developed in the fourth century, as Constantine sought to use its skills to govern his empire.

Clericalism, whose negative influence Berise Heasly analyses with such passion in this book, is a product of an institutional elite seeking to maintain its power in society. Jesus himself struggled with that attitude within the religious establishment of his own day, as revealed by that warning of Jesus (Matthew 23:9), 'call no man father, because you have only one father in heaven'. This did not stop a clerical elite from seeking to assert the authority of a single church. This in turn provoked many disappointed Christians to choose an ascetic life in the deserts of Egypt and elsewhere, imitating the example of John the Baptist and the Essenes in their pursuit of a more authentic following of the gospel. Religious orders, especially of women, have often challenged the clerical order.

It is not often realised, however, that in Latin Christian tradition (at least prior to the Council of Trent) bishops are consistently described as chosen 'by clergy and people'. This phrase itself recalls the Roman republican ideal (which never fully disappeared) that authority was vested 'in the Roman Senate and People' (SPQR: *Senatus populusque Romanus*). In practice, lip-service was paid to this idea of a social compact within the church. Popes tended to be chosen by the ruling families of Rome, or the Holy Roman Emperor, with the people having no say in the process. In 1059, Pope Nicholas II, previously bishop of Florence and a friend of Matilda of Tuscany, rejected the practice of popes being appointed by the emperor, when he declared that the pope should be chosen 'by clergy and people'. He also ruled that the people should avoid attending churches served by unchaste and morally dissolute clergy – a ruling that subsequently morphed into a prohibition on clergy of the rank of deacon or above from getting married.

In practice, this phrase about bishops being chosen 'by clergy and people' referred to a small elite in medieval society, not the people as a whole. The pope's role was to confirm rather than initiate episcopal appointments (quite different from the system established only in the last two centuries, of bishops being appointed directly by the pope). The choice of a bishop was always a matter of high politics in the medieval period, as an episcopal candidate would be put forward by the leading canons of a cathedral, often connected to the local ruling family. Nicholas insisted that the election of the pope was to be conducted by cardinals, whose role was to represent the Christian community of a particular community, whether at the level of deacon, priest or bishop. Being a cardinal is not a rank in 'holy orders', but rather an appointment to an electoral college.

Quite often in the twelfth and thirteenth centuries, the people of Rome were at war with a pope chosen by pro-French cardinals, that they often supported an alternative pope, favoured by the German Emperor. Papal elections tended to be dominated by competing interests among the cardinals, more often promoting the interests of a few noble families than the people as a whole. Cardinals could be more powerful than the pope in terms of the financial resources at their disposal.

Voices did emerge, however, to challenge tradition. Francis of Assisi, respecting the words of Matthew 23:9, insisted that within his Order all friars should be called brother, regardless of whether or not they were ordained into holy orders. Following the reforms promoted by Vatican II, this practice has been re-asserted within religious orders. In mainstream catholic tradition, however, the title of 'Father' is still used as an honorific, unlike protestant pastors, who prefer the term 'minister'. Catholic terminology has moved away from ideals of catholicity. Instead, it serves to reinforce the power of a privileged elite, concealing abuses of clerical power over women, children, and the larger community they have been called to serve.

Reform is always possible. Just as Nicholas II sought to restore the role of clergy and people in electing a pope, so Pope John XXIII sought to re-assert the notion of 'the people of God', as a counter to a clericalised vision of the church. The sexual abuse scandal provides an opportunity to redefine chastity, not as celibacy, but as a moral ideal of fidelity and respect, relevant to all people, both celibate and married. Francis is renewing this struggle with the clericalist values that have still not disappeared. He broke with tradition in choosing to adopt the name of a saint who resisted clericalism as a stain on the gospel. What impact Pope Francis will have in challenging clericalism in the church still has to be seen. His emphasis on 'synodality' reflects this vision. The Greek word *synodos* literally means 'the path together'—just as the early followers of Jesus travelled together in small groups to promote 'the way'. Universal synods, from the Council of Jerusalem (50 CE) to the Second Vatican Council (1962-65) have always been moments for listening to different perspectives, and finding a common path. Too often, however, they became clerical talking-shops. There is an urgent need for cardinals to be chosen to represent the voices of the laity, in particular of women, within the church, and have them involved in choosing the next pope. Looking back at the long history of the church, in particular at those holy women and men who sought to break down bastions of clerical privilege, we can find inspiration in exploring new paths to reform and renewal. As Berise Heasly argues, only through discussion, not demonisation, can we go forward.

Constant J. Mews
Fourth Sunday of Advent, 2018

Introduction

As an introduction to what follows, it is necessary to explain the raison d'être of this project. In an effort to read the signs of the times as Pope John XXIII indicated when setting in motion the Ecumenical Vatican Council ll, this is an exploration of the existence of clericalism today in the Catholic tradition. It is addressed from the perspective of a female member of the laity, a mother, a teacher and a musician: as one of the People in the Pews, within the voices of the *sensus fidelium*. This term: 'People in the Pews' refers to those battered and embattled cradle Catholics, some of whom have gritted their teeth, trying to negotiate their various ways through the contradictions from the hierarchical structures of the suddenly global Catholic Church. It also includes those who, through a variety of circumstances and traumatic pain, have walked away in varying degrees from the continuing connections and communal observance of parish life. This term People in the Pews is, of course a somewhat different concept to the term People of God of Vatican Council ll, which signals the various sections, cults and movements under the mantle of Catholic Church. It could also signal by extension inclusion of the wider humankind to whom John Paul ll initiated the call of the new evangelisation.

The title of this project is taken from Matthew 23:9. An inspired reflection based on extensive research is presented, so that the elements of what Matthew has Jesus say, are able to be identified. This is necessary in order to gather the threads of all the nuanced and uncomfortable realisations that are addressed in this exploration of clericalism in the Catholic tradition. It is inescapable that the accruing of titles and prestige was anathema to Jesus, to Matthew and is, but needs to be, to the People in the Pews. This surely also includes the conferring of sainthood in double-quick time for people including popes whose influence held identifiable heavy negativity and harm as well as certain saintly elements on a grand scale.

Importantly, this project will offer content seeking how we can be true to the message of Jesus but accept the need for an honest paradigm change. That paradigm change will be anchored securely in the tenets of our faith, but changes in emphases and inclusion of current knowledge, skills sets, and expanded understandings will aid in the search for 21st century ways to adhere to the message of Jesus: his way, his truth, his life. In application, this means identifying the presence of faulty thinking, and allowing for the limitations of this process. Augmentation of these thinking processes through a change of paradigm, means expanding our ways of thinking, without losing either the skills of all patterns of thinking, or the value of the historical content of the Catholic tradition. The outcomes of these new and very productive thinking skills sets will be explored and evaluated during the passage of this project.

The book cover photograph is a faithful reproduction of the normal Holy Saturday Vigil liturgy at the point of the Ceremony of Light. The celebrant intones three times: 'Christ, Our Light' and the lighting of candles from the Easter fire burning outside the back porch of our little church, begins to spread through the congregation from the back of the church to those in the front seats. The softness, the gentleness and the welcome that spreads, also brings a stillness and reflective prayerfulness experienced by all present.

So this project begins with the Gospel of Matthew. It proceeds through a many-hued exploration of the elements of what is to count as the bones of clericalism in all its variations. It offers three educational change processes for 21st century consideration, meant especially for a refreshed profile of what is needed in the preparation of candidates for priesthood, called throughout this exploration: the ordinand. In particular, and in view of the investigations world-wide of the appalling criminal behaviours of paedophile rings, lone abusive operators, and the systematic, ignominious, and callous hierarchical cover-ups, the examination of what is to count as priesthood and the position of an ordinand of every diverse background must be made. Signposts, recommendations, conclusions and pitfalls to be faced complete the vision, as we look to the Holy Saturday liturgy: Christ, Our Light, through the auspices of the Holy Spirit.

There will be a nuanced element present in the text, meaning that personal experiential learning is included in the practical theology underlying each section, and which includes a firm but not strident feminist perspective. It will be emphasised that this project is wide-ranging in its scope, but is also a direct response to the silence and resistance of the hierarchical figures presently tasked with higher levels of leadership, transparency, accountability and advanced levels of governance, but who appear to be paralysed by either defiance, resistance, fear – or all three.

This book is divided into four sections. First, there is a need for an introductory opening up of our understanding about how broad and complicated the whole concept and practice of clericalism really is. This is supported by Voices of the People in the Pews (voices within the *sensus fidelium*), followed by an attempt to uncover deepened understandings of the theological elements within which clericalism is embedded. Second, there is the logical requirement of exploring three vexed areas of today's dilemma, clericalism, for the church: clerical sexual abuse particularly of children and vulnerable others; then the entrapment of gay priests and their subsequent experience as priests; and the phenomenon of a series of papal figures whose authoritarianism or emotional ineptitude has verged on apparent distortion of some tenets of faith.

The unfortunate outcome of each of these three phenomena is still providing resistance as hierarchical efforts too often infantilise the faithful with a consequent utter contempt for much of human lived experience of the People in the Pews. This appears to be because of hierarchically preferred reliance on dogma inserted by power, edict and control, coming in-between any person in relationship with our loving creator and Triune God. This tendency cuts across and contradicts the integration and interaction of the myriad of elements which make up the global Catholic Church under the dome of the message of Jesus: his way, his truth, his life. This dome will feature often as we come to terms with the metaphor for the global church, which is made up of many living cultures and national groups – all under the 'dome' of the Catholic Church.

The third part is my response, in which a description of three educational change processes is offered, with indications of their relevance to the present representations for the church of the future. This section relies on a serious change to be investigated, analysed, developed, shaped into 21st century curriculum and instructional design for the ordinand and is based on an enormous expansion of knowledge, supported by an urgently organised new curriculum in thinking skills already available today. Of course, this implies that the education of the laity and the existing band of priests in all countries will need to be sensitively developed in parallel to that of the ordinand. There is, therefore, an authentic theological connection between the Leuven research on Catholic Identity, Paul Sharkey's (2015) educational work and the considerations in this book, and much work for the People in the Pews. Teams of experts are already working towards this goal and their work must not be dismissed.

The fourth section is an effort to take into account the findings of the Australian Royal Commission and the effects of institutional damage, due to abuse of children and vulnerable others by some criminal priests, brothers and sisters. A strenuous effort is made to understand the theology of the body as outlined by John Paul ll in 129 presentations over a five-year period. This understanding is expanded in part as an effort to change the emphasis away from a seriously simplistic approach to sexuality. By broadening the emphases to include the integration of maturity in physical, emotional, social, intellectual and spiritual elements of personality, it is possible to propose a theology of personhood rather than present the mechanical and disengaged underpinnings of a theology of 'the' body. Theologians, therefore, have much work and many challenges to address.

Some reference to similar situations in other cultures emerges, but stringent and careful efforts are made to find conclusions, further questions, implications for the future, and to address the undeniable resistance of some members of the existing hierarchy around the world to the possibility of change. Those implications will need to include new metaphors to better understand the organism called the Catholic Church and a significant metaphor offered here and which pervades this project is, as explained, that of the geodesic dome. The geodesic dome is a structure familiar in medicine, biology, architecture, engineering, and increasingly in education - in which the push-pull factors of diverse parts of the whole help each other to keep the whole structure together. The geodesic dome leads us to the concept of tensegrity, allowing the application of this concept to the Catholic Church of today. Tensegrity as a concept allows us to extend the idea of the geodesic dome to inspect the many diverse areas and influences with their many energies and developments to remain integral to each other as parts of a whole. I introduce the concept of theo-tensegrity, as an authentic substitution for adversarialism so visible in our ranks, or what is termed polarisation in some theological perspectives. Theo-tensegrity will rely on developed and advanced patterns of thinking embedded in the three change processes introduced in Part 3.

The audience for what follows will encompass a potential series of interest groups. Written from the perspective of a teacher of almost four decades' experience in secondary teaching of religious studies and allied disciplines in Catholic and Christian secondary schools (including some years doing the Year 11 and 12 Units for VCE), a personal influence will pervade particularly the three processes for change which are offered in Part 3 of this project. Concerned parishioners particularly in Australia, but perhaps also in UK, Europe, USA and NZ may find elements which resonate with their own particular cultural experience as Catholic. This possible relevance for other cultures and nations is not further explored here as the canvas is too broad to be efficient or effective, and would not engender excellence in the present Australian milieu. However, it does indicate the long process and the urgency of the tasks ahead.

As an exploration of what is needed to aid our battered but beloved church, some theologians, philosophers of religion, sociologists and others may also find connections and echoes which can be inserted into their considerations. The extensive reference list identifies the levels of research used. This will provide ballast for the explorations and the adjustments needed in so many areas to rid ourselves of the negative effects of the cult of clericalism, including the pantomime of effusive use of incense and medieval dress. This was so noticeable when Pope Francis celebrated Mass in Abu Dhabi in early February, 2019, to a combined audience of Catholic, Christian, Jewish and Muslim participants.

We, a mature Christian body of believers, offer our knowledge, our wisdom, our experience, our pain and our scandalised faith to the long process which must be endured by the followers of Jesus in the 21ˢᵗ century. We must cope, with the humility and courage necessary to offer our own expertise, as a result of a broad palette of excesses that include the narcissism and disdain of some members of the various Bishops Conferences as well as the clerical sexual abuse of children so rampant in the last 150 years. However, we find some clarity and an invitation to explore further the process of change when O'Loughlin (2012) outlines some considerations of the journey of the church from Christendom to Pluralism and concludes with some thoughts on Spirituality for the Future.

It is also necessary, in order to lay the foundation of this project with clarity, to identify that this is not an angry book. Binary ('either/or' patterns of logic) thinking has haunted the development of dogma and theology in the Latin tradition of the Catholic Church and has led to adversarial attitudes which are bent on control by the privileged over the other. My subtitle reads 'Countering Clericalism' not 'Confronting Clericalism'. The concept of the various elements of meaning embedded in the term clericalism; the meanings attributed to this perspective today by many; the existence of clericalism in real life; all this is real and must be honestly faced. The global subtleties of what the term means in different cultures; the difficulties inherent in the existence of clericalism in all forms in many cultures; the consequential damage is already apparent. It includes the personalities of all sides of the present conversation (or is it schism?); and the identification of needs for 21ˢᵗ century living. All will at times be part here of the various areas of research as linguistic and liturgical meanings, important understandings and indications of signposts emerge to flag the way forward. That way forward is full of meanderings, if we allow that the Holy Spirit takes charge and forges new channels in God's own time. As faithful followers of the Jesus message, we can't expect answers and change to happen quickly. The pendulum must swing in both directions, then in circles, as the Holy Spirit wills. We can but contribute our hope-filled considerations and allow the presence of God to pervade all our concerns.

What is clericalism?

We need to recognise that the best possible understanding of the deepest nuances of the verb 'to counter' is required if we are to plan efficiently and authentically. Regarding how best to address chronic clericalism and its partner narcissism is paralysing particularly the Latin-rite of the Catholic Church. This development is needed to clarify the elements of what this project is providing for the social and theological debate regarding clericalism as a concept. We need to ask the question: what in the practical life of the church can release us to become faithful to the message of Jesus in lived experience: in his way, in his truth, in his life? It is certainly not a synonym for clarification only, or for some angry adversarial divisiveness in the political and moral codes of the Catholic Church. So the title is Countering, not Confronting Clericalism, and the project is a careful exploration by an author embedded as a cradle Catholic in the People in the Pews category: the laity, one of the voices of the *sensus fidelium*.

What is clericalism today? Many voices are heard in chapters 1, 2 and 3, as we try to broaden our understanding of this concept. The layers of clericalism, in strata, in entitlements, in exclusivity, in questionable and corrupt behaviours, in cover-ups, abound. By extensive research, it has been possible to find a broad perspective of meanings attributed to the practices of clericalism. We study how Wilson, Storer, Faggioli and others explore the extremes of behaviours based on careerism, narcissism, princely daily life, exclusive entitlements to so much, regardless of the rest of the world. We analyse the phenomenon of the explosion of ecclesial communities like Opus Dei, Focolare, Neocatechumenate, Liberatione e Communione and their urgent push back towards the vision of John Paul ll, with special note of the tragic ruin of a young man's life (Urquhart, 1994). We note the exclusivist character of such movements and their reliance on a claim of being exclusively consecrated men and women. It is important to note that each person baptised is exclusively consecrated; there is no further exclusive claim possible to a higher form of consecration, only a deeper recognition of what it means to be a consecrated person.

What is clericalism from a theological perspective? A number of authors, including Wilson, Alison and Martin, give us a nuanced and sometimes complicated palate. Unconsciously, and perhaps from utter ignorance, many fissures and misunderstandings have emerged. We have a clear example that communicates the flawed theological perspective emanating from Pope Paul VI, whose dithering and betrayal of that Committee of 72 focused on generous People in the Pews. They gave time, effort and worked with him prior to the completion of the encyclical *Humanae Vitae* which made such a mockery of consultation with the People in the Pews.

The extraordinary development we now discover is that the pope whose betrayal of women and men – the People in the Pews – who caused such widespread scrupulosity, trauma, rebellion, broken marital bonds, dismissal of efficient regulation of childbirth, and mental as well as physical and spiritual anguish, is now canonised. It is a trauma revisited for many who lived through that time in the church. That betrayal of the People in the Pews who relied on the papal message in an already communicated intention to clarify this vexed question was shattering. What was to count as the sin of artificial contraception and what therefore was considered a sin of mortal proportions by many of the harassed and oppressed husbands and wives, was monumental in its consequences for the bonds of marriage. This same set of consequences also ruined the priestly lives of many a pastoral parish priest, as so many compassionate priests struggled and tried to aid the traumatised couples who sought support.

Elements of clericalism

Three elements of clericalism emerge: first, the existence of widespread clerical child sexual abuse and the extraordinary lengths to which hierarchical figures, including those at the top of the pyramid, stretched their consciences. Secondly, the trauma attached to the intrinsically-disordered tag used to stigmatise members of the priestly caste who knew they were not heterosexual. Thirdly, we noted the burgeoning of papal authoritarianism and its inevitable consequences for the People in the Pews. It has spelt anguish for the heroic and hidden lives of the pastoral and priestly men who ministered to the People in the Pews as best they could despite the arrogant constraints imposed from Roman Centrale.

Clerical child sexual abuse and the cover-ups, and the Royal Commission findings: the binary thinking that allowed a mandated oath at ordination to keep silent in the face of criminal activity, also contributed to the aim of what here is called *Reductionism*. This term infers that pope and hierarchical prelates know the mind of God – and so the sin of presumption is widespread. Importantly, reductionism is as close to heresy as it is possible to travel: by using cover-ups and requiring oaths from ordinands as they are presented for ordination to defend the church-as-institution at the expense of any person. It seems to reduce the People in the Pews, in descending order, to the status of inferior beings, not quite human, with a reducing hierarchical status showing hierarchy first, priests next, men after that, women somewhere beyond, and children hardly recognised as human. The tragedy of reducing the message of Jesus

Introduction

to a simplistic, even ignorant misunderstanding of what we mean when we talk about a human being – one that God has called good – contradicts the Apostles Creed, and the Nicene Creed *and* the Book of Genesis.

The 'intrinsically disordered' tag and the entrapment of gay men particularly from the last few centuries: the binary ('either/or') thinking that allowed the abuse of the diversity and differences in men presenting for priesthood, also inflicted grievous psycho-sexual harm on all members of the priestly caste. James Martin and James Alison have much to say about the ignorance of one after another of the hierarchy, especially papal and curial figures, about the mystery and complexity of the human psyche and about the diversity within humankind. The history of callous and cruel harassment and dismissal of homosexuality in favour of heterosexuality is the opposite of the respect, compassion and sensitivity that every human being is given by our loving Triune God. It seems that living in the enclosure of the Vatican, these hierarchical figures are disengaged from the realities of the world and make the presumption that they know what is meant by the Jesus message in the private world of the marriage bond. They don't appear to understand that they do not have the knowledge or expertise to claim an authority over the People in the Pews. The claim, knowing the mind of God, is the essence of reductionism, and it crashes into ignominy and humiliation when a pope wishes to canonise a founder of an ecclesial movement even though that man specialised in founding a regime of financial corruption, sexual harassment of his followers and founding also two separate families.

Authoritarianism, historically in the Catholic Church, includes the Australian context: Pope John Paul ll set out to bring back to the practice of what he deemed to be best for the whole global church and used ever more authoritarian measures during his long reign as pontiff to achieve his objective. Conservative US Catholic author

Matt Nelson (2018), having decided that he knew what was needed, wrote a short expose of what he believes the Catholic Church should be, while Cardinal George Pell, over a lengthy career in Victoria, in Australia and in the Vatican special squad of Pope Francis, used every possible avenue to shape the Catholic Church as he believes it should be. The binary thinking that allowed the strict observance of moral codes at the continuous expense of the Jesus message also turned the Catholic Church towards another phenomenon called *Restorationism*. This term refers to the blunt demand to conform, to turn back towards, to the simplistic and passive practices of Catholicity belonging to a Eurocentric framework of the 1940s, promoted as being humble and holy.

Requiring the whole of the Catholic world in all continents to somehow translate this demand into going back to previous post-World War II practices, led to ecclesial movements that smack of extremism, ideology, psycho-sexual dilemmas, and to the spectre of many People in the Pews walking away. A strong example of what is considered the rightfulness of an authoritarian pope, exaggeratedly called Pope St John Paul the Great by Matt Nelson, is a case in point. Here, Reductionism is partnered by Restorationism. To restore young people back to the faith is presented as a simple matter and a series of ecclesial movements have been promoted to achieve this extraordinary aim. Cardinal George Pell wrote with apparent sincerity and confidence that he did admire the man Wojtyla, his life and his doctrinal emphases.

What is the meaning of tradition? What is the Catholic tradition?

Has there been a change in the historical meaning of tradition? These are not two rhetorical questions in the sub-heading being fired out into the ether. Each question has deep relevance for the processes the

Catholic Church must face in the third millennium of the history of God's people – the People in the Pews. Subsidiary questions set off our detective work in each chapter, as we begin to deepen our existing knowledge, stretch our conceptual understandings, and find new steps to fuse with existing scenarios to give the Holy Spirit the space to direct our reflections, our subsequent questions, and our new understandings. This becomes a continual spiral process which provides a chance to expand again and again how we respond to what is to count as fertile and authentic realities of historical and future import within the Catholic tradition.

Do we recognise the dependence on diversity that is implied in the lived experience of a tradition? A tradition is helpful only when a people, like the People in the Pews, have the skills sets and the opportunities to examine what is to count as particular traditions in particular places. Argumentation regarding cerebral concepts of syncretism and relativism need to be analysed to find deeper meaning by every local and national ecclesial community otherwise confusion stops the People in the Pews from offering their collective or individual wisdom. An example comes to mind: Australian Catholics of the post-World War II period were astounded and Australian-born cradle Catholics were scandalised to find that their understanding of the central practice of abstaining from eating any meat on each Friday of the year was so different to the relevant beliefs and practices of people then called New Australians. Suddenly, we were confronted with some European Catholic peoples who abstained from eating red meat only.

Which is tradition? Is it perhaps enculturation? Michael Morwood (1997) was asking questions then about beliefs and practices, trying to bridge the gap between doctrine at the turn of the millennium and the essential gospel stories of the message of Jesus. We note: 'Jesus understood his ministry in terms of setting people free. We need to be clear about this. His life and death were not concerned with changing God's mind or winning back God's friendship. Rather, his living and dying were about changing people's minds and hearts'. Matthew's Gospel indicates that the church must not use pomp and ceremony, edicts and authoritarianism to intrude between God and humankind in relationship.

Are we aware of the cultural differences and the tribal influences implied in any religious tradition? It is so important to allow for the practices of our own tribal group which may not be parallel to other national and cultural groups. The salutary differences of the lived experience of Celtic Christianity and European Christianity were starkly in relief when tourism took off in the last half of the 20th century. Australian Catholics, especially the younger generations, found many differences in spirituality as we came to terms with Ignatian, Franciscan, MSC, Carmelite and other spiritual traditions. They were little known or taught in many Australian Catholic schools of the 20th century. Many of the People in the Pews knew nothing of the existence of communities like the Taizé in France, and the various religious movements so promoted by John Paul II. This situation also highlights the futility of importing men from widely variant foreign cultures to minister in Australian parishes.

What is the value of the linguistic meanings we could attribute to our project of exploration of clericalism? Can we explore the civic traditions of the Constantine era with the princely and Roman traditions of privilege and power, control and constraints placed on women? The resultant exclusivities of certain eras in Catholic history, especially as a Eurocentric church only, fester with injustice, distortions and even rampaging narcissism. An example: many were the women tortured and killed, being called evil witches, because of their knowledge of herbal remedies for better health of all. Deemed expendable by the clericalist and exclusivist attitudes of papal authority, those people were killed with enthusiasm in public arenas as criminal or heretics. We must do better in 21st century terms as we stretch ourselves towards the authentic living of the message of Jesus: his way, his truth, his life. Reference also to the confronting episode described by John Bossy (1991) about the Dominican preacher Giordano Bruno whose contact with Elizabeth 1 of England took place during the time of the deliberate obliteration of Catholics in England is another case in point.

Can we build or expand the meaning of tradition by checking out the historical elements of church history? A sustained effort to answer this question pervades this whole volume. In each century since Jesus walked the laneways of that country we may call the Holy Land today, extraordinary people have emerged to become prophetic voices as the Holy Spirit guided, shaped, propelled, splintered open, and challenged the People in the Pews. In the first millennium, we emphasised perhaps the mystery and work of the Creator God, as popes and prelates developed an institutional church modelled on their own strategic requirements, both politically and religiously. In the second millennium, the emphasis placed on the embedding of the message of the redemptive nature of the life, passion, death and resurrection of Jesus, the life-giver himself, seeped into the consciousness of the faithful believers.

Now, in the third millennium, we are being prompted to become agents in the co-creation of the now-global focus of the Catholic tradition, with emphases on the baptismal responsibilities of the People in the Pews. We need to step up to add our creative wisdom by building a nuanced and subtle expansion of understanding of whatever is understood as God's plan for the universe, especially taking account of Joachim of Fiore, who first introduced us to the picture of the influence of the Three Persons of the Triune God within the three eras of history. This is a potent sign for the Australian nation, called four or five centuries ago The Great Southern Land of the Holy Spirit.

Sociologically, are we able to add nuances that are perhaps secular in nature but valuable to our deepening religious understanding, so that new insights emerge? When Galileo first used his scientific eye to add a new element of knowledge to Europe's understandings of the universe, he paved the way for so many others. Unfortunately, we now realise that the emphases within the Catholic tradition rested only on the existing belief, leaving out a whole dimension of the reality of God's extraordinary creation. Cosmology today teamed with anthropology, archaeology, continuing education and the huge expansion of knowledge of what **is**, has been seen within the ranks of papal perspectives as somehow secular, and stained with the disdain of being outside the norms acceptable to the Catholic curial tradition. Instead, we now find that science and religion together give us a new foundation for belief in a benign, infinitely creative and loving God, who walks with us without the burdensome boundaries of secular versus religious realities. To separate secular from sacred is a specific form of clericalism.

Given that there will always be politics in a loosely organised entity like the Catholic Church, we need to pursue the various strands of catholicity often termed liberal, conservative, feminist, liberationist and other such labels. Since the Enlightenment, politics and religion in Eurocentric nations and beyond have been plagued by war, persecutions, corruption, and even calumny and detraction: what in many places today is called fake news. Why is this so? Providing porous and imaginary boundaries between the various strands of belief systems, we find ourselves as the People in the Pews confined by edicts, pronouncements, exhortations, encyclicals, bounded by creeping infallibility of an earlier reigning pope and traumatised by the cavernous and yawning chasm represented by clericalism. The practice of exclusively binary thinking which allows only one point of view to be right, also means that any other or the opposite is always wrong, and seemingly always sinful. Further, the practice of silencing those whose courage allows them to test the theological possibilities of deepening certain elements of faith is logically ridiculous. Damning them as heretics because they don't conform (or silencing them without due process), to the reigning curial charisms is unrealistic, pompous and also wrong.

It is important too that we understand terms like an ideology, a philosophy, a faith, a denomination, *ad intra* and *ad extra* (terms of the Latin-speaking ruling Curia). The boundaries and overlaps, as well as a canonical or moral code must be clear so that we know precisely what is to count as heresy. Why are all these considerations important? The tendency to remain in the practice of very early centuries before education became more prominent and widespread has done considerable and unnecessary damage to the faith of the People in the Pews in the last century.

Eventually, this phenomenon has led to universally available knowledge in most continents in a global form of catholicity, and can be seen still in the disengaged nature of the administration of the church in Rome. How the hierarchy of the church can persist with illogical and contradictory requirements emanating from the Curia is beyond the ken of the People in the Pews. Ideology meant to keep the power and control, the pomp and ceremony, the apparent authority within the exclusivity of hierarchy, precludes the opportunities for honest attempts to learn each from the other. Adversarial stances that result in these 'ad intra' and 'ad extra' boundaries imposed on the whole People in the Pews, not only should, but must, give way to the voices within the *sensus fidelium* and must be addressed with transparency, accountability and truthful responses.

The false but firm boundary that separates ecumenical issues from inter-faith matters does damage to the discipline of theology. Tradition can *not* be maintained without responses to existing dilemmas. Change can *not* be processed without the recognition of the response-ability, i.e. the ability to respond. This needs to be built on knowledge and skills sets of all teaching personnel in every corner of the existing Catholic world. Process can *not* be attempted, until coordinated responsibility for existing difficulties is accepted and addressed by those whose damage has been such a scandal today. It is not justice to plead that somehow we did not have the depth of knowledge that is available now. The responsibility to recognise both intended and unintended consequences of one's decisions and one's actions is a mark of maturity, already accepted by the People in the Pews, in both a secular and a sacred sense. The formal ruling of papal decisions that criminal paedophiles, or those whose sinful omissions are called cover-ups, must go into seclusion and lead lives of penance is infantile in its response. Criminals in today's jails have monitoring regimes to shape their future. The injustice that accompanies the accommodation of offending hierarchical figures in lives of apparent calm and quiet, with no efforts made to personally redress the appalling damage to victims, survivors, adjacent family members and truth-telling whistle-blowers, needs immediate review. There is a necessary and specific aim of requiring these penitents to demonstrate transparently every day for the rest of their lives, their responsibility to serve individuals, victims or other similarly-placed oppressed peoples – and to learn remorse, to accept guilt and to spend their time practising humility.

Three change processes to replace seminary and seminary formation

We must recognise at this point that the three processes of change which will be examined in the chapters of this book originate out of the discipline of education. In Australia, there have been six decades of educational change in the lifetimes of today's People in the Pews, which are significant in the secular development of best practice in student learning and student study skills sets. Each of the three change processes uses the means to deepen student learning, to enhance educational research and to guarantee the opportunities of promoting best practice into the present experience of the ordinand in the 21st century. The importance of understanding the possible presence of indoctrination, especially the practice of thought control, in the enclosed experience of seminary 'formation' today must not be ignored.

The first of the three change processes advocated here is the *Community of Inquiry*, which is a central plank of Matthew Lipman's philosophy in the classroom, and which refers to the study of practising practical logic, of asking questions, and a number of other thinking skills. The second is the use of reasoning based on gathering answers and options for those questions, and shaping the thinking skills towards decision making and towards the *development of conscience*. The third is the *entrepreneurship education* which allows for sustainability and proper skills sets which would be available to the ordinand for work in ecclesial communities.

Reductionism, restorationism, regenerationism and reform: what is ahead?

We now recognise and examine connections between concepts of conscience, discernment and indoctrination. This is necessary to begin the personal thinking and reflection needed to imagine with the help of the Holy Spirit how the profile of the priest must change for the 21st century needs of the People in the Pews.

What emerges? We explore the earmarks of reductionism and the simplistic though aspirational notions meant for the People in the Pews. The unfortunate mistake, made by hierarchical figures focused only on Rome and similar aesthetic centres of holiness, is that education with new knowledge is already at the fingertips of the People in the Pews. The members of the laity are quick to identify when they need to find information digitally to aid in their daily experience of life. We explore restorationism and the illogical effort to force the People in the Pews to somehow find ways to function within the values and practices of much earlier times when life was considerably simpler. We are challenged by the realisation that going back is illogical because cultural boundaries have changed immeasurably. It is not possible to achieve this outcome successfully. What happens instead causes spiritual stress, spiritual abuse and emotional trauma. We explore the possibility of a concept of regenerationism with its huge agenda, and we must not push outcomes impatiently, without allowing for the influence of the Holy Spirit. So are we preparing the way for reform in God's good time? And will elements of that reform vary as differing processes of change emerge, offer some important improvements, and then fade as cyclical processes emerge?

Looking towards the future

What are the questions? A list of question-starters is set out in later chapters. They are crucial to address the possibilities for the new ordinand, and consequently for the People in the Pews, who will be the community experiencing the message of Jesus through the aegis of the ordinand. During preparation in the last years before ordination, the ordinand needs to have made a quest to decide how those questions will form the basis and foundation of the work to be done in all the areas of responsibility that the pastor of a parish must address. This is an enormous agenda, but it is exciting as we feel the impact of the presence of the Holy Spirit.

Introduction

Where do we begin without re-inventing the wheel? The list is a long one: careful planning and inclusive action for synodal activities; actual and immediate appointments of lay expertise to all levels of the administration arm of the church and immediate insertion of in-services are needed. Such moves will be covering every area of what is to count as the skills sets of a 21st century priest: whether male, female, married, celibate, gay or eccentric. The steady rearrangement of existing priests closeted in Vatican corridors being appointed to positions of service in every continent of global Catholicism will bring their skills sets to the People in the Pews. The immediate, deliberate and measured endorsement of females must emerge in every area of daily life within the Catholic Church of the future. The inclusion of People in the Pews as adult and mature individuals will follow as a necessary adjunct to the well-being of the whole Catholic Church. Authentic contributions to our moral codes will interpret the message of Jesus with integrity, compassion and care.

Why is all this necessary now? Why not just proceed as we always have done? Given the parlous state of the Catholic Church in the first two decades of the 21st century, it is obvious that we are the laughing stock of politicians, world figures and in the scenario of the secular and inter-faith milieux. It is obvious that many Catholic figures have scandalised the whole world with the stain of corruption, bribery, gross claims of entitlement, and undeniable evidence of criminal behaviours in the duplicity of so many supposedly holy men in the church. The People in the Pews will not accept that proceeding as we *were*, is possible. It is not acceptable to allow the resistance and defiance of the official hierarchical pyramid of the church to overtake the needs of the faithful in a way indicated by an earlier papal comment: that those who might walk away will leave a small number of real followers of Jesus! Unfortunately, the intrusion of the institutional church, in the form of clericalism practised for generations but reaching its zenith in the last seven-eight decades, identifies that power and control in the form of resistance and silence (supposedly till the noise from the People in the Pews dies down), will not be countenanced.

Who is involved? Who is challenged to listen, hear, attend and allow for the input of many experts in many continents, in many parishes, in many particular Christian communities? We are all challenged to collaborate, consult, clarify, communicate, comfort and support each other, negotiating the shoals and pitfalls and mistakes and blind alleyways that will confront us as the decades go by. We are all called to respond to the possibility that Jesus was a Wisdom figure in the mould described by Bourgeault (2008), or of Johnson (2015). This realisation brings excitement, awe and wonder as we try to deepen our relationship with the mysterious but loving figure of our Redeemer and Life-giver.

We are called too towards facing some current issues in theology which, as Tanner (2010) outlines, start precisely from her thesis that Christ is the key to our pilgrimage and our questions. She outlines the urgent longings of us as creatures for God, in a foundational focus on a covenant between God and creature: 'The desire for God as an absolute truth has the power to drive us forward in constant dissatisfaction with any form of knowledge short of absolute truth'. And herein is the challenge for today. Tanner's exploration is a long, long way from the scandal and pain of clericalism and clerical child sexual abuse.

The administration of the Vatican has led to centuries of political action inside and outside the boundaries of what we call the church. Adversarialism, or adversarial behaviours, seen as somehow normal, has led to serious disruption and heretical behaviours in the various church eras. Binary thinking has allowed successive popes to promote one interpretation over all others pertaining to various contentious matters as the right way: a one-size-fits-all approach. This chosen stance is considered to be harmoniously in line with what is contained in the message of Jesus. The corollary of this is that the opposite point of view is disparaged as wrong, as heresy, as against the mind of Jesus, and the persons involved are deemed heretical – with dire consequences.

Papal power and control is promoted as the authority vested in the church by Jesus himself. Difficulties, because of this adversarial approach to the governance of the church of yore, have caused pain and torture within the church – called the 'ad intra' business of administration of all countries regarding faith matters. Serious and provocative adversarial stances regarding those not within the fold of the Holy Mother Church –those not baptised into the One True Catholic Church – those who are outside the boundaries as 'ad extra' categories, have been treated as inferior, as evil, as fodder for war and pillage – supposedly in the name of Jesus.

What can we change? What are the authentic reasons for change? In the first place, we can *not* change the essence of the message of Jesus. We cannot change the tenets of faith pertaining to the mystery of the passion, death and resurrection of Jesus so long ago. We can *not* change the internal understanding of the Triune God as Creator; Teacher, Life-giver and Model; and Spirit of Wisdom. As Creator, we believe in the One who has created humankind of which we are a part in the early decades of the third millennium. As Jesus, we believe in the Son, both divine and human, who has taught those he knew in the land of the Hebrew ancestors. As the Spirit, we believe in the One whose creative wisdom is the foundation of how humankind sees the message of Jesus, and who prompts us all to respond to the love, care and compassion we experience in abundance in our lives.

We can, however, find the time to investigate the neuroscience surrounding the concept of the Triune Brain within Paul MacLean's theory of how our human brains work (Shields, 2018). If ever there was a significant contribution from the secular milieu to help us understand, without changing the essence of church teaching, about the Triune God of the Catholic tradition, it is the examination, the exploration, the evaluation and the ethical concepts in 21st century theology, and MacLean's discipline certainly contributes much. The question of the likelihood of change means asking the question of what we can change. We can change the interpretations of what is to count as right and wrong according to new knowledge emerging from the studies of history. We can use anthropological evidence regarding the world in which Jesus lived, in the application of new knowledge. These considerations have been emerging from the remarkable expansion of knowledge uncovered today. We are alerted to the complicated and mysterious elements of the Cosmic World, unfolding through science, of the wisdom in some of the People in the Pews, who are the salt of the earth and whose daily experience is authentic and truthful.

How can we and how do we accommodate these new perspectives? It is urgent that we revisit the documentation of the unfinished Ecumenical Vatican Council l. Efforts to achieve this goal are examined. Losing the adversarial attitudes of the past in favour of collaboration and coordination of what is already known and what is unfinished is the starting point. The regional and world wars of the 20th century in which successive popes were involved in various ways must be inserted into the expansion of the historical critique of the influences that swirled around the Catholic Church of the 20th century in particular. As science and religion grew close or splintered apart, much relevant new knowledge was uncovered, and must now be incorporated into the bigger picture of the profile of Catholicity at the pivot point of the millennium. This includes the various political pressures internally and externally by the time of Ecumenical Vatican Council ll. Exploration of these many strands of belief means that experimentation and retraction must be honestly assessed and by degrees provide content to aid in the many questions we must face. Much has already been done but so much more is needed. Leaving power, control and privilege behind, we can address this well.

When do we change? It is a sad indictment that this question is seen as a challenge by many. So much in the scenario of today is good, true and Christlike. But so much must be reviewed, and in some cases changed immediately. In education scenarios, change is embedded in curriculum and instructional design which is constantly refreshed, updated, rearranged, piloted and reviewed regularly in an efficient, effective and excellent manner. Catholic theory, practice and praxis could also be treated in a parallel fashion. Seminary formation, equality of women, mandated celibacy, married priests, ideology parading as moral considerations, ignorance of applied knowledge in many disciplines: all this is in the mix for the inclusion in an exciting future shaped, sifted and developed by teams of lay and priest researchers from all existing levels of the present hierarchy, partnered with expertise within the ranks of the People in the Pews. A mammoth task, but we have the foreseeable future to make careful steps in the areas indicated by the documentation and development of what is to count as a result of the three years of Ecumenical Vatican Council ll.

Which liturgical and other practices and which tenets of faith do we need to revisit? In every culture, and in every nation, there will be change and experimentation. The pendulum swings, and the circles of development will provide those steps, imbued with the listening to the Holy Spirit which is the bedrock of that future.

What if we do any or all of this? The existence of hope is very important here. Hope is not just optimism. It must be part of that bedrock of belief with a focus on the sign posts examined in the last chapter of this project.

Those sign posts are:

1. Compassion, community, and collaboration
2. Entrepreneurship, energy and ethics
3. Transparency, truth and trust
4. Accountability, accommodation and action
5. Governance, God and growth.

We now proceed to the shaping of the project, confident that the Holy Spirit is present in all our deliberations. The task is overwhelming if we don't allow for discernment which emerges from our labours. Patience, resilience and humility will accompany us as we proceed.

> 'A clergy/lay distinction was foreign to the consciousness of early Christians. ... all were God's people (the laity) and all were "heirs according to the promise (the kleroi, the called, the "clergy"). ... Not everything that the early church did is neatly transferable to the present day. But when its understanding of ministry, put in modern dress, seems so well tailored to address the ills of our present ecclesial condition, perhaps the time has come to look again at the wisdom of the first Christians, imbued as they were with the Spirit, too young in the faith to be hide-bound by custom' (Lakeland, 2002).

CHAPTER 1

What is clericalism in the Catholic tradition?

It is important to recognise that the daily life of the People in the Pews has been fed an unrelenting diet of extreme dependency on what papal authority, curial power and promulgated control has considered appropriate for everyday life. This has led to the most stringent efforts made to achieve holiness and perfection. Perfectionism is a consequence of this extremism – a term today controlled by reference only to Muslim fundamentalists who use brutality and violence to subdue all other ways of life. Perfectionism is promoted by our church as a way to achieve holiness, sainthood and heaven. Apart from the effect of this cultured program leading so often to scruples and unbalanced emotional landscapes, perfectionism is an offshoot of a gnostic attitude. This attitude postulates that continued efforts must be made towards extreme personal submissiveness to unwieldly recommendations about calming an officious, angry and offended God. It is based on a seriously flawed perception that we can presume to 'know' the mind of God at all times.

Is it in order to title this phenomenon as the sin of presumption? There seems little opportunity for accepting the responsibility to become a balanced, mature individual, dependent or independent or interdependent according to life's vicissitudes. As each believing person balances out personal efforts to live according to the Jesus message, the support and knowledge of members of the community that were called at the time of Vatican ll, the People of God, is today paramount. In today's world, four generations, popularly known as the X-generation, the Y-generation, the Millennials, and the Z-generation, have lived a different childhood to earlier generations (Mackay, 1997 and his Australia Day address, 2019). It is therefore obvious that elderly men locked in an isolated hierarchical curial scenario, with a cohort of narrowly focused hierarchs strategically placed in Papal Sees globally, are far from daily contact with the huge diversity that is normal in family life, in whichever continent such families reside. Becoming disengaged therefore from reality in the 21st century, they seem to rely on paradigms somewhat unconnected to lived experience of the People in the Pews, and instead are locked into a mindset of dogma, ritual and formality.

Harris' fine drama – sociologically clarifying clericalism

In 2016, Robert Harris published *Conclave*, his finely drawn narrative thriller in which he provided a probable timeline, a realistic process, and a remarkable knowing insight into life in the Vatican. The connections of steel which surround the hierarchical figures we subsequently were faced with trying to understand, left us shocked when the Australian Royal Commission into Institutional Responses to Child Sexual Abuse uncovered the ongoing and past details of the clerical sexual abuse of children in Australia. Yes, *Conclave* is a fiction, but like the Gospels themselves, it is the truth behind the narrative that arrests our attention. It is the predictive quality of the story and the connection to the subsequent details within the installation of Pope Francis and the present crises reverberating around the Catholic world right now, which gives an authentic ring to Harris' storyline for any member of the People in the Pews.

The assumption of holiness that pervades the telling of the story needs to be analysed. Saying prescribed aspirational prayers that accompany even the vesting for ritual is seen as the means of attaining that ephemeral state called holiness. Even the blurb on the promotional cover states: 'They are holy men. But they have ambition'. And they have rivals, and therein we see in part the foundation for the growth of clericalism. As the story unfolds, we are witness to the authentically drawn characterisations of many of the leading figures of this narrative: the personalities and the vulnerabilities are well drawn and it dawns on the reader at different times in the reading of the whole narrative just how difficult life in such disengaged and rarefied conditions is for each individual character. It is not too much, therefore, to apply that understanding to the real figures in the various dramas unfolding around the world, two to three years after Harris' book was published.

The actual process of choosing a new pope also unfolds as the narrative develops. The utter secrecy that envelopes the preparations; the security measures that are applied; the jockeying for position; and the politicking that gathers momentum, are secretive in the extreme. The major tragedies that engulf several of Harris' leading contenders for the papacy are dramatic in content. Without revealing its final outcomes, it is possible to posit that compassion is sparse, judgmental opposition is central to the outcome, and justice is dismissed as inconvenient at particular and significant points of the storyline. Power-and-Control is central to each of the main characters, whether they use such measures benignly or viciously. It becomes clear that clericalism is rife, but this is not seen as detrimental to the way of life or to the operation of the conclave itself. Not much sign of the message of Jesus floats to the surface.

The reader can't dismiss the undercurrent of adversarial attitudes of each of the persons within Harris' narrative. The playing of politics is paramount even as a reigning pope expires. Sorting out whether their pope had a heart attack, and whether there were warning signs; who knew what, before and after the discovery of the dead pope, is dramatic. The predictive quality of the prelates who were present in the pope's apartment trying to decide what action to take; the planning of how to address the media about the momentous news, and the anxiety about how the Curial personnel would respond, were central to how the establishment of the official timeline of the whole episode was to be plotted. Even in the responses of the various cardinals at this most vulnerable time, Harris has one say of another: 'There was a careful theatricality to his movements. He was always conscious of his dignity. A true prince of the Church.'! That particular lens on the members of the Curia seemed to focus on the overall power and control expected to be used as a way to manage and manipulate the various conditions surrounding the truth of the pontiff's death. This is very strong in the narrative.

Harris – politically clarifying clericalism

One interesting curio in the early part of the storyline is provided when one cardinal expected to be called according to the manual on procedures on the death of a pontiff, sooner than he was. Another cardinal had taken over. The reason given was disturbing, given the present indications of inaction and bafflement of so many hierarchical figures today: 'but I felt that as Camerlengo (i.e. the person in charge when a pope dies) that my first responsibility was to secure the integrity of the Church.' and the revealing comment: 'You only have to remember the tragedy of Pope John Paul I – we've spent the past forty years trying to convince the world he wasn't murdered, and all because nobody wanted to admit his body was discovered by a nun'. There are disturbing echoes here of the vicious in-fighting that is emerging from mid-2018 regarding entitlement and prestige, particularly in the halls of the Vatican administration.

The extension of the political scenario referring to John Paul I and his unexpected death included refusal of normal medical procedures like taking an X-ray or performing an autopsy. The reason stated was on the grounds that it was too intrusive and that those present thought that such measures demeaned the man as pontiff. Another cardinal present some hours later objected to any move to publish the news to the public. The reason was to do with the dignity of the office and so his recommendation was that they should wait till daylight. It is reminiscent of the real situation of John Paul II and his demise, that there were these archaic responses to what members of the People in the Pews would see as usual procedures and not in any way unexpected. To treat the body of the man himself as somehow so different that normal rules and procedures would not apply is the bones of clericalism. Is this a conglomeration of the ontologically-changed syndrome, perhaps?

Later in the storyline, preparations of the Sistine Chapel were in full swing so that formal voting would be in line with an age-old process. This process had been in operation for so many centuries, highlights the dilemma for those present at the real conclave. Somehow, somewhere, in this story, the question of worthiness of each cardinal was being canvassed. This led to the description of one important cardinal as having 'made his reputation at the University of Eichstatt-Ingolstadt with a treatise on the origins and theological foundations of clerical celibacy'. This appeared to be a central focus in the judgment of others about the possibility of a relevant candidate for the pontiff's hat. Was the author pinpointing it as an idolatry of celibacy that placed this man's worthiness in the centre of the considerations?

A certain degree of disapproval appears when the late pope was remembered as having 'gone too far with his endless harping on about simplicity and humility' and further, 'An excess of humility, after all, was just another form of ostentation, and pride in one's humility a sin'. An exploration of these responses is really important because it highlights the business of how one demonstrates the state of holiness. Apparently it is not wholeness or responsibility that is needed. There is a ring of unbalanced emphasis about the meaning of both humility and pride in the statement which needs development, insight and understanding. And today, we must address this urgently, to avoid the pitfalls of clericalism.

Harris uses one cardinal as the central character of the whole narrative and the reader is privy to the cardinal's thoughts and feelings continuously. He must lead and manage the whole process of the conclave. His papal title is Camerlengo. In preparing and praying for God's help in leading the whole consistory, he reviews his past life as Cardinal-Bishop, as Cardinal-Priest, and titular Archbishop – and feels deeply inadequate: 'But one could be the grandest prince of the Universal Church and still lack the most basic skills of the common country priest. If only he had experienced life in an ordinary parish, just for a year or two!'

Once again, the spectre of clericalism is in evidence. If this is even half the degree that career priests are expected to experience when taken into Vatican service, this is a quite extraordinary situation. Responsibility for the welfare of the whole People of God, the People in the Pews, rests with such men – and their ignorance of, and lack of respect for, the norms of daily life. This has been catastrophic in the last century and a half, and possibly since the promulgation of *Humanae Vitae*.

As the security arrangements were completed and the threat of terrorist attack was addressed, we see the almost ludicrous other traditional regulations that were in place. As the procession of two cardinals together in pairs – the whole one hundred and eighteen of them – moved across the piazza: 'a member of the Swiss Guard in his plumbed helmet walked with them carrying a halberd. It might have been a scene from the sixteenth century'. A series of colourful Swiss Guards in uniform accompanying each pair of cardinals might look great and contribute to the solemnity of the occasion, even make the deliberate connection with the lengthy tradition of the unbroken line of ritual harking back even to Constantine, but in modern times, it is quite impotent, and unfortunately defiantly irresponsible in view of today's need for public security.

As the long description of the 118 cardinals processing over the piazza progressed, there is comment from Harris' pen on many individual prelates until finally: 'there came that and most rarefied species of cardinal, the two dozen members of the Curia, who live permanently in Rome' but 'they lacked the precious gift of *awe* he had detected in those who travelled from across the world. Good men though they were, they were blasé'. Sins of vanity, intrigue, malice, gossip, authoritarianism and incredibly, with regard to the Americans, Harris has the late pope say: 'They are so innocent: they have no idea how bribery works. Did you know that the going rate for a beatification is said to be three quarters of a million euros?'

Conclave – morally clarifying clericalism

Without slavishly following the full narrative to its incredible end, it is possible to recognise so much here that indicates elements of the living out of clericalism. Careerism, narcissism, unconscious cruelty, deliberate malice, disengagement with culture and diversity, and possible lack of realistic maturity all mix and wash together in a toxic lifestyle. It seems based on a narrow almost fanatic emphasis on doctrine, on extreme profiles, on entitlement and on privilege. When it is then the unenviable task of the ordinary bishop back in home territory, or the priest in his parish trying to do the workload carried in previous centuries by a team of co-adjutors and parish curates, we find that the clash of contradictions is unsolvable.

The subconscious comfort, which comes from the story of *The Blessed Virgin, Untier of Knots* (Lewis, 2013) is the first response for us, the People in the Pews. Walking on eggshells, trying to manage the various dilemmas and paradoxes which appear unexpectedly in daily life, and maintaining loyalty to the parishioners as well as to the Curia and to the pope, means anxiety. And exhaustion dogs the life of the priest today. As priest and laity come closer to understanding each other in stronger and digital communication today, it becomes obvious that Harris has done the Universal Church a significant service in highlighting these matters without denigrating any individual cleric alive then or now.

George Wilson's Analysis – from the theological perspective

George J. Wilson is a Jesuit, who in 2008 set out to analyse the concept of clericalism in the broadest and most careful terms. The underlying aim of Wilson's analysis is hopeful, in that his thesis is couched in what he expects is as balanced a manner as possible. He maintains that both laity and clergy have unconsciously collaborated in the growth of the phenomenon of clericalism as it appears in the 21st century. His hope is that by degrees, the church, both hierarchical and the People in the Pews, will accept a transition towards a culture that looks for a restoration of a genuine priesthood couched precisely in a stable future truly united in Christ. The dedications he chooses at the beginning of his text highlight a familiar theme: we are a chosen race, a royal priesthood, in a culture marked by sin. He quotes John Paul ll as indicating our needs to be healed, ennobled and perfected *(Redemptoris Missio)*.

Central to this thesis is Wilson's clarification of two terms: priest and cleric. They are not synonymous in meaning (Wilson,

2008). *Priest* is a 'religious term, pointing us to the transcendent or numinous or sacred dimension of life, to the holy'. By contrast, Wilson describes *clergy* as a 'sociological term that names the fact that society recognises a certain segment of its members as having recognisable social features and norms that distinguish them from the rest of society'. If, therefore, we mix or confuse these two separate entities, 'we reduce our lay faithful to passive recipients of the holy actions of the ordained, diminishing the dignity that should rightly be theirs by virtue of their baptism and confirmation' (his Introduction).

A very telling comment of Wilson will be addressed often in the following chapters: 'Unless we wrestle with new forms of expression in order to tap into the energies of new insights, the language of the past will continue to trap us within its walls'. Intended and unintended consequences of our actions cannot be ignored or dismissed. 'If we continue to *talk* in a certain way, we will also continue to *act* in the ways that those expressions have made comfortable. And as a result, we will perpetuate some bad stuff'. It becomes obvious that the institutional boundaries that are titled in Latin as '*ad intra*' and '*ad extra*' within the Catholic Church become barriers that perpetuate the diminishment of the People in the Pews by ignoring the reality of daily lived experience of family and individual life and the covenantal relationship of each to the Cosmic Creator, as personified by Jesus as teacher, life-giver (Bourgeault, 2016) and saviour, under the aegis of the Holy Spirit.

It is, therefore, of vital importance that we pinpoint exactly the difference in the two terms: priest and clergy. As an organisational theory specialist, Wilson clarifies that priesthood includes; 'priests, ministers, rabbis, imams, and shamans' (p. 11). In consequence, 'society' begins to develop nomenclature that corresponds to group. 'A name is assigned, a class is constituted: physician, lawyer, soldier, minister. The treatment accorded to members of that class begins to be stylised and turned into custom. A clergy has been created' (p. 12). We begin to realise that there is now a deeper layer of meaning that we may have blindly ignored in the norms of our familiar sociological paradigm. The paradox is that there was no collection called 'laity' until there was a class called clergy. They came into existence together, states Wilson. On this basis, we can acknowledge Wilson's conclusion: 'Academics are clergy; lawyers and physicians and military officers are clergy; the ordained are also clergy'. But, we need to differentiate one more consideration. Wilson highlights: 'The term "cleric" like the term "clergy" implies no value judgment. It does not carry the same negative meaning as 'clericalism'.

It is important, therefore, in the face of this realisation that we look deeply at the consequences of this clarification. Unintended consequences of a dangerous kind, including instant personal status, are encountered by the new ordinand, with attendant potential for good and harm, sometimes simultaneously. Wilson asks further about the 'seeds of clericalism' – whether that automatic status prompts the ordinands towards potential harm. We must also ask whether the response of the ordinand, usually aged in his twenties, includes being aware and being able to distinguish whether the sudden status is earned, assumed, bestowed, demanded, attributed and by whom? – And for what actual objective? If the ordinand has not had broad opportunities to develop emotionally, psychosexually, intellectually and socially, then the spiritual dimension of his life may be jeopardised.

Wilson takes us through a small learning strategy here and uses it a number of times to highlight where sociological blindness may be present. The expectations of various groups in society often generate an *'Unexamined Attitude'*. His example at this point is significant: 'Because I belong to the clergy I am automatically

What is clericalism in the Catholic tradition?

credible. I don't have to earn my credibility by my performance' says the ordinand. 'There is a diploma on the wall so I can put my trust in her (or him)' says the laity! – so the expectations are cemented through the acceptance that ordinands and priests can look forward to the elevated status 'through distinctive dress, address and perks' (p. 16). The expectations of careerism, entitlements, generalised but unearned respect, high social status and a possible lack of humility are dangerous territory.

The severest impact according to Wilson, is another unexamined attitude: 'The laity accept these manifestations of privilege so they must be deserved' and the laity's response: 'It's showing respect for the cloth' (p. 19). Further, these cultural patterns may well result in losing touch with reality. Defensive responses then by individual members and by the collective group tend to assume that all are special. This results in the lack of honest critique and self-reflection. Group loyalty ends in the growing existence of secrecy. Protection of the group image and resistance to change accompanies a tendency towards superiority and narcissism. This scenario emerges as the seed and the cult of clericalism, because the gap and the isolation of the ordinand is so complete that he is perhaps unaware of the existence of the unreality towards which he may be hurtling.

One particular element of Wilson's efforts to deepen our understanding of the phenomenon of clericalism in today's Catholic tradition needs special analysis. Wilson's identification of the practice of being accountable to no-one, to no regulation, to no law, to no member of the laity, leads often to no practice of the respect and the niceties of the culture within which we all live. It seems that civility becomes a practice of isolated actions and spoken conversation which stay on the level of trivial response. This outcome deepens that sense of difference, of superiority, of disengagement with the concerns, the worries, the sufferings, the oppressive moral code enforced on the laity. As Wilson comments 'the harm to the community of the faith is great indeed' (p. 30). Add to that the underlying knowledge that the individual ordinand is ontologically-changed (whatever that means) and the scene is set for a wide range of responses in the new ordinand.

It raises for the People in the Pews the question as to why the sacrament of Holy Orders is so different from the sacrament of Baptism. Surely the person baptised is ontologically-changed in exactly the same way? And why is the Sacrament of Eucharist any different? After all, we believe we are receiving the deepest connection possible in the Body and Blood of Jesus: his way, his truth, his life! And does that mean that the sacrament of Marriage, which consecrates a particular man and a particular woman to a lifetime of devotion to each other and to the children of their union, somehow not mean that the receivers are ontologically-changed? The incoherence of this vexed area of understanding of what we really mean, when we title these experiences as sacraments, is apparent.

Referring to the experience of being ontologically changed by the sacrament of ordination, John Paul ll did not explain the resultant questions about the depth of the impact of each sacrament. This is an area of the faith needing immense reflection about meaning, for the church of the future. Curial officials would be serving the People of God fully if this concept were to be minutely and specifically developed, rather than the present efforts to hammer the codes of ethical conduct and moral theology as it presently stands. To address this matter would mean that Curial teams would need augmentation of qualified People from the Pews, whose skill sets, knowledge and experience provide insights so obviously far from the experience of the curial world. And perhaps the vicious in-fighting for power and control and stifling of cultural boundaries can be consigned to the ether as a consequence of a choice of addressing meaningful questions for the future of a chastened church. The leadership in

Rome may, finally, reluctantly be persuaded by the realisation that they are *expected* to follow in daily practice the service embedded in the message of Jesus: his way, his truth, his life.

That lack of accountability and sense of separateness, of possibly living in a bubble, especially in a seminary, exists because the ordinand is having little experience of the different forms of friendship and degrees of intimacy, whether of a sexual or altruistic texture, normally experienced by the maturing individual, as the People in the Pews find familiar. There is no sign of journeying together, walking in the shoes of another, as that person experiences new and sometimes challenging or fearful situations. It is beyond the experience of those ordinands bent on an exalted career in the church. Such a secret world is impenetrable. 'Transparency does not come by easily, even when what might be concealed are clearly criminal acts' (p. 31). It seems that Wilson is highlighting that on ordination, there was for the ordinand 'no medium to hold him accountable for anything' except perhaps for 'blatant heresy' (p. 32).

When an ordinand identifies himself as a Catholic priest, the listeners immediately conjure up a complex profile of power, prowess, access to divinity, and bearer of a holy heritage, with a life commitment to God and to the People in the Pews. An aura of respect and social capital accrues. Enough, one might say, to tip a vulnerable young man into a false or assumed sense of worthiness. Add to that, the writings of Pope John Paul ll and others insisted that at the point when the sacrament of ordination is administered, he is ontologically changed. But no process seems to exist to help the ordinand or the People in the Pews towards a realistic assessment of what all of this actually means. It is easy to recognise that humility, respect, compassion, mercy, let alone understanding of the vicissitudes of daily life of the People in the Pews, is needed: that is a huge challenge.

In the mind of the new ordinand, everything must be addressed, and it puts that person in a quandary. On the one hand, he must take up duties in a busy domain where the Bishop expects him to manage immediately. On the other hand, he is expected to be totally independent, separated from most previous support systems, and expected to give everything to his parishioners – often on call each twenty-four hours. It is obvious that everything must be simplistically reduced to a manageable proportion for his daily life to proceed. It is easy to understand just how overwhelming such a situation is. Everything is reduced to the many regulatory pronouncements of the milieu in which he must function, and to some extent he will not have much opportunity to identify consequences of the many decisions that must be made.

He may be unconscious of intended and unintended consequences. In a situation where confusion may appear to mistake the overlap of the gifts of Baptism, he may be so focused on managing the situation, just because he has been gifted also with the wherewith-all of ordination. He may not be aware just what this means fully. So the royal priesthood of the faithful People in the Pews loses ground as he uses all his strength to contribute the fruits of his gifts at ordination. That somewhat simplistic approach, necessary as it may appear to him, must apply to the sayings of Jesus, any other scriptural content, and impinges on the undeniable responsibility for personal conscientious decision making. That royal priesthood is assumed within the priestly caste in the Catholic tradition, and the inevitable result is the submissiveness and dependence of members of the laity, who are told what their sins are.

Wilson puts it bluntly: 'Priesting is a way of living a *life*' (p. 43). 'It is not a state but a process unfolding through appropriate action' (p. 44). This appropriateness includes living the Jesus message, within his role, giving real service to his community, on a pilgrimage towards God. Wilson makes much of holiness as a goal in life for both priest and people. However, in an effort to understand how clericalism has intruded into the Catholic tradition, it is worth exploring the meanings we attribute to the concept of holiness.

Jesus left us a message to follow his way, his truth, his life. He did not imply that this meant perfectionism. There is no such state as a perfect human life, as God created us all as unique people, different from every other person, full of potential and with the series of innate gifts which will be the foundation of that way, truth, life that will take us on a journey towards God, not towards the idolatry of perfectionism. Perfectionism can imply careerism, and the possibility of veering very close to heretical thinking patterns. God is perfect; humanity, whether priest or people, uses appropriate action including prayer and compassionate behaviours, to reach towards wholeness, not holiness.

The church over the centuries has made much of holiness and there is room to develop understanding at a deeper level of the concept of wholeness, rather than holiness, lest we fall into a cult of pietistic behaviours without deepening the intention and attitudes that keep us close to the message of Jesus. It is a condition of clericalism that highlights the *aim* of a person to become a pope or a saint! It is possible that we don't acknowledge the possibility of a cult of holiness for its own sake – and that is close to heresy. That extreme overdrawn aspiration perhaps tempts the ordinand, and the people, towards individual and exclusive acts at the expense of the communal aspect of the Jesus message.

This can lead to compartmentalisation of thought, intention and action. It becomes clearer that a new paradigm, based more precisely on the full implementation of the Jesus message, must include that praxis, practice and possibility of sharing, which the Eucharist exemplifies (*Lumen Gentium*). If we change the meaning in the text from systematic submission to many exacting and overemphasised individual acts to the fuller understanding of the overall effect of living the Jesus message in a sustained and balanced manner, we will be living always in the consciousness of the presence of the Holy Trinity, and we will find ourselves able to connect the way of life promoted (*Lumen Gentium 39, 40*) by Wilson (pp. 45-46).

It is worth giving full attention and careful reflection to Wilson's descriptions of holiness-based-on-relationship: 'That Gospel call means acknowledging the fact that I have been and still am being created out of pure love by a God whose love always precedes any action on my part to earn that love' (p. 47). It is a 'demanding discipline' to relate all the time, to all those around me. Reminiscence here is paramount as we remember the Jesus call to love God with our whole self and our neighbour as ourself.

On ordination, Wilson states that the candidate becomes 'clergified'. 'In the case of the ordained clergy, when clericalism is allowed to flourish (and remember that both the clerics and the laity contribute to the process), the impact can be devastating not only for the individual's faith journey, but also for the whole faith community and the mission it proclaims to the broader society' (p. 54).

Wilson raises another question regarding the maintenance of rigid use of ritual, some of which harks back to medieval times and beyond. When extracted from their rightful milieux, these rituals emphasise the divide between the cleric and the lay person. This was indeed noticeable when Pope Francis celebrated Mass in Abu Dhabi. When insistence on promotion of these practices at the expense of creative and careful liturgical actions happens, that emphasis promotes this clericalism which is employed for almost narcissistic purposes. It is likely to be the result of another unexamined attitude, whose zenith leads to creeping and complete papal infallibility. This phenomenon is authoritarian in texture and cuts down altogether the necessary pastoral and teaching function of the church. It forces a stereotypical thinking pattern, which operates on the edge of, or outside of logic, and becomes the idolatry of ideology rather than a faith-based response to the Jesus message.

It is urgent at this juncture to look again at the concept of wholeness because it is important to distinguish it as something to be worked at, developed and evaluated. Wholeness does not happen. Neither does holiness. Relationship with a loving Triune God may result in others discovering that holiness may have existed in the life of a particular individual.

Wholeness is the practice of continually becoming the best and most mature adult we can be. It means gathering our personal resources, evaluating challenges and paradoxes we meet, practising resilience, being patient, prudent and prayerful each day. It means consciously recognising personal response, response-ability and responsibility within every aspect of our daily lives. This is the essence of an informed conscience as we deepen and understand the virtues and values we learn from Jesus through our parents, in our secular culture, within our Catholic faith community and according to what the Gospels have shown us of the Jesus message.

By contrast, holiness seems today to be an outcome of perfectionism, which pays homage to the earliest forms of extremism. Before the advent of ISIS-plus, extremism paid attention to the practice of the inferiority (not humility) of the laity. This was accomplished by a steady diet of sacramental practices, good in themselves – like the Nine First Fridays, the Five First Saturdays, prayers for the dead (all of whom were assumed to be in Purgatory for aeons), daily rosaries, and participation in sodality life. Outcomes of these practices so often included scepticism, serious scrupulosity, hidden depression, fear of death, dread of dying without the sacrament of Extreme Unction (called Anointing since Vatican Council ll). The profile of a God who demanded extreme forms of repentance for even a cultural mistake, (but who, it was said, loved us), was a contradiction anxiously accepted, because Jesus, as God, had died a death of awful torture. This resulted in the familiar term of Catholic guilt. There was no relief for those who lived this torture.

Richard Storer – and English clericalism

Richard Storer has written an overview of the excoriating issues faced presently by the English Catholic Church. He is realistic in assessing the progress of change for his country. In an article for *The Tablet*, 16 June 2018, Storer's final assessment is a stinging one: 'The good work of safe-guarding professionals in the Church should be commended, but in the absence of a more profound process of change I fear we will still be where we are now in a few years' time' (p. 7).

The English Independent Inquiry into Child Sex Abuse (IICSA) hearings 'provide an opportunity for a deeper examination of some of the issues, and a review of the progress the Church has made in its response to the abuse crisis, or the lack of it' (p. 6). Storer goes on to commend the hearings for uncovering 'some stark realities' and states plainly: 'the hearings revealed disturbing evidence that the attitudes and culture that allowed abuse to fester for so many years still persist in the Catholic Church' (p. 6). Amazingly, Storer records that 'Police complained of repeated obstruction, and significant records documenting safeguarding concerns about specific monks, previously undisclosed, were discovered in brown envelopes during police investigation'. In one monastery school, the abbot stated: 'I am not having child protection policies in the monastery'. And the corollary of this issue is: 'there is nothing mandatory and nothing enforceable, there is no accountability with safeguarding in the

Catholic Church, it is all on a goodwill basis' and Storer concludes that there is emerging evidence of a 'systemic problem' (p. 6). Echoes abound here of Joanne McCarthy's extended discoveries of cover-up, lies and evasions she found in the Hunter Valley in Eastern Australia in 2017.

One element of this manifestly gargantuan problem is highlighted by Storer: 'Thickets of policies and procedures can make it difficult for clergy and lay people alike to understand in simple terms precisely what should be done and by whom' (p. 6). As Storer suggests (and it is familiar in Australia): 'The Church seeks to be a moral beacon for the world around it, yet clerical abuse cases and the scandals surrounding them powerfully undermine this claim'. One interesting sidelight is worth exploring here: 'All too often this leads to a cognitive dissonance. A culture of victim blaming is created' (and) 'reputational pressures may still discourage external reporting: a problem seriously compounded by safeguarding policies that still sometimes say should, rather than must, report abuse to statutory authorities'. As Storer indicates, it currently leaves 'wriggle room' for those who prefer to keep everything private.

A very significant point included that the hearings 'were replete with instances of clerical abusers being protected from accountability by a distorted concept of forgiveness' (p. 7): 'Looking at the Catholic Church from the outside, it seems to combine an unhealthy exaltation of the clergy with a serious neglect of their emotional well-being, (talking about) the clerical arrogance that equates the Church with God'. Storer includes comment on the sense of superiority, saying clearly that 'the battle against clericalism in the Church has to be more than merely rhetorical. Abusive priests are often the product of a culture'. Tragic to read his next comment: 'it has been obvious for decades that the all-male institutional environment of the seminary can infantilise' and 'many priests continue to face the terrible choice between the emotional loneliness of celibacy and the secrecy and guilt of illicit relationships'.

The rhetoric regarding social justice is strangely absent in these considerations, as no effort is made, either logically or morally, to recognise that restorative justice means adjusting to the unendurable pain of the victims of sexual abuse, and the requirement of restitution for both intended and unintended consequences. Well may prelates claim that they are sorry, but life-long damage to victims, to victims' families and friends, and to the truth-tellers called whistle-blowers, seem easily dismissed. Resistance to change, and defiance in the face of undeniable evidence of life-long psycho-sexual suffering particularly of victims, is not the Jesus way, and must be called unequivocally by its truthful title.

This causes the People in the Pews to wonder why clerics from the higher echelons of the hierarchy are told by the pope to retire to a suitable place for a life of prayer, reflection and penance. It would seem more appropriate if these men are strictly monitored as they serve the poorest of the poor by staffing soup kitchens, tending the homeless, supporting the refugee, listening to the prisoner every day for the rest of their lives. That way, the offenders learn about the pain and deprivations of the poor, as Vatican ll indicated: an option for the poor.

Scorer's stark final comments highlight the absence of women from the church power structures, noticing that women would be more inclined to act firmly on abuse cases, but naming the historical elephant in the room in the last few decades: 'the *group-think* that so often underpins abuse scandals and their cover-up' (p. 7). He is not confident that the required 'profound process of change' that is needed will be sufficient or developed enough to improve the situation in his country. He states categorically that 'the time has come to impose mandatory reporting requirements, backed up by legal sanctions'. He is very clear that those profound changes must be systemic; must be mandatory; must be universal; must include attitudinal change; and must be heart-felt in its sincerity, transparency and authenticity.

Underlying his exploration of the situation in England and Wales, where he was intimately involved in the hearings of the Sex Abuse Inquiry, is a significant clarity of description about the concept of clericalism itself, and the widespread culture which sustained the abuse of children. The superiority factor of the priestly cult seemed so broad that no consciousness of the effects on the victims and the total disruption of young lives were ever entertained. The contradiction between the spoken word, the ritual and solemnness of liturgical celebrations with the evil and predatory behaviours, the criminal assaults and emotional wrecks they left behind, is breathtaking in its enormity. It is worth noting therefore that real and severe damage has been apparent in the universal church in the authoritarian style of evangelisation manifested in the last century. Clericalism, with its emphasis on leading the People in the Pews back to a semblance of the European Catholicism of monastic and pietistic times, is a tragic failure to live the message of Jesus.

Unrealistic expectations or ignorant edicts handed down, at the same time as Europe and the whole Catholic world, of the 20th century endured and survived horrific warfare, led to assumptions of their own brand of authority by some church leaders. Their underdeveloped understanding of the concept of authority led to brutal rendering of what the message of Jesus was intended to be. Into this confusion came the appearance of the emphasis on the priest and the prelature as ontologically-changed during ordination. Next came the papal demands that Vatican ll was to be interpreted in its narrowest sense. The uncertainty, which would naturally be a prelude to examination of new situations normally expected to be the basis of balanced decision making, was dismissed as against the will of God. The presumption that any human, no matter how holy, could or would or did fully know the mind of God was apparent for many decades and led to severe papal and hierarchical strictures. The sin of presumption was present for the last half of the 20th century and in retrospect can be seen today as close to heresy. After all, humankind is not divine, and was created by God to be of the best humanness possible. We each were meant to become a loving person full of compassion and mercy but not meant to assume the place of God in that most private relationship which exists between God and self.

The Legacy of Vatican II

The difficulties that assail the Catholic Church today seem to rest particularly with the strands of thought which insist on a no-change or a real-change approach to what is to count as being a true believer within the Catholic tradition. The vexed and wilful efforts of those who wish to push their own agenda, tend to make tradition a very elastic term anchored in fuzzy logic. It remains for theologians to dismantle the fuzziness and clarify the meanings of the Catholic tradition and the effects of some individual traditions. There is much work for theologians, and the lead is already being taken up. The latest includes the theological gem of Francis Moloney (2018), in which he examines the disconnect regarding the evolution of Eucharist.

Faggioli (2012) begins a careful exploration that seems to hinge on the spectre of sublimely unconscious perspectives of some hierarchical figures who do not recognise the difference between the Eurocentric version of the Catholic Church as an entity, and the burgeoning expansion of the Catholic Church as a world phenomenon, with a measurable array of responsibilities to provide clarity and modelling of the message of Jesus (His Way, Truth, Life) within 21st century daily living. The contentious attitudes of so many popes highlight the binary thinking patterns used to establish opposites: right or wrong – with no recognition of the need to teach, only to declaim. The Battle for Meaning was the consequence.

The adversarial tendencies and rigid authoritarianism model instead a refusal to respect the need for questions, for exploration, for graded teaching, resulting in the one-size-fits-all effect which emanates from the publication of encyclicals, apostolic exhortations and papal letters. It is important to understand the laziness as well as the disrespect which is inherent in promotion of the one-size-fits-all syndrome. Faggioli has detailed a historical and theoretical process worthy of our careful exploration. He looks at the Second Ecumenical Council with its debate on how to discern the will of the Holy Spirit, questioning even the legitimacy of the whole of the gatherings and their considerations. Was the Catholic Church in need of renewal, as Pope John XXIII indicated when he widened the institution of the Ecumenical Council to Catholics, Christians and people of good will? Of course, but the use of binary thinking patterns was never going to produce much change.

Faggioli refers to the Opposite Extremisms (2012 pp. 19-20): 'traditionalist Catholics – that is, from the extremes of 'sedevacantists (who claim the Papal See has been vacant since the death of either Pius XII in 1958 or John XXIII in 1963) to the more moderate advocates of the Latin Mass – have grown much more vocal in denouncing the council as synonymous with disaster and chaos in the church. Their negative view of the results of the liturgical reform could be applied uniformly to all of the major developments of Vatican ll (ecclesiology, ecumenism, religious freedom, and the church and the modern world) without altering their level of outrage'.

Faggioli has taken us through a historical process: 'to show that Vatican ll was a paradigmatic event of the new era in the history of the Catholic Church: not only for what happened *at* Vatican ll but also what happened *after* Vatican ll as well' (p. 139). He refers particularly to Thomas S. Kuhn and the 'Structure of Scientific Revolutions' and the question arises then about whether the ability of the members of the hierarchy as well as the People in the Pews can be open to the Holy Spirit, who seemingly wills us to consciously be of this world (John 17), not the ancient exclusivity of being in the world and not of the world. This is a stance which today does not make much sense – if it ever did make sense. Arguments about Augustinianism versus Thomism, Faggioli tells us, are the new two tendencies. This is binary thinking again.

There seems to be no understanding of subtlety and nuance, no degree of depth, no recognition of respect due to each other's convictions, and this evokes a firm resistance to the possibility of learning from each other. So it is worth ventilating the six principles for sound interpretation of Vatican ll, which according to Faggioli, Avery Dulles paraphrased as follows:

'Each passage and document of the Council must be interpreted in the context of all the others, so that the integral meaning of the Council may be rightly grasped'; 'The four major constitutions of the Council are the hermeneutical key for the other decrees and declarations'; 'The pastoral impact of the documents may not be separated from, or set in opposition to, their doctrinal content'; 'No opposition may be made between the spirit and the letter of Vatican ll'; 'The Council must be interpreted in continuity with the great tradition of the Church, including earlier councils'; 'Vatican ll must be accepted as illuminating the problems of our own day' (pp. 84-85). There is therefore much ongoing and detailed work for theologians to develop, declaim and to teach. It is important for the People in the Pews that this be so.

It is important here to recognise that the great tradition is a nebulous phrase which can be made to mean whatever the believer wants it to mean. Unconsciously perhaps, depthing the meanings of many of the concepts, beliefs, cultural practices, moral codes and other important considerations will not happen while each 'side' clings to the fact that they are right – which, of course, means that the other is wrong. Conceive of a person who stands in the countryside crossroad, where four roads come together. If the person faces one road, then it is possible to see three tracks, but not four tracks. Always it is a movement of turning and changing direction which allows that person to see and come to terms with the fourth track. And so it is for the endless discussions, books, lectures, and other communications which we must wade through, in order to be sure we have some sort of balance of what exists within the matter at hand, e.g. like the proposal of a change in liturgical form, before we reinterpret the various relevant questions which help us to discern with the help of the Holy Spirit, what paradigm change might mean for the People in the Pews.

It is a relief to discover that the editorial staff of *America* (2018) can offer from their archives a significant statement regarding change: 'The right of Catholics to express disagreement with their leaders is a right as old as Peter and Paul, though dissent from papal teaching is obviously not the normal posture of the Catholic. But dissent is possible when the teaching in question is still in a state of development, and when those who dissent have listened with open minds and hearts to what was said, and in the end have found grave, solidly grounded reason for disagreement' (Editor, 1968).

Clericalism will resist the possibility of being open to change, because comfort zones are being challenged. If such comfort zones include the infantilised emotional development implied by formation in a seminary milieu, then confusion reigns. Then when concepts which have hardly ever been studied, like actual care of the environment, rather than dominion over the environment, again confusion reigns. Clericalism, in its rigid disregard for persons but favouring of dogma, leaves little room for the engendering of the classical virtue of hope, as distinct from optimism about the future. The deliberate infantilisation of the People in the Pews, the voices of the *sensus fidelium*, is apparent in the continual flow of edicts, apostolic exhortations, encyclicals, and other communications directing the faithful.

No understanding of the various and subtle skills of teaching of students from early primary through to upper levels of tertiary studies is exhibited in these documents. They do give us particular explanations, connections, regulations but no suggestions of a teaching praxis. The latest Apostolic Exhortation of Pope Francis is a case in point. The suggestions about prayerful actions of a very simplistic nature are useful as ideas for primary and sub-primary children, but this is nowhere near enough for the present generation who are fully familiar with digital technology, world-wide internet capacity and teaching practice within daily experience of the classroom in first-world countries. Neither should such suggestions be any different in the educational development of people in third-world countries. To do so is dangerous because of the pitfalls of exhibiting racism and other exclusivities with no basis in reality.

The idea, previously promulgated that the world is so complicated, so astonishing, so much the venue of our Cosmic Lord, is one which seems to escape the reality of what humankind has done to the natural environment in the last few centuries. The underlying knowledge of the People in the Pews regarding such matters swirls around the reductionism, the restorationism and the resistance of those who can see no value in recognising that reality is so very different today from any decade or century past. That reality goes even back to when Jesus walked the lanes and paths of Nazareth, Capernaum, Jericho, Bethsaida, and eventually Jerusalem and surrounds. So we are obligated to listen to the prophetic voices around us; we are obligated to educate ourselves about historical concerns regarding belief without labelling those with whom we disagree as heretics.

> 'The Church needs a new direction, one pointing not upwards but *forward,* not towards "heaven above" but a *new future* of healthy relationships. Beatrice Bruteau describes a shift in consciousness from a domination paradigm to what she calls a "Holy Thursday" paradigm, marked by mutuality, service, and Christian love. To be "in Christ", she writes, "is to enter into Holy Thursday by experiencing some death and resurrection, letting an old modality of consciousness die, and seeing a new one rise to life. It is to abandon thinking of oneself only (in) terms of categories and abstractions and seeing oneself as a transcendent center of energy that lives in God and in one's neighbors – because this is where Christ lives, in God and in us". We need to come to terms with the fact that Christianity is less an historical religion than a religion of the future.' So says Ilia Delio (28/8/18).

CHAPTER 2

Voices of People in the Pews

The disaster emerging from the various investigations around the world now engulfing the Catholic Church because of the brutal practices of clerical sexual predatory assaults on children and young and vulnerable people is a presenting problem for today of the deep and cancerous presence of clericalism. In the past, as George Wilson indicates, the People in the Pews have been submissive, and they and we unconsciously contributed to the evil behaviours that were covered up. Pompous attitudes in arrogant prelates whose perspectives were based on the 'ontological change (?)' allowed them to disregard civil law and criminality. Presently, Royal Commission findings and relevant and remarkably similar rulings in many countries have finally emboldened us to speak out from within our enduring anger, disgust and sense of betrayal served up by those, whose disdain allowed them to believe that they could stay silent and wait patiently for the furore to dissipate and go on their way as usual. It was almost as though the then Australian Prime Minister, Julia Gillard, had given us permission to say what we had been thinking for so long.

If we are to understand the responses from People in the Pews, we need to canvas widely. There are people who are hurting badly from being actual victims of sexual abuse: family members who feel impotent about the betrayal of their family member and the secondary consequences of being victim through the destruction of family life. There are whistle-blowers, the truthtellers, who were and still are victimised for their valiant attempts to address the brutalising effects of personal assault and the aftermath suffered for the effort to move on behalf of the victims. There are some priests and some bishops who also courageously highlighted the callous behaviours uncovered and who also paid a huge price in physical and psychological consequences at the hands of hierarchical figures in a systematic cover-up, in a wall of secrecy and in a vicious system meant to keep control and power in the hands of prelates far removed from the message of Jesus: 'Suffer the little children'.

It is important to recognise that the People in the Pews have suffered from the predatory behaviours of paedophiles in a variety of ways. Any kind of physical abuse, whether of women, young men or children, is a suffering mostly misunderstood by so many in the clerical caste. The reality of assaults on the victims is compounded physically: the shock and dread as well as the overall discomfort, pain, trauma and turmoil for the individual so assaulted. That shock and dread emerges emotionally: the dogmatic regulations which ignore confusion, psychic suffering and sense of despair as outcomes of ongoing assaults. Negative effects appear socially: the scapegoating of the victims by those who blame each victim rather than engage in compassion and care. There is also the hammering of the truth-tellers (whistle-blowers) who dared to speak out. The pain is felt intellectually: the contradiction of the dogma which insists that God is a loving God, but the reality of life is that the victim is condemned to secrecy and a life of repeated violence. Unforgivably, there is also a penalty spiritually: the overall experience of overwhelming control and the intrusion of power demanding perfection and submission in the face of arrogance and narcissism. Finally, there is the intrusion of predators whose brutality all but obliterates the presence of God for the victims.

Imagine two examples that may highlight these consequences in the life of a victim.

A) *A woman in an unsatisfactory or violent home environment pushed to have sexual encounters by a partner whose demands result in yet another pregnancy.*

> The physical abuse is the requirement of accepting the inevitable outcome of reduced health and ability to function as a wife and mother. The emotional abuse is nine months of serious physical and emotional stress of the pregnancy itself and the inevitable demands of the continual stream of attending to the needs of existing children. The social abuse is the lack of understanding and support of her plight by an uncomprehending church whose published documents describe her place as in the home (translation – having babies). The intellectual abuse is the arrogance and ignorance which the woman faces, when the contradiction between logical responsibility to manage her family in the face of a wall of unreal religious and cultural expectations designating her as inferior and ignoring her varieties of skill sets. The spiritual abuse is the subtle emphasis on the priority of church requirements under pain of dogmatic edicts based on medieval or outmoded knowledge of how a human being called woman is created. And there is no relief. The double-jeopardy element is found in the abysmal ignorance of a disengaged clericalised church and the reduced ability to reach God for relief. Church dogmatics intrude and the woman must make the best of her potential and failing health because her children must be responsibly reared.

B) *The boy who is violated by clerical paedophilic behaviours and must face contradictory demands of the abuser, who imposes secrecy, psychic confusion, physical pain, lies and brutal behaviours.*

> The physical abuse is the sexual assaults and the dread which accompanies, and which may continue ad nauseum. The emotional abuse is the confused nightmare, the emerging hate and revulsion coupled with ongoing fright, utter vulnerability and hopelessness of knowing there is no rescue but the almost impossible suppression of these memories. The social abuse is the isolation, disengagement and the inability to make friends, find support, achieve in education, and failure of trust in personal relationships. The intellectual abuse emerges as the victim struggling to become a maturing person, often mistakes boundaries in communal or commercial scenarios. The spiritual abuse becomes apparent in the blinding anger of the victim who knows he is not believed, or is doublecrossed and betrayed by clerical figures who claim to represent a God not of love or compassion or justice but a brutal, betraying, overwhelmingly unjust Being incapable of giving one's personal trust.

Monsignor Tony Doherty (2013, p. 3) provides us with a telling statement from Bryan Doyle:

> 'But Catholic is my language;
> Catholic is the coat I wear,
> Catholic is the house in which I live.

It is a house that needs cleaning,
A house in which savagery and cowardice thrived,
Where evil has a room with a view,
Where foolishness and greed have prominent places at the table.
But it also a house where hope lives,
And hope is the greatest of mercies,
The most enduring of gifts, the most nutritious of foods.
Hope is what we drink from the odd story
of the carpenter's odd stepson.
When we eat his body in the ludicrous miracle of the Mass,
We hope in him, and with him,
Forever and ever,
World without end,
Amen, Amen, Amen.

The Storm Bursts

Importantly, voices from the People in the Pews have finally begun to become a resounding choir demanding justice and change. What follows is an example from People in the Pews, who have raised their voices on behalf of those reduced to misery by their circumstances of abuse, and the cruelty of 'Mother Church' by disregarding them. But the People in the Pews are also making their judgments on the obviously slack governance, the lack of transparency, the absence of a sense of accountability and justice, and their furious response to the slaying of trust by those who claim the right and the privilege to lead, shape and nurture the relationship between the individual and the loving God, who created us, redeemed and gave us life and inspires us today.

For readers who have an interest in the public dialogue of recent date, the reading list attached, details a lengthy choice of relevant, but not all, statements of People in the Pews, who have pursued a careful conversation in the columns, features and correspondence of *The Tablet*, in other blogs and online conversations, and in many relevant writings about how to understand the complex nature of the scandals that are eclipsing the current hierarchical levels of the church and the corruption of some prelates in recent decades right up to today.

Eric Hodgens, retired parish priest of the Melbourne Archdiocese, has stated quite clearly: 'The priesthood itself is divided' (2018). In a separate paper commenting on the disastrous consequences pertaining to the betrayal of the People in the Pews when *Humanae Vitae* was promulgated, Hodgens makes it clear that 'Officialdom leading people away from God's reality' was the tragedy that became 'a watershed moment. Paul VI meant to settle the matter but, instead, began a movement that put conscience, reception and sexual taboo under the microscope. John Paul ll laboured for twenty-seven years to bag the cat again – but lost' (2018). Hodgens writes separately on the theology of clericalism: 'Knowing the history helps to work out a solution. Theology follows practice and is an attempt to provide a rational explanation of that practice. The theology of the Constantinian Church was formulated in an intellectual climate of the philosophy of Plato and Aristotle and in the Greek language. Much of it does not speak to today's world'. He decries the church-as-institution today and the phenomenon of clerical sexual abuse, inspecting pastoral practice and states: 'Theology tends to ramp up the status and certainty of its models and theories so that what starts off as a theory morphs into unquestionable truth' and 'the theology of the seal (of confession) has passed its use-by date. A priest is no more sacred than any other baptised Christian'. Internal digestion of the whole of the Hodgens' meanings leaves us as People in the Pews thankful for his insights, but no closer to solving the ills of this beloved and embattled church, and facing confusion, pain, and a great deal of disgust and shame at the enormity of the actions of paedophilic figures and their shameful cohorts who secretly ignored and covered up their crimes.

Peter Johnston, who has led a Coalition of Concerned Catholics from all parts of Australia, has even conceded that it may be necessary to take drastic action regarding the seal of confession. 'Most Australians would hope that any citizen would bring to the attention of the police any knowledge of criminal plans to harm society, be it the sexual abuse of children or a terrorist plot to blow up the MCG on Grand Final Day' (2018). In an Open Letter to the Catholic Bishops of Australia, Johnstone (2018) states: 'Most Australian Catholics have long been aware that the structures of their Church are autocrat; most were brought up accepting that Church decision making is unaccountable and often secretive, that bishops are remote from their people in their decision making, and that the views of laypersons count for little, particularly if they are women. Catholics have increasingly questioned this dysfunctional governance; many have walked away and many have witnessed their children walking away. The widespread disillusionment of Catholics has peaked with the revelations emerging from the Royal Commission into Institutional Responses to Child Sexual Abuse.'

Michael Kelly SJ sets out the description of painful mismanagement of church decision making and governance and states: 'Even if all Bishops and Religious Leaders at a given date signed up to offer commitments to the Australian people, these would not, and could not, bind their successors. That is the governance problem at the heart of Catholicism.'(2018). He goes on: 'And that is precisely where the international ramifications of the Australian enquiry will have the greatest impact if what is declared to the Commission is heard beyond Australia... In all parts of the world, the Church's government operates according to the principle of "subsidiarity", the medieval political principle that has matters handled by and decided at the smallest, lowest or least centralised competent authority. What the Church as a global community has to face now is that this principle has actually led to gross abuse and extensive damage to people'.

After all, many centuries ago when sailing ships carried intrepid explorers from the northern hemisphere to the southern hemisphere, people like the sailor Velasquez named Australia the Land of the Holy Spirit. We Australians need to live up to that indicator, and allow ourselves to accompany the Holy Spirit, making efforts adjusting to the space, the time, the focus, and resolve we need to walk in companionship and dawning wisdom into the expanding future of God's Cosmic World as the People in the Pews on their pilgrim journey.

Unfortunately, a blatant contradiction exists for us as pilgrims because walking in the companionship and dawning wisdom as People in the Pews has not been fully operative. The authoritarianism (Collins, 2018) of a series of recent papal decrees has resulted in creeping infallibility; and this without taking any of the subsidiarity concepts flagged by Vatican ll into account. Confusion and anger within the People in the Pews is fuelled by the resistance and defiance of some local bishops who don't seem to know how to proceed, so no action is taken, and they retreat into defiant silence.

John Warhurst takes up a wider lens: 'Let's talk about the Catholic bishops. The Catholic bishops are by institutional design the centrepiece of the Australian Catholic Community. This means a lot is happening in the name of ordinary Catholics whether they like it or not because the perception of the wider community is that the bishops represent all Catholics' (2018).

Terry Laidler is scathing in responding to a radio interview with one Australian archbishop, who had stated that clericalism is an important cultural factor that contributed to the appalling scale and nature of abuse. Says Terry: 'Asked about absolute confessional secrecy, and the ordination of women, (the archbishop) said correctly that current practice in both regards was "non-negotiable", but he did not go on to say why. I will – they are non-negotiable because a group of male clerics who have power in the Catholic Church say so. No matter what others within and without the church hold different views, no matter what evidence might show that each contributes to the disease at the core of the problem, these things cannot be spoken about or better alternatives found. And those who try to broach the issues are ignored or ostracised or simply wrong. This is what clericalism is.' (2018)

Anthony Hogan has analysed further the ventilation of defence by two Australian archbishops in June/July 2018 when they responded to the public conversation which led to the comments within this chapter. 'On the Law and the seal of Confession' Hogan explains an apparent anomaly: 'The Church's position against such laws is based on the arguments that: People basically don't confess such sins anymore so there is no issue; that children would not be safer; the priest has taken a holy vow to keep confidential what is heard in the confessional, and that the practice of confession is a religious freedom and as such, that what occurs within the practice of religion is somehow outside the law of the land.'(2018).

Having set out an analysis regarding this statement, Hogan is explicit: 'at ordination priests do not take a holy vow to keep confidential what is heard in the confessional. At ordination, a priest promises, for example, to celebrate faithfully and reverently; the Eucharist and Reconciliation. During the same ritual they also make a promise of celibacy. Respecting the so-called seal of the confessional is a matter of convention, of obedience to church law. And it is a law that only came into existence in the early 1100's.' Hogan goes on to describe the third rite of reconciliation in which no-one is closeted alone with a priest – called a community rite of reconciliation. Hogan is worried about the amount of hierarchical oxygen being used to defend a redundant rite when real leadership and compassion and respect would manage the problem so much more lawfully and less power-driven.

The editorial on Catholicism in the United States in *The Tablet*, 27 October 2018, gives a clear history on the activities of Archbishop Vigano, who has three times changed his story regarding the accusations that Pope Francis should resign because of supposed culpability in cover-up of activities of Theodore McCarrick. Details of the history of the three attacks are outlined by Christopher Lamb (*The Tablet*, 2018). The archbishop was contradicted by another prelate, that 'Pope Francis must be the first to set a good example for cardinals and bishops who covered up McCarrick's abuses and resign'. When accused of serious misdemeanour as a result of that accusation, Lamb advises that Vigano 'is taking a different tack, denying he is in an "open and scandalous rebellion" against the pope. 'The second shift is over the restrictions he said McCarrick had been placed under by Pope Benedict XVI. The implication of the earlier Vigano testimony which Cardinal Ouellet sought to refute, was that Benedict XVI enforced formal sanctions of prayer and penance, which Francis ignored. In his latest testimony, the archbishop insists that he told Francis on 23 June, 2013 that McCarrick had been ordered to a life of prayer and penance by Benedict XVI and writes that McCarrick 'continued to enjoy the special regard of Pope Francis and was given new responsibilities and missions by him'. Vigano maintains his insistence that written claims about McCarrick were lodged in 2000, 2006 and 2008. Vigano is maintaining also that the conflict is due to homosexuality which 'has become a plague in the clergy, and it can only be eradicated with spiritual weapons' (Lamb, 2018).

The very serious nature of the editor's analysis under the heading of 'Vigano and the Political Agenda' makes an attempt to recognise just what is happening. The first attempt was in August, 2018: 'Vigano alleges that Francis deliberately facilitated the appointment of homosexual clergy to senior positions in the Catholic Church, and that the root cause of the sex abuse crisis is "the scourge of homosexuality". There is no evidence for this causal connection'. The editor states firmly that 'Pope Francis instead pins the blame on "clericalism": a culture which places priests on such a pedestal that they are beyond criticism, and which puts the protection of the Church's reputation above the safety of children. Archbishop Vigano rejects this. There is a distinct aroma of a homophobic conspiracy theory about his argument.' The long history of the two perspectives (clericalism and catholicity) is laid out by Constant Mews at the beginning of this volume.

Referring to what he calls 'almost an undeclared schism', the editor advises the change in the appointments in United States church when progressive clergy were replaced by socially conservative ones. 'That policy has been put into reverse. Vigano is clearly unhappy about this.' Stating that the 'culture wars' in the United States include economics as well as sexuality as circular issues, Vigano has been heard loud and clear in political circles, as he and they question how state intervention in business and in welfare, 'is perverse in its effects. That is not the doctrine taught by Pope Francis, nor was it ever taught by Pope John Paul ll, or any of his other predecessors. It is a strongly individualistic creed that downplays solidarity and regards economic success as a mark of divine blessing'. In US church circles, it has become 'an inflexible Jansenist/Calvinist approach to human weakness, with more emphasis on judgment than mercy, and a fondness for strict rules. If this lies at one end of the spectrum, Pope Francis is at the other.' And so the binary (black-and-white) thinking and the entrenched resistance to learn how to listen to the People in the Pews, can now be expanded to include adversarial clouts by those in minority who do not accept the teachings of Vatican ll, as implied by the editor's paper.

John Carr, a member of the laity but involved in much of the developments in USA about the almost universality of clerical child sexual abuse, has written a sad paper for *America* (2018) in which he says he has been haunted by this dreadful phenomenon, for five decades. His lessons which he recommends for us to learn alongside him include eight particular points. In regard to sexual abuse, he says that the first lesson is that there are never enough parents in the room to balance the investigations and prevent the defiance and resistance when evidence is produced which is undeniable. A second lesson stipulates that lay people need to be much more involved, but they need to provide independent responses but not allow clerical influence to overcome their efforts to protect children and the vulnerable. He goes on to pinpoint that many bishops are so isolated from the weft and web of daily lives that they don't hear anything about the anguish of survivors and their families because of the wall of institutional protection, general isolation and lack of connectedness.

His fourth point is indelible: 'There have to be independent, credible and effective ways for bishops to be reported, investigated and held accountable for their behaviours, abuse of power, actions and non-actions with regard to sexual abuse'. His fifth point echoes the underlying message of this volume: 'Institutional protection and clericalism can blind us to protecting the vulnerable. Beware of those who seem to use the suffering of survivors to settle old scores or to advance their own ideological agendas, left or right, or their opposition to Pope Francis' – stark common sense about an evil which is truly the elephant in the room! Carr has several warnings for which we would be wise to reflect on carefully. Defending past choices is no substitute for owning and personally apologising for past actions that harmed the vulnerable. Silence in the face of attacks may be spiritually defensible but is pastorally harmful. Silence makes things worse and is not an option for any of us (Carr, 2018).

Confessing when recently reporting that he had suffered abuse, his last reflection draws compassion from us as we try to understand that because he kept his troubles secret, he believes that he may have somehow allowed sexual harassment to be visited on others. The anguish that encircled him and many others is a sample of how many people suffered secondary stress and anguish, as well as the terrible suffering of the victims and survivors. This, of course, included the truth-tellers who tried to act but met silence and resistance, the parents whose families were split, broken and wrecked as a direct consequence of the appalling fate delivered by abusers. Carr worked with cardinals Law, McCarrick and Vigano, so he was faced with lies, betrayal, broken trust and severe entrenched clericalism on a long-term basis.

Countering clericalism – how?

Allowing humbly for listening and the discernment that all this implies, three processes of change are offered for the ordinand. From the perspective of the discipline of education, these three processes are offered for Catholic education to be reviewed from the primary, secondary and tertiary levels of the teaching-learning journey. Inserted into existing educational theory, practice and praxis, these three processes can become (and in so many educational milieux already are) a methodology meant to teach the ordinand. These processes are able to support existing parish clergy, and to close the gaps of exclusivity that are sailing so close to schismatic perspectives now so pronounced in the Catholic Church in the first couple of decades of the third millennium.

It is important to register immediately that each of the three proffered processes, laid out in a later chapter for the consideration of the reader, is already in existence in many ways and in many places. It is this recognition of the patterns of thinking skills recommended for primary, secondary and tertiary student learning in Catholic schools that can underpin the series of skills sets, knowledge concepts, relevant understandings, and efficient aims to be collated in a single overall curriculum for the ordinand. The strength of this project will allow possibilities and processes to emerge. It is important to recognise immediately and commend at this point the heroic lives of so many pastorally-oriented parish priests who have resisted the excesses of this clericalism, forming the central considerations of ongoing research and efforts to understand throughout this book.

If these three educational processes are to be offered, then it is ethically urgent to provide recommendations, reasons for inclusion in the exploration, and indications of differences in outcomes that must be available to the People in the Pews. As the institutional church begins the urgent task of taking responsibility for the clerical sexual abuse scandals, it becomes apparent that changes to governance, to the transparency needed, to the lack of accountability for past culpability on a massive scale, must be urgently implemented. The various models of church, which are familiar to us, require the subtle development of applied knowledge surrounding expertise in thinking skills. The foundation for such development of applied knowledge begins with the metaphor of the geodesic dome to the understanding of what is to count as the Catholic Church in the 21st century. These explorations do not admit the presence of indoctrination, no matter what convenient other title like 'new evangelisation' we might use to further the ideological agenda present in the political arm of the church. This focus requires that the People in the Pews, who are part of the secular world every day, will also be able to contribute. We are told in Genesis that God said that all this including us, was good (Genesis 1, 2). The multiple contributions needed, will come from the various wells of knowledge, disciplines, expertise and skills sets to augment the limited nature of the ordinand's skills at ordination. Ordinands may not necessarily have been provided opportunity to develop quite a number of skills needed in parish work in 21st century but those seven present years of formation need immediate augmentation – especially as 'formation' is a term which has echoes of indoctrination and induction into the experience of groupthink!

Rather than indulge in the isolated binary thinking that has bound the Catholic Church in chains for so long, an honest attempt to name areas of contention; dilemmas for hierarchy; new perspectives from the People in the Pews; and care for the whole Catholic Church is a paramount task in this book. There is no interest in adversarial bullets, political infighting, or point-scoring, though contentious matters will surface. It is so important to allow the incoming influence of God to surface even though mistakes may occur. Explanations are helpful; regular conversations and consultations are needed; and conclusions will emerge as we take up a listening stance attributable to the presence of the Holy Spirit.

So what is clericalism?

It is also useful to pursue the best and most precise meaning of what the church means by the title of Catholic. If it means universal, there is a need to redefine what parts of the monolith we see are to be universal. If it means conformist, there is a need to explain in minute detail exactly what we are to be conformable about. If it means monocultural, then there is a need to set out how this is to be planned, how it is to be effective, and how this aim brings the People in the Pews closer to the message of Jesus. If it means unchanging, then it is necessary to find a way to define the starting point from which we must provide the means to bring this non-change into 21st century living conditions, and provide channels to bring this to fruition. If it means male and celibate, then it does not follow the Jesus invitation to all: Jew and Gentile, male and female, slave and freeman to follow him. Are we starting from the essence of the message of Jesus? Are we starting from the momentous times of Constantine? Are we starting from the mission journeys of Paul? Are we choosing the times with a misplaced romanticism consonant with an infantilisation of the People in the Pews? Uncomfortable as these inter-related questions may be, they underline the complexity of the present scenario. It is imperative that courageous and sustained action takes place.

When we dissect the implications of what the term clericalism actually means in the Catholic Church today, it becomes apparent that power and control is wielded by a small number of male celibates situated in Rome but who claim the right to call the shots on all areas of life for the whole cohort of the People in the Pews. Obviously, these aims are not achievable. When rules and regulations, codes and commands are more important than any individual in any part of the world, and decision making of all sorts means bending the People in the Pews towards the will of those in Rome, we have strayed a long way from the initial invitation of Jesus: Come, follow me.

It is necessary then to explore where the notion of clericalism has invidiously invaded the emotional landscape of both ordained and non-ordained individuals, baptised into the Catholic Church, aided and shaped by papal encyclicals, apostolic exhortations, and dogmatic rulings emanating from various popes and councils of the church. Creeping infallibility, contradictory rulings, ignorance of the skills sets of the People in the Pews, and resistance to the logic of primacy of conscience sets up confusion, suffering, spiritual abuse and callous disdain for the People in the Pews – those whom Jesus called.

Some contributors to clericalism

Some major contributors to the excesses of the cult of clericalism being uncovered in the second decade of the 21st century include a long list.

The utter public condemnation by the church of gay men to the shadows, especially the intrinsically-disordered tag which has dogged the footsteps of gay clergy, and is addressed honestly in a later chapter through James Alison. The extraordinary evil of priestly paedophilia and the official criminal cover-up activities of the relevant hierarchical figures within the church, is hiding behind the official papal secrecy code, explored carefully by Kieran Tapsell (2014, 2018) and Kathleen McPhillips (2018). It includes the excessive use of power and control, and the creeping infallibility of the edicts issued in authoritarian style from the Curia under the pen of individual popes and highlighted by the defence of John Paul ll by George Pell (2007) and Matt Nelson (2018). Evidence shows in the remarkable efforts of Curia, certain papal incumbents and members of the hierarchy to flatten and silence any kind of enquiry, in a centuries-old tradition of thought control, resulting in our failure to think. This is whimsically addressed in *America* by David J. Michael, as he describes Alan Jacobs' extraordinary output of writing, and includes 'How to think: A Guide for the Perplexed' (Spring 2018).

There are four convenient profiles of the church in the Catholic tradition, which have historically existed sometimes in isolation and sometimes in parallel to one another. Signposts of each profile include a number of features.

The Perfect Society

Gospel accounts, of course, have been chosen decades after the death of Jesus the Christ, as is other early literature from witness bases and developments (century by century) of doctrine, dogma, beliefs, regulations, rituals. There has been steady emergence of the sacraments and an annual formal liturgical pattern. There is also a pyramid style of power and control, feudal in nature with a human society built exclusively on the feudal concept of a king with power over a powerless and vulnerable mass of unnoticed human creatures. Coexisting is an elitist and self-styled holiness in a seemingly hybrid concept given the title of 'discernment' in which the seemingly authoritarian clerical caste is engaged in choosing what was dogma, and the unidentified masses called the People of God are being groomed to accept and obey. This is a pyramid within which a descending assumption of complete power of princes of the church, seen to be the embodiment of God (though God is acknowledged on the one hand as divine) on earth. Unfortunately, there is also a growing disdain for those outside the church, sometimes given the exaggerated title of heretic. This is accompanied by a rigid and public punishment system for those who voice dissent, or who are deemed to be in error. There seems also to be an elastic set of boundaries, which have been of political as well as religious import to provide certainty in addressing public or private dilemmas, problems, difficulties and mysteries.

There is a firm reductionism in which the mind of God was assumed to be known by the clerical leaders of the tradition, allowing complete control physically, intellectually, socially, emotionally and spiritually of the believers. There is a hybrid concept of Tradition, in which, due to the pontifical secret and the duplicitous evading of Canon Law dictates, the faithful has understood: 'Do as I say, not as I do' as a firm assumption promoted by popes, Curia and hierarchy. The process of papal edict or considered judgment or church-approved Doctors of the Church, that the Catholic Church was always right, is promoted as correct and beyond criticism. By contrast, anyone presuming to question or to criticise is plainly wrong. The clerical caste has been the princely leadership frequenting the triumphalist halls of kings and royalty, particularly in countries of Mediterranean proximity.

Examples like burning of women as evil witches, and the excesses of the Spanish Inquisition have highlighted the power and control by the perfect leaders over sinful faithful, who must be rescued from evil. The inevitable consequence of this spiritual and emotional abuse is the punishment by the assignment of sinfulness. This has led to assumptions that any time and without notice, the princes of the church could demand total control of prayer and penitence of the hapless believers. Many have accepted that such entitlement meant indulgences which would result in eternal relief from the privations of this life. The emphasis on sinful humanity, bound by regulations to pursue penance and adoration of the Real Presence in the monstrance rather than (not as well as) frequent reception of the Real Presence in the Eucharist has meant that intrusion of these practices obscured the message of Jesus, rather than enhanced it, and highlights the presence of clericalism.

The Mystical Body of Christ

Idealised and ideologised concepts of the person of Jesus, divine and human, highlight instinctive visualisation of the person of Jesus being seen as pale skinned, blue eyed and northern European in appearance. Emphases point to the life hereafter, founded on pious daily practices of particular piety like novenas, first Fridays, Five Saturdays, lectio divina, coupled with the emphasis on the doing, rather than on the being, in relationship with the Triune God of the Apostles Creed. Focus is always on the submissiveness of Jesus, who submitted to the Will of the Father, through the aegis of the Holy Spirit, in acceptance of the burden of humanity's sin, in acceptance of his passion, death and resurrection. Jesus as redeemer and life-giver is to accept the pain of man's (sexist language here is offensive) rejection through sin, through ignorance. Pyramidal governance has been built on a monarchical system of acquisition of lands, art, artefacts, understood as God's will, even though lack of skills and silly decisions result at times in mismanagement. Practice of the monarchical caste is that of encouraging the ordinary man (not including women, who rarely rated separately) to reach for holiness through aesthetic lifelong practices, especially the wearing of scapulars and other sacramentals. Emergence of special saints is at times idolised as well as idealised, as a means of modelling how to maintain a shaky relationship with Jesus Christ, knowing always that Purgatory awaited, and Hell might be close.

At times, there seems to be an impetus with an emphasis on the appalling approach of enduring penance at the will of an angry God who nevertheless was supposed to love us. Discovery that papal infallibility meant doing just as the pope directed, included acts of penitence for little children in foreign lands, to hopefully attain closeness to God, thereby putting a myriad of boundaries into daily life to avoid sin. Scrupulous acceptance of the details of rules and regulations regarding reception of all sacraments, has meant hoping to somehow win or earn God's approval. It has also meant handing over to the clerical caste the choices of how we, the people, live, pushing excessive generosity to maintain the priest, the school, the parish. Papal promotion of mystical figures like Terese Martin, the Little Flower, along with Bernadette Soubirous, the Fatima children, Maria Goretti, has modelled the preferred behaviour of good Catholics, especially women and girls. Promotion of Mary's apparitions in Ireland, Portugal, France, Mudjegorge and beyond, has been seen as preferred channels and attitudes of prayer. Examples also of ideology turned into faith like the self-flagellation and other extreme penances and privations of the ecclesial movements favoured by Pope John Paul ll, were to help us to gain a place in Heaven. The utter absence of the understanding and the respect due to each person as a creature of the Triune God, has not left us imbued with the responsibility of becoming the very best human being in the Jesus manner that we are capable of being. The overall impact has many times been akin to oppression, depression and suffering to be endured (rather than an approach towards a real relationship with a loving Triune God), highlighting the intrusion of clericalism.

The People of God

More emphases has been applied to laity and their faith journey, emerging, approaching and around the time of the Vatican Council ll. Maintenance of the pyramidal governance in structures of centralised control has been in the hands of the pope, then the Curia, then the hierarchy, *downwards* to the local parish priest and this structure had the power to dispense sacraments, provide educational opportunity, and allow formation of conscience of the laity. There was also the power to withhold those sacraments without recourse. Emphasis on the priesthood in which the candidate was ontologically changed, somehow above the laity, on the way to being more than human, was believed to be rather closer to being divine. An obsessive focus was placed on boundaries between the sacred and profane, religious and secular, consecrated and professional, philosophical and theological, male and female, heterosexual and homosexual, Christian or other. Distorted theology of the body, not psycho-sexual reality, appeared amid the categorising of those we labelled as acceptable or disordered.

Emergence of the secret and separate life of the clerical caste pointed to emphases which were on power and control. There was a lack of acknowledgment of pastoral need, theological application and suffering resulting from callous clerical behaviour, both sinful and criminal. This behaviour showed no inkling of the damage done to generations of children and vulnerable adults or the existence of the ripple effect on those surrounding such victims. Damaged hierarchical figures controlled all cultural preferences for uniformity through authoritarian edicts and harsh silencing of theologians and truth-tellers. Duplicity in governance was demanded by submission to papal requirements regarding bans on women's ordination and laicisation of priests and the total abrogation of any responsibility in consequent dilemmas, problems, social tragedies. Misogyny and sexist behaviour favoured no respect for difference, diversity, women's wisdom or the plight of children and vulnerable adults so callously abused. This phenomenon existed with a matching disdain for addressing the damage. Refusal to accept responsibility for the diminishment of the laity in favour of the privileged position of all levels of the priestly caste, highlighted yet again the presence of clericalism coupled with a defiant resistance to admit a need for self-analysis as Christian leaders. Unfortunately, this has been coupled with a breathtaking narcissism that allowed entitlement and prestige to take centre-stage at all times.

And today, there are the People in the Pews

As a recent phenomenon to the authoritarian impulses and obsessions of mid-20th century distorted theology, response by educated, ethical lay people, particularly surrounds the creeping infallibility claimed for the reigning popes of the last century and a half. This shows in resistance by the People in the Pews to the thought-control efforts of authoritarian edicts surrounding the dilemmas met in the secular world, especially when addressing vexed questions demanding maturity of conscience and balanced ethical decision making. The emergence of liberation theologies becomes a means of localised support for oppressed and distressed peoples, dismissed by the clerical caste, whose ignorance, lack of compassion and narcissism has been plain to see.

Response to the lack of justice, impatience with clerical ideological explanations of the need for restorationism, appears to be a preference for the control of the faithful. There is a prolonged silence as defence from many of the hierarchical caste. Their attitudes rest on the belief that eventually resentfulness of the noisy faithful would be reined in, and the hierarchs could resume their centuries-old traditional practices as before. There is a similarly impatient response from the laity to the unmasking of the corruption, lack of transparency, duplicity and betrayal experienced as the extent of the clerical child sexual abuse scandals has erupted in so many countries. We are conscious of the expanding influence of educated laity, firmly embedded in an ethical experience of the secular world so scorned by many of the clerical caste. Their influence surfaced as knowledge of daily living understood as God-given. This is the opposite of the ridiculous papal direction about *how* to be 'in the world, not of the world' (John 17). We recognise the acknowledgment of the laity of the emerging responsibility to manage the extraordinary leaps in scientific achievement, even though church terminology still disdained this as secularism, relativism, heresy and the like.

We try to manage around the arrogance and narcissism behind the curial and papal practices of silencing practical theologians, while simultaneously promoting reductionism, restorationism and a distorted view of sainthood to the People in the Pews. We try to be balanced with the parallel practice of obsessive behaviour patterns which were promoted as holy, evidenced by the sometimes distorted understanding of the title of discernment as a practice. We reach carefully towards deepened listening and reflection between the Holy Spirit and the individual. The response to the sufferings of those whose lives were irreparably damaged by callous church practices bent on cover-ups of people in privileged positions, not only but centrally in the world-wide clerical child sexual abuse scandals, shows confusion and pain.

The contrast of being ontologically challenged rather than ontologically changed must emerge, as responsibility for trails of damage and cruelty paraded as holiness, are encountered. We see the tsunami of examples of appalling criminal cover-ups of ongoing clerical child sexual abuse, that are coupled with the resistance to owning responsibility and refusal to initiate the smallest changes for the purposes of restorative justice. This matter is evidenced by the assumption of clerical promises of martyrdom or jail rather than restructure of the seal of confession. We try to respond in the emergence of laity groups who have begun to take full responsibility for regeneration of our ailing church, focusing on a demand for repair of the existing practices of governance. This is in partnership with the responsibility for developing relevant and appropriate practices for faith, hope and love to surface as the main channels we need, to follow the message of Jesus Christ, without the intrusion of the evil influence of clericalism in all its forms.

As Francis, Bishop of Rome, has stated (and we forgive the unconscious sexist comment!) in *Misericordiae Vultus*:

We need constantly to contemplate the mystery of mercy. It is a wellspring of joy, serenity, and peace. Our salvation depends on it. Mercy: the word reveals the very mystery of the Most Holy Trinity. Mercy: the ultimate and supreme act by which God comes to meet us. Mercy: the fundamental law that dwells in the heart of every person who looks sincerely into the eyes of his brothers and sisters on the path of life. Mercy: the bridge that connects God and man, opening our hearts to a hope of being loved forever despite our sinfulness (Francis, 2017).

CHAPTER 3

Theological sign-posts of clericalism

In general, we must look for the theological substance, the Christian mores, and the cultural practices that have been familiar in a Eurocentric Catholic Church over the last few centuries. People in the Pews may not be familiar with the highly technical and closely argued points in many a sacred concept and moral claim, but they certainly know when they are presented with unbalanced or contradictory communications which are titled as church teaching. Now, the church is in such a world-wide crisis that it threatens to overwhelm the whole institution, dimming the message of Jesus, and causing schism, whether declared or undeclared officially. People in the Pews may not be able therefore to articulate the evils, spoken and unspoken, that threaten by spiritual abuse to damage the whole church. So we must rely on investigations, on research, on recognised existing expertise to aid in clarification of some of the confusion surrounding the way forward.

A careful examination of the Irish scenario, by Claffey, Egan and Keenan (2013), gives us an opportunity to identify some theological signposts in Australia of clericalism. If we are to counter clericalism, not just confront it in daily life, we need cool logical approaches and careful analyses. These editors have brought together authors whose expertise provides scope for reflection, recall and remembrance in our own experience. Distinctions which signpost clericalism in their milieux include many startling points from the Irish experience.

Too many new Orders have been founded since Pope John Paul ll provided and promoted this channel as bringing the young back to the Catholic faith. This was also echoed by Australian Professor Des Cahill whose monumental work paralleled that of the Irish scenario, in a presentation in Melbourne, Australia, on 2 August 2018. Restorationism which means restoring the elements of what existed in the past, is a contradiction in terms, as x-generation, y-generation and millennials were mostly never there to come back anyway. Z-generation young people, however, exhibit almost no understanding of loyalty and see no reason to bestir themselves with an age-old controversy seemingly outside their interest and consciousness, as they retreat into their more familiar virtual communities.

One distinction needed is to be sure that 'public opinion' is not seen as a synonymous term for *sensus fidelium* (Claffey et al, 2013). In ensuring that the voice of the laity is heard in structural planning in liturgical, financial, moral theology, cultural understanding, we must promote and facilitate wider theological reflection on what the Holy Spirit is promoting (Claffey et al). Structural improvements need to include formal channels of communication between hierarchy, curial and lay personnel on regular bi-annual calendars, with equal co-responsibility for listening, understanding, accepting, respecting, recognising all views and perspectives without coercion, not pushing aside minority concerns as negative. All perspectives must be included as this channel aids attitudinal change and provides distinctive reasons for modifying personal perspectives as we learn from one another. Truth is served as those consultations are accompanied with prayer and authentic discernment. Obstruction, exclusivity and dismissal, all of which model arrogant claims to truth, cause alienation, disintegration and stalled progress, but so does a false reliance on consensus without thorough critique.

Patience, leading to hope is one channel that allows movement and expansion of perspective. Theological perspectives as stated, using 'see –judge –act' (the Cardijn –YCW way of last century methodology) has three identifiable consequences: first, we can listen carefully to the voices of victims of sexual abuse, of brutality, of oppression, of cruelty; second, we can provide interdisciplinary academic analyses of the various situations; third, we can address theological reflection in order to discover a way through the morass of pain, anger, shame and betrayal. The intention surely must be to provide for the flickering of hope to expand beyond the broken faith of a whole people. Clericalism is seen as an aberration by the Irish authors as it brought abuse of power and a wide malaise within the local Irish church, as it has done in many other national churches including Australia (Claffey et al, 2013). The authors are hopeful that this is a Kairos moment.

No quick fixes (Claffey et al, 2013) exist but new insights and structures are needed and are being provided now. Concern for survivors must be central and ways to handle perpetrators still vary between extreme vengeance and letting go too soon and this is echoed in the presentation of Des Cahill. Cahill explained (2018) that the levels of depravity and depth of distorted emotional landscape of perpetrators rests on a spectrum of abuse. Many paedophiles will say that they firmly believe God made them that way, so no guilt exists.

So we are faced with the dilemma of what possible action can be taken that allows for restorative justice to be central to the deliberations. These sentiments have highlighted many elements. Not included are the expertise and expanded knowledge and academic prowess existing within the laity. Many notables in hierarchy are so dismissive that they don't appear to know how much they don't know! Nineteenth and twentieth century preoccupation with making education universal highlights the cultural change from when humble peasantry had individual experience only. The priestly caste that spawned clericalism identified, interpreted and insisted that they knew the mind of God.

In one paper, one of the editors, Joe Egan, refers to the 'brokenness' of all Christians: 'vulnerable, divided among themselves and visibly disheartened by hypocrisy, double standards and manifold failures in discipleship and in leadership' (Claffey et al, 2013). Egan ends with the wish that 'with enduring trust and resilient hope', the church, – that is all of us – can face the task of renewal, regeneration, responsiveness and repair that faces us.

The renowned journalist, John L. Allen Jnr looks carefully at hierarchical authority, priesthood, Church and State relations and attitudes towards the world with a paper titled 'Between Reform and Realism' (Claffey et al, 2013). He notes a list of specific phenomena certainly worth our careful examination: impact of sexual abuse on Mass attendance; defections from the Church; evangelical prospects of Catholicism in 21st century; seminary formation as presently practised; present state of the discipline of moral theology; liturgical and spiritual practice; and emergence of new liturgies for repentance and healing, specific to the sexual abuse scandals (Claffey et al, 2013). He defines his role as a journalist from America, with a focus on the Vatican and global Catholicism plus an intention to identify currents and global phenomena relevant to the current crisis. 'A new Catholic geography is coming into focus, one in which leadership and vision will no longer be concentrated primarily in the West' (Claffey et al, 2013).

In examining hierarchical authority, Allen describes the two prevailing elements: 'the appalling abuse itself and the systematic failure of Church authorities to correct, choosing rather to hide it all'. Allen contrasts sexual abuse crisis and breakdown with the systematic failure of authority to correct the problem. When the response in the *Melbourne Catholic* archdiocesan magazine (author unidentified) offers an article about child safety, at least it highlights: 'We need to create a culture of safeguarding children, led from the highest levels within the Church and adhered to by every single adult in the archdiocese'. It is to be assumed that the writer here is referring to all adults rather than single but not married adults.

Allen's own two fantasies are contrasted: the possible wiping out of authoritative church structures with the belief that the church can put this crisis aside and return to status quo, meaning things as usual. He contrasts a list of concerns: democratic revolution with monarchical restoration; episcopal power to censure priestly faculties or a lay-led corporate-style body to do the same function; top-down movement (curial-based?) with bottom-up challenge. He contrasts papal infallibility with the voice of the *sensus fidelium*; hierarchical freedom in financial and governance procedures with tighter controls in all matters beyond faith and morals. He advises that all this is called 'ad intra' as distinct from 'ad extra' in which pressure is from the secular world i.e. media, lawyers, police, prosecutors and the like. This, he indicates, is exemplified by the American bishops' 'zero policy regarding paedophilia, but where 37 priests active in ministry are facing current charges of such abuse'.

We are alerted to an anomaly now. So when Cardinal Ladaria in his capacity as Prefect of the Congregation for the Doctrine of the Faith, 'recalls that when Pope St John Paul ll taught in his apostolic letter, *Ordinatio Sacerdotalis* of 22 May 1994, that priestly ordination is limited to male Christians, he did not teach ex cathedra. John Paul ll invoked what has been called the infallibility of the ordinary, universal magisterium- to be held definitely and absolutely' as in *Lumen Gentium*, 25 (*The Tablet* 9 June 2018). This is in line apparently with the ad intra category. As the writer of *The Tablet* article, Gerald O'Collins SJ alerts us: Is it a clearly established fact that the bishops around the world have been unanimous and constant in teaching that women should be excluded from priestly ordination?' (O'Collins, 2018)

Allen has identified a number of outcomes about a confused hierarchy: the claim that local bishops are not agents of the Vatican, but have their own jurisdictions. The psychological impact of the enormity of this crisis has made bishops less deferential to Roman influences in some places. Some bishops acknowledge prevailing scepticism to their traditionally-wielded authority, accepting at least some blame for today's scandal regardless of the norms of apostolic succession (in Claffey et al, 2013). Allen called this 'ferment over authority'.

On the impact of the world-wide crisis in the priesthood, Allen highlights: 'a devastating impact on the public image' of priests, who all are suspected of active paedophilia. This is in spite of increases in candidature in Africa and Asia. Bishops and priests now operate on uncomfortable levels of trust because bishops have used 'draconian measures' (in Claffey et al, 2013) on priests, but minimised their own culpability. Lately, information from Africa about the 'use' of nuns as comfort for bishops and priests wishing to avoid contamination of HIV/Aids, has surfaced. The blame game extends to pointing to the Curia, to Pope John Paul ll and separately to Pope Emeritus Benedict XVl.

Theologically, the family concept of pope, hierarchy and the laity is currently at a very low ebb (Claffey et al, 2013). Pastorally effective priests now see themselves as the butt of the whole crisis, as their rights seem to be ignored: 'there is a conviction in some quarters that Catholicism has reacted to one injustice with another' (Claffey et al, 2013), even to the move by Benedict XVl to laicise priests without a judicial process. Such major confusion in the hierarchy, who have persisted in claims that they are entitled exclusively to command the lives of the People in the Pews, and this with little respect for primacy of conscience and with expanding areas of infallibility! Rescue in the form of the voices of the *sensus fidelium*, who in some cases, like with the promulgation of *Humanae Vitae*, do not receive the content because of serious flaws in moral, sexual, biological and logical knowledge.

Confusion, says Allen, over all the various forms of what is to count as sexual abuse is rife in the corridors of Catholicism include actual physical contact by a priest with a minor; pornography about children; too intimate conversations; inappropriate sexual humour and other similar matters called 'boundary issues' (in Claffey et al, 2013). Resistance to change regarding the celibacy issue is central to Catholicism, seen as a Latin-rite requirement, and believed to be free of suspicion: 'priestly celibacy is a visible hallmark of that identity' and also that no evidence points to celibate males are more prone to paedophilia than other males.

This is echoed by Joanne McCarthy, whose article in the Melbourne *Age* (22 September 2018) highlights church leaders grooming of adults: 'The Catholic Church had to take responsibility for clergy who preyed on vulnerable people as it had been forced to acknowledge child-sex abuse' stating also that research in USA found that 'four times as many adult women and twice as many adult men were sexually abused by clergy than children' . Challenges to mandated celibacy for the male priesthood of today is clearly warranted because McCarthy uses Australian research from the Australian *Encompass* program which suggests 'at least 5000 men and 10,000 women had been in secret sexual relationships or interactions with Australian Catholic clergy over decades, with "horrendous" consequences for some'.

In the matter of Church/State relations, Allen highlights the existence of what is called secularism, in which the Western world is considered godless but the Catholic Church is seen as very separate and godly in its perspectives. Allen claims there are several ways that clashes will or have emerged like raids by State authorities looking for secret documents. Such expressions regarding accountability of the church rather than cover-up activities are viewed positively by some, but as authentic Catholic hostility by others. Though thoroughly dualistic in approach, they are seen as new flashpoints at this time (in Claffey et al, 2013).

The church can *not* now be a voice of conscience. 'The crisis has put a serious dent in that situation, and funding is now an issue at diplomatic levels – a serious credibility gap. The church is not 'above the law' (Claffey et al, 2013) as it wrestles with two important issues: autonomy and accountability. Allen asks: Does this amount to the State compelling the Church to revise its theology of priesthood? The dualistic approach of the church involves a fortress mentality of Vatican Council 1, and an open-door policy of Vatican Council ll, and it is contradictory, adversarial and based within the concept of clericalism. Hostility, tribalist approaches and ideological stances are evident. These stances range from controversies about liturgy to moral questions, to the autonomy of conscience and more, but they could highlight a credible diversity if couched in respect, positive attitudes, non-judgmental listening. Too often communication is stilled, guarded, and controlled, thereby dulling our efforts to live and love according to the Jesus message.

Allen maintains that political stances of one group namely doctrinal dissent, inadequate priestly discipline, relativism and moral decay are matched by political stances of the opposite namely celibacy, a negative view of sex, patriarchy and authoritarianism. Nowhere does clericalism emerge in these profiles as each splinter group gropes for the media spotlight. Allen suggests there is a need for a renewed spirituality of communion. Can we stay among the comfortable tribal scenarios of yesteryear or will we choose to meet and communicate with honesty those whose diversity makes us uncomfortable? As Allen comments: 'all Catholics must think of themselves as (they are) the architects and evangelists for this spirituality' (in Claffey et al, 2013). So where do we go from here?

Another significant paper by Irish theologian Geraldine Smyth OP is titled: 'What lies beneath? From Purity and Power to Crisis and Kairos'. Smyth claims urgently and at once that there is a need to probe beyond settled opinion (in Claffey et al, 2013) in church, society, culture and public policy. Of course, this presumes that we are not still trying to work out the contradiction fostered by early theology to live in the world but not of the world (John 17). Theologically, we must (not just should) examine fixed doctrinal formulations and non-doctrinal 'factors and power relations in the Church's life and its various orders and agents'.

Many questions erupt as a result for Smyth and we must (not 'should') also examine each of the questions deeply and thoroughly. What lies beneath what seems to be? What is to count as truth and loyalty? What lies beneath current theses, praxis, and practice? What informs any world views today? What informs our ideas on perfection? What do we mean about a need to change? Smyth identifies from a theological perspective 'our easy dichotomies': sin and grace, clerical and lay, sacred and profane, church and society. She connects what lies beneath to the 'spirit, motifs and thought structure of the Gospel', highlighting the 'perennial dysfunction between conformity and hypocrisy, between purity of identity and purity of heart'.

Her very significant question: 'How do we correlate any of the preceding questions with faith in the Holy Spirit who renews and makes all one? Referring of course to the worldwide crisis of clerical child sexual abuse, Smyth suggests that through analogy, we can learn more deeply of the past and its present pain. Through listening to untold narratives of sufferers, we can try to understand that suffering. Through giving space and time to this learning curve, we can engender compassion and remembering. Through careful understanding, we can learn how to use expressions of genuine repentance and then to begin honest mourning. Through recognition of the distortions of cover-ups and powerful hierarchical dismissals in the past, we can begin the gigantic challenge of restorative and restitutional justice.

We must face as much as it takes (remembering Jesus' comment about forgiving seventy-seven times, not seven times); recognising that the victims' needs are diverse and deeply painful. They may eventually try to progress towards a point where they can contemplate the possibility of forgiving perpetrators, church institutions, and those on their journey who did not respond. Through humility and deep regret, we must recognise and address the possibility that for some sufferers, we will never be forgiven. We must accept that response without criticism or anger. Through careful planning, both personally and institutionally, we must work to right the wrongs with generosity, with compassion and with ongoing honesty. Through trilectic thinking patterns (meaning the practice of including as many options as possible for finding balanced responses), rather than dualistic contrasts (meaning two extremes only), we must always include the bridge between the two ends of the relevant spectrum. In this way, we allow the indwelling of the Holy Spirit to help us to discern, to manage options, to identify mistakes, to patiently balance theory, practice and creativity so that we manage to inform ourselves as we approach the paradigm change indicated by Vatican Council ll and further directed by Pope Francis.

This must be done through exploration of writings of a variety of theologians, including feminist and liberation theologians, where we must critique carefully the previous separation of private and public spheres. Comfortable resorting to binary thinking patterns limit our ability to be listening to the Holy Spirit, so it is authentic and accurate discernment that will flourish rather than be limited by ideology parading as faith. If we apply these approaches to this aim, we will find that by careful conversation by theologians and the People in the Pews, we can find understanding of the various diverse perspectives. This will lead to the expanding of our own perspective to include the value for all cultures in our global church of elements of each of the theologies which have been dismissed by recent papal edict as wrong therefore heretical. The power of including all these diverse perspectives as we stop to listen to the Holy Spirit is what tensegrity means. This power can hold the elements of the whole of the Church together as we strive to follow the message of Jesus: his way, his truth, his life.

Smyth comments that 'two legacies in Ireland of untruth, suppressed pain and injustice are not unrelated'. The chorus of communication by Australian groups trying to induce Australian bishops into conversation is not unrelated either. Current comment throughout this project from the People in the Pews is undeniable evidence.

Church doctrines have allowed a list of very contradictory behaviours to thrive in our Catholic tradition. The practice of unalloyed violence as exemplified by the methods of the Spanish Inquisition and by torture and killing of women, some with healing knowledge in their villages, as evil witches come to mind. So does the 'barefoot-and-pregnant' phenomenon of Catholic history by deliberate oppression of women through dismissal of unjust behaviour within marriage. So does the clerical abuse of children covered up in favour of the apparent right of MOTHER Church (irony indeed!). This is accompanied by dismissal of the existence of homosexuality as part of God's creation. So it is obvious that false civility, obstruction, untruthful distortion and authoritarian mindsets white-ant the message of Jesus, says Smyth.

'That culture has infected our political, familial, social and religious institutions and relations with neighbouring countries.' Thus hassled, over many centuries since Constantine, towards deliberate use of war and deception, this has induced powerlessness of the People in the Pews. So has the papal edicts using all manner of concepts like limbo, indulgences, excessive promotion of pious practices meant to support that ideology of being in the world but not of the world (John 17).

'There is a lingering cult of glorified violence, sacrifice and martyrdom in the cause of purity and freedom; the myth of violence as cleansing is not far from the surface. It is time to relinquish this religio-political imagery of self-sacrifice – a soteriology of blood mysticism and of violence as necessary and redemptive – given the transcending cause. The deeper soteriological implications here also need to be engaged critically by revisiting theologies of salvation that sacralise human suffering – via sacrificially-focused readings of sin and atonement theology – a hermeneutical enterprise' says Smyth.

She reminds us: 'It was Aquinas who made the breakthrough in reinstating nature at a time when the prevailing teaching overlooked created nature in favour of an Augustinian emphasis on sin infecting grace'. So the application of the continuum here shows us sin on the one hand, nature as the bridge and grace on the other hand. Again the People in the Pews are faced with the internal divisiveness and binary thinking when Augustine and Aquinas are pitted against each other as though the whole future of the church belief system relies exclusively on this dilemma.

We might take issue with Smyth, perhaps, when she claims: 'it is God's purpose in creating, saving and sanctifying us, to make us more than human – indeed, divine – in and with our bodies. We are called at once in and beyond nature to be made utterly new'. Aquinas' vision is the 'teleological dynamism in creation', she points out. Is it not, though, that we are called to co-create through the aegis of the Holy Spirit, using human frailty, understanding and connection, to further the divine purpose, rather than to aspire to become somehow divine? There is an important distinction to be made here: that humankind is created in imago dei, in the image of God, rather than the human being as divine.

Reference to the work of neuroscientist Paul MacLean (2018) yields information regarding new knowledge of the brain of every human: there is the reptilian brain, the mammalian brain and the neocortex. The use of the term, triune, by MacLean brings echoes of the Triune God emerging as evidence of our humankind as creation, as in *imago dei*. Yes, there is 'the paradox of human knowledge and freedom as connatural with the divine purpose' (in Claffey et al, 2013). Smyth's point, that 'human nature, however sinful, weak and liable to great evil, is created in imago dei for the self-transcending end of union with divine glory' (Smyth, 2013), does not necessarily imply that humankind becomes divine, only is joined with the divine, through the love and compassion of our Triune God. Would that these considerations were to occupy the research, the discernment activity, the content for prayer, rather than the pomp, privilege and power structures so beloved of those mired in clericalism. Chan and Chia (2003) give us much to study about the business of genetic science and humankind, so the idea of a theology of personhood begins to solidify and the questions begin to be shaped in the backs of our minds. We must rely on theologians to point the way forward towards deep understanding of the new elements that challenge us today.

Our little parish experience when a previous archbishop came some years ago on the official parish visit highlighted clericalism as a case in point: representatives of many groups in the parish were called to meet with the archbishop as we were told that he wished to hear how the parish worked. The conversation consisted of various individuals who commented on their own areas of pastoral involvement and inevitably we were expected to evaluate the success of the parish priest in this process. The supercilious nature of the hierarch's replies, regarding the remarkable work of our parish priest, showed that he could not quite accept the quality of the leadership shown to us, and he was consistent in using the tone of dismissal, including his comment that he was in the habit of driving past our church when Mass was in progress to check to see whether the patronage of the parishioners was still at maximum levels, which it was. The tone was parallel to the supercessionism of clericalist Christianity towards the Jewish traditions, except that it was supercessionary of the exalted prelate towards the humble parish Eucharistic celebrations each week.

Inevitably, consequences of such distortions include: 'The truth falls casualty in a culture of complicity in idealised constructions of the family and Church, with actual toleration of domestic violence and violent abuse as the lesser evil to damaging the patriarchal ideals of marriage or clericalism. The cognitive dissonance fails to register. And no-one takes responsibility' (in Claffey et al, Smyth, 2013).

A Ministry of Listening

In a 'Faith and Reason' paper for *America* (2018), John J. Strynkowski has given us food for thought in which he indicates how bishops can help heal the church in a time of crisis. Seven separate crises are listed and the author immediately asks for serenity and clear thinking. 'The nature of the human mind is to seek answers and solutions as quickly as possible. The nature of conscience is to slow down the mind in order to gather facts before reaching a judgment and then proceeding to a gradual and communal deliberation that precedes solutions and action. Unfortunately, all too often the urgings of conscience are ignored and the deliberation that can also be called discernment is short-circuited'.

This is a form of reductionism, and as such, can *not* provide decisions and action suitable for 21st century milieux. Without the insertion of the principles first of the Community of Inquiry, described in a later chapter, in which all persons can listen and learn from each other, from the Church, and from the world environment in which they live, we must face the possibility that reductionism will expand, and mercy and compassion will become a diminishing behaviour. Without the added inclusion of the conceptual complexity of theo-tensegrity, and the intended and unintended consequences of not understanding the harm we do, a responsible option for the poor is unattainable as a response to the message of Jesus.

This also emerges as restorationism, because the resistance to change of paradigm means that we will always be burdened by the edicts and cultures of pre-Vatican ll boundaries. The unavoidable consequences mean that the Holy Spirit has little opportunity to support those whose faith asks for succour and relief in anguished circumstances. We don't have a right to deprive children, vulnerable adults, People in the Pews or vulnerable priests and bishops of the support of the Holy Spirit. Often, their road has been dotted with harassment instead of the lived experience of the message of Jesus.

The second area for listening that Strynkowski describes concerns the need that 'the laity must be increasingly involved in the discernment leading to solutions and action' (2018). This would actually be a manifestation of what Pope Francis has called the constitutive synodality of the church. The word synod means journeying together, he says. The author insists that 'the pilgrim people of God is called to constant walking together in order to discern how our history and tradition can be used for its evangelising mission today'. Attitudinal change comes slowly, but with the insertion of the message of Jesus in various democratic life experiences of the young, the vulnerable, the People in the Pews have a set of tools that can at least signal a beginning for the pilgrim journey. 'Circularity: that careful, mutual listening among all the members of the church (laity, women and men in consecrated life, clergy) gradually and hopefully, leading to a consensus on decisions to be made by those charged with governance (pastors, bishops, pope)' is part of the author's indicators for this aim. 'Thus, the laity become fully active participants in the journey of the church, the process of discernment and evangelisation', says Strynkowski (2018).

The third area of listening concerns the concept of affective collegiality which is a distinct change from the autonomy of pre-Vatican ll days. 'Affective collegiality ranges from the spiritual bond of communion to the various levels of contact between bishops, both informal and formal, and culminating in special events with possible juridical consequences, such as synods and ecumenical councils. These latter are known as instances of effective collegiality because of the effects they may have on doctrine and pastoral practice' (2018).

The next signpost for listening concerns the concept of 'unity in diversity'. 'Prelates who attended the Vatican ll deliberations were mired in Vatican I thinking with closed and binary strategies, unconcerned with the suffering of the People in the Pews, who it was seen needed to be shown their evil ways. Those men arrived to be given documents prepared in the same thinking pattern before they arrived. It was called Neo-Scholasticism' (Strynkowski, 2018). However, 'As the bishops embarked on their synodal journey, they came to know each other (affective collegiality), the challenges to the church in different parts of the world (e.g., atheism in Europe, poverty in Latin America, the effects of colonialism in Africa, the fragility of Christianity in Asia) and the renewal in scriptural, liturgical and theological studies' (2018). What a challenging agenda, and what a need for cool heads and careful collaborative thinking. As Strynkowski states: 'in the course of their four-year walk together they chose renewal and approved almost unanimously in every case documents that have provided reform and guidance to the church since then'.

When a proposal from the German bishops regarding the organising of an internal forum for conversation about couples in irregular living circumstances was accepted within the Synod of 2014-2015 on the Family, two thirds of the bishops accepted and a minority resisted, voting against the internal forum. Strynkowski points to the 'minority of bishops who have taken issue with this act of the *ordinary magisterium* of the bishops and have failed to give the religious submission of intellect and will demanded by Vatican II'. This has been scandalous for the People in the Pews, but the situation needed firm counselling, careful understanding, dismissal of provocative defiance and general politicisation of dissent. Care and compassion for minority positions does not mean giving way or allowing 'simplistic denunciations of a teaching' (2018).

An interesting feature of the concept of affective collegiality is that 'the bishops are not only not accountable *to* one another and *to* the pope, but also not accountable *for* one another'. Because there is no presence of the People in the Pews, it is very easy for this focus to lose momentum and fall deep into the very cult of clericalism that has contributed to the disengagement of the hierarchy. So networking on a regular basis must accompany the best qualities of what affective collegiality is meant to be. This obviously means careful, ongoing, open-minded listening. It includes walking the journey of the Other, and ensuring that priorities are not unbalanced in a vain attempt to privilege the point of view of the hierarchical position. Strynkowski acknowledges that it is possible for a bishop to disagree with the pope, but recognises that 'what is not appropriate is the use of media and partisan cliques, in an effort to 'win' some obscure matter or to induce a certain caste of mind in the People in the Pews'.

We sense the internal stress of Strynkowski when he concludes that short-term solutions are not enough today. 'Issues like seminary formation, clericalism and polarisation – indeed, the very ordering of the church – demand long-term solutions that are best addressed by gradual discernment leading to broad consensus on the part of the college of bishops'. It is of course important that while these matters are being discerned, we, as church, as pilgrims, as seekers, as the People in the Pews, are not led into side issues that confuse, complicate and thereby control the outcomes needed, before the Holy Spirit responds to the listening and begins to fuse grace, compassion and internal connection to the sacred community of the church in the 21st century.

We would do well to heed the connection made by Ilia Delio as we listen, too:

> Now let us ponder and move with the image of the Trinity. Picture God ... loving justice and what is right ... being One in whom we place our hope. Envision Jesus, the one who is perhaps more human ... "I am with you always" ...Third, imagine the Holy Spirit, who moves in and among us, helps us grow, change and develop as better Christians ... Living trinitarian faith means living from and for our magnificent, all-merciful God, living with and for others, as Jesus taught and did, and trusting in a Spirit that moves throughout our bodies, our communities, and our world. (Delio, 2016)

CHAPTER 4

Three vexed areas of complexity in clericalism today

James Alison's explanation from inside the priestly cult
So many People in the Pews were affected by the emergence of the phenomenon of homosexuality into the public arena in late 20th century. Families, parents, siblings, had to come to terms with the truth, the lies, the ignorance, the vicious tongues, and so much more as adjustments within families were made – supposedly in line with what 'Mother' Church directed. The title of mother in relation to the experience of the People in the Pews, of church behaviours, is a travesty.

A vocation to priesthood meant, for a young gay man, a chance to give meaning to his life. This provided a channel for a relevant future by delegating the uncomfortable shame of being different or not normal, or coping with dismissal as inferior and sinful with the consequence of alienation and ostracism. The serious shutting down of an individual emotional landscape often led to emotional and sexual immaturity, and meant compartmentalisation and a double life. Isolation from the home community and the home parish *and* exclusion from normal cultural communal activities led to desperate efforts to find relief and acceptance in some sort of community milieu. Safety seemed to reside in seminary formation where emphasis on moral theology, ethics, ritual, study of biblical texts was paramount. This, however, was without the exegesis and interpretation available through research methodologies, particular writings of certain doctors of the church. An implied compartmentalisation of emotional confusion led to the slow realisation of emerging sexuality and the trap which meant living that double life.

Eventual relief in traumatic acceptance of a personal homosexual nature was managed without having a way of leading an uncomplicated service to the People in the Pews, but declaiming the Vatican emphasis regarding the evil of homosexuality – a contradiction indeed. That crushing oppression of coping with the intrinsically-disordered label, led to the splintering of personality and consequently to dramatic decisions about lifestyle, personal relationships, fractured parish responses, and total assigned shame. The concept of mandated celibacy of priests drew some gay men because it promised a safety net which seemed to provide acceptance, safety, structure, and a pathway past that assigned shame and the accompanying attribution of guilt.

Trust, respect, connection, inclusivity were believed to be within reach so with warm and healing hearts, priestly vocations expanded till the strident echoes of the papal edict: 'intrinsically-disordered', crashed into their lives and the trap that James Alison (*The Tablet*, 4 August 2018) described, was complete. Inevitably, living daily life became, therefore, an existence on two levels, where managing his private life became a contradiction because that edict required continuous public assent to the homophobia inherent in the intention and outcome of a pope's 'infallible' encyclical.

Unforgivably, connections were constructed between gay priests and paedophilia. Even now, decades later, this furphy has not been totally stifled (Snipe, 2018). Homosexuality and paedophilia are opposite as part of a condition within one personality. Consequently, detailed and long-term education for hierarchy, priests and the People in the Pews must be established urgently. Perceived and apparent dangers emanating from the conflicted state that impacted individuals discovered recently has resulted in psychic suffering. 'Coming Out' is studded with pitfalls because the People in the Pews would be, and often are, scandalised. A whiff of suspicion surrounding the gay priest would mean that the carefully crafted future in a career within the higher echelons of hierarchical splendour would recede or disappear. A priest in the family was traditionally treated by family as an honour, and it has been understood as the family giving the candidate to God, so the conflicted gay man is faced with a sentence of the life-long penance of alienation and loneliness. It was learned – sometimes harshly – that the condition of celibacy as a future lifestyle contained rules and regulations, codes and specific culture, bounded and constrained personal discipline, in ever-increasing circles, and that this scenario must never be breached. The People in the Pews had little idea that such harshness was deliberate and ongoing.

Outcomes of such dangers enclose the gay man inside an iron loyalty within the condition we now call clericalism, as a means of psychological survival. Consequences for the mature gay man included keeping the rules down to the most precise form of aspirational piety and ritual. Eventually, does life seem to be a round of prescribed and proscribed mechanical moves? Robert Harris (2016) seemed to think so. Do these requirements provide no attention to the personal feelings, psycho-sexual health and possible nervous exhaustion for a gay man who may well have believed, or have known, that his vocation is real, but whose experience of hierarchical edict has shattered this belief?

It is important to attend at a deep level to the experience and knowledge of James Alison, who wrote for *The Tablet*. We must recognise and understand what this gay priest and theologian tells us of his understanding of what is undoubtedly the scourge of clericalism. We are indebted to him for his honesty, his insights and must learn from his knowledge, understanding and experience. In the first of two extensive *Tablet* feature articles (4 August 2018), Alison explains what he has titled 'Caught in a trap of dishonesty'. He highlights the ingrained hypocrisy and the double standard, well-known by clerics and hierarchs in the Roman Curia as well as in his home country. The first significant element of clericalism is careerism: 'plenty of people in authority sort-of-knew what was going on, and had known throughout the clerics' respective careers. The informal rule in the Catholic Church – the last remaining outpost of enforced homosociality in the Western world – is strictly 'don't ask, don't tell' (Alison, p. 10). And the People in the Pews knew nothing of these phenomena.

The second significant element of clericalism here is the demand, which became popular in conservative circles from 2002 onwards, in some individual countries and not others, that the priesthood be purged of gay men. Alison identified that investigative journalists were to identify informal gay networks of friendship, patronage – and potential for blackmail.

The third significant element of clericalism is the 'massively disproportionate numbers of gay men in the clergy, but highlight the refusal of the Roman authorities to engage in any kind of publicly accountable, adult discussion of this fact' and so collective dishonesty and psychosexual immaturity dogs the lives of all gay clergy.

The fourth element of clericalism that Alison wants to record is the 'rage at a collective clerical dishonesty that renders farcical the claim to be teachers of anything at all, let alone divine truth. Jesus becomes credible through witnesses, not corrupt party-line pontificators'. Alison thinks that particular interventions, whether by civil authority or papal mandate, are always going to run aground.

Incredibly, Alison records for us the various delicate diversity of situations of gay clerical culture needing to make precise 'distinctions: between innocent friendship, sexually charged admiration, abusive sexual suggestion, emotional blackmail, financial blackmail, recognition of genuine talent, genuine love lived platonically, genuine love lived with sexual intimacy, sexual favours granted with genuine freedom, sexual favours granted out of fear or in exchange for promotion, covering peccadillos for a friend, covering graver matters for a rival in exchange for some benefit, not wanting to know too much about other people's lives, or obsessively wanting to know too much about them. Let alone the usual rancours of break-ups, career disappointments, petty jealousies, bitterness, revenge'. Alison laments 'the issue of a gay cleric's personal relationship status – single, partnered, widower, serially available' adding 'A stably partnered and emotionally balanced priest can no more be publicly honest than a deeply tortured one with many partners' and 'Of course, we know that the partnered ones are the healthy ones'... 'In the clerical closet, dishonesty is functional, honesty is dysfunctional, and the absence or presence of circumspect sexual practice between adult males is irrelevant' (Alison, p. 12). The People in the Pews can only acknowledge and begin to support the physical, emotional and spiritual suffering that he is chronicling for posterity.

Explosively, Alison states: 'A far, far greater proportion of the clergy, particularly the senior clergy, is gay than anyone has been allowed to understand, even the bishops and cardinals themselves'. He explains that Pope Benedict XVl commissioned a report which delivered a serious shock: 'Part of their shock has to have been their fear at how the faithful would be scandalised if they had any idea. They were right to be afraid, and the faithful *are* going to have an idea as the implosion of the closet accelerates'. And the People in the Pews are scandalised, not about the condition of homosexuality but by the hypocrisy, the duplicity, the defiance of the hierarchy to maintain control at whatever cost to the priests in the parishes, whichever category they had been assigned.

Another element of this complicated scenario is the thrust to 'weed out the gays' because 'The clerical crusaders in this area turn out to be gay themselves – in some cases, so deeply in denial that they don't know it' and a very tragic comment added by Alison: 'Some are very sadly disturbed souls who cannot but try to clean outwardly what they cannot admit to being inwardly. These can't be helped since Church teaching reinforces their hell'. Alison laments: 'For honesty is effectively forbidden by a Church teaching that tells you that you are an intrinsically heterosexual person who is inexplicably suffering from a grave objective disorder called "same-sex attraction"'.

Alison has not mentioned gay aversion therapy, but to be immersed in such a program would be absolute hell. Alison shows also that the clerical closet is not influenced by the 1960s liberality or the culpability of Vatican ll bishops or the blame-the-gays mentality prevailing late in the last century. 'The idea was that the new breed of John Paul ll hardliners would sort it out', commenting also 'This is not a matter of left or right, traditional or progressive, good or bad, chaste or practising; nor even a matter of twenty-five years of Karol Wojtyla's notoriously poor judgment of character, though all these feed into it'. The People in the Pews need the voice of Alison to help us begin to understand.

His conclusion is stark: 'It is a systemic structural trap, and if we are to get out of it, it must be described in such a way as to recognise that unknowing innocence as much as knowing guilt, well-meaning error as well as malice, has been, and is, involved in both its constitution and its maintenance'. So whatever the chinks in Alison's perspective as he tries to describe this situation within our clerical caste, we must respect, listen deeply and have real compassion for the people whose lives he has described and which is experienced as entrapment.

Authoritarianism: John Paul ll, Benedict XVl, George Pell and Matt Nelson

John Paul ll was a complex and large personality whose early life was marred by the evil of communism in Poland, and the loss of each of his parents very early in life. He was so familiarised with intrusive behaviours and insistence by communistic authority from vicious and niggardly Russian and Polish satellite rulers, that he may not have realised the extent of his own authoritarianism.

In some ways, Benedict XVl seems to have made a commitment to follow the safe direction of his predecessor after the student riots in his own country in the decade that followed the deliberations of Vatican ll. However, the silencing of some 500 theologians during his abruptly ended papacy distinguishes him in a negative and nasty way as being unable to see the good or the important content of any work of theology not fully in line with his own views. Neither man seems to have exhibited any insight into or understanding of the norms and stresses which accompanied the responsibilities of being a married couple, or of the unpredictable elements of health, mental anguish, or general suffering in daily life. Total emphases on moral edicts built on binary thinking patterns (where everything is viewed as black and white) with no recognition of the intended let alone unintended consequences of the promulgations of their many exhortations, speeches, rulings is evident. So is the ignorance of medical and psychological knowledge available, exhibiting abysmal ignorance and quite callous disregard for the People in the Pews. Authority, for both these popes, enveloped in medieval traditions of Church Militant and Church Triumphant and even the eternal truth of church (institutionally), was exclusively formulated towards this direction to the past. No understanding, no mercy, no compassion, and no justice on behalf of the poor, vulnerable or distressed within the ranks of the People in the Pews, meant that some princely prelates were induced to follow this same path.

George Pell (2007) is a case in point. Essays in his book *God and Caesar* highlight the considerations identified here. The editor, Michael Casey, recommends: 'One of the central themes adopted by Pope John Paul ll but brilliantly developed by Cardinal Pell turns on the culture-of-death that these pontifical politics encourage and support. Pell states, 'The example and writings of Pope John Paul ll also sustained and encouraged me, and countless others, to persist in the struggle in the culture wars, in the battle of the "culture of Death" (p. 3). This preoccupation with a warlike attitude shows further: 'One temptation is to remove the vertical dimension of religion. This was one of the dangers of liberation theology which Pope John Paul ll successfully opposed in South America' states Pell.

There seems to be a contradiction by Pell in the assessment of John Paul ll: 'John Paul ll was the first pope to give a thorough critique of culture'. Pell says the pope was portrayed 'as being driven by an interest in specific and tough moral norms ... despite his powerful encyclicals on public life and the economy. But, one of his central preoccupations was the topic of freedom and responsibility' (p. 47). If such was his preoccupation regarding freedom, why then was the matter of women's ordination ordered to be taken out of any church considerations by a personal ban?

Interesting that Pell could describe the mind and intentions of John Paul ll: 'God-given law is not some legalistic imposition but consists rather of truths meant to help human persons make good moral choice - freed from subservience to arbitrary feelings and obsessions in a free choice of the good' thus implying that the understanding of John Paul ll was the only measuring stick of the tenets of the catholic faith as a superior approach (pp. 47-48). Pell asserts that the church's 'clear preference for modern democracy and its commitment to human rights as a proper goal of democracy coexist well with a traditional Catholic approach to faith and morals – they certainly do so in the teachings of Pope John Paul ll' (p. 60).

Importantly, we need to evaluate what exactly Pell is promoting here. 'Our teaching on rights is coherent with our anthropology, with the natural law tradition of Aquinas, and with the moral principles with which we approach bioethical, sexual and other human issues, such as social justice' (p. 61). The underlying thinking patterns can't quite disguise the deliberate prioritising of privileging what the church says (whatever is meant by that, when he has been talking about culture wars) over the stark truth of everyday lived experience of the People in the Pews. His view of the historic elements, which Constant Mews has highlighted, seems very limited.

In particular, it is noticeable what Pell says about conscience. Referring to John Henry Newman: 'In all Newman's examples, conscience is not left as an unfenced equivalent of secular autonomy but is closely defined and linked with a proper understanding of Christian, indeed Catholic, teaching. In strictly theological language, the claim to primacy of conscience is a cliché, which requires only preliminary examination for us to conclude that it needs to be refined and developed to have plausible meaning at all. I do not even favour the substitution of the primacy of informed conscience, because it is also possible that with good will and conscientious study, a devout Catholic could fail to recognise some moral truth and act upon this failure. It is truth, or the Word of God, that has primacy, and we have to use our personal capacity to reason practically, that is, exercise our conscience, to try to recognise these particular truths' (p. 164). Somewhat incoherent language and logic underpins this stance.

So it would seem that Pell would favour the intrusion of his version of truth into the relationship between the individual and the Creator. The presumption that he knows that even the informed conscience of a person is not suitable, is breath-taking in its arrogance. Pell's whole chapter reeks of reductionism, in which the individual person is not important, as he talks exaggeratedly about 'one opinion is held to be as good as another' (p. 165) pertaining to nothing in particular. 'The idea of culpable moral blindness is discussed as infrequently as the pains of hell' (p. 165), and one wonders at the bold generalisation and how such a charge could be sustained. These narrow thinking patterns pervade the whole text, and one wonders again at his next charge: 'Just as conscience is claimed to have primacy over truth, rights are claimed to have primacy over *justice,* in the full sense of that word as it is understood in the Catholic tradition' (p. 169). Pell talks of 'decisionism' with little evidence of subtlety and insight. He speaks of 'blind choice' (p. 172) stating 'The crucial question is whether a mere decision, even a deadly serious decision, in favour of human rights is sufficient to sustain the commitment and action necessary to ensure that rights are consistently respected' (p. 172).

What does he mean by 'mere decision'? This is a disdainful comment that shows no respect for an individual wrestling with complicated problems. The last judgment in his text highlights his emphases on the culture of death, and he displays a confused understanding of those people, different from himself, who struggle to achieve maturity in daily lived experience. 'But just as the *scientia* in conscience, knowing objective truth, has been replaced by preferences, feelings, and the invention and construction of moral obligations or options, so too human rights divorced from a proper understanding of the dignity of all persons can be used to further the culture of death and damage the civilisation of life and love'

(p. 174). Such black and white thinking leaves no space for growth in a person's expanding understanding of the opportunity to develop a unique relationship with our Cosmic Lord.

For sheer simplistic reductionism, Nelson (2018) provides a spectacular example: 'Man exists to worship God and is obligated to do so, precisely because man is man and God is God. We cannot avoid it: we will all worship something. That is, we will all accept *something* as our highest good. Why not accept the Highest Good as your highest good? Because if there are good reasons to believe that such a being exists, this is the only reasonable option. *For man becomes like whomever he worships;* and in that simple statement is the secret to why religion matters' (p. 80). The unfortunate sexism of this language as late as in 2018 leads to the most revealing untried black and white thinking that exemplifies the shallow reductionism of the whole text. Even the sub-text of the book's title is disdainful of those he titles as spiritually indifferent and the generalisations which are scattered throughout the text include: 'It should be surprising, then, to say that one of the most difficult aspects of converting to the Catholic faith is conforming one's life to Church teachings – whether one fully understands them, or likes them, or not' (p. 135). He seems unaware of the sweep of history that pinpoints the existence of clericalism beside catholicity, already explained.

There does not seem to be a realistic understanding of the process of conversion apparent here. There is also a breath-taking contradiction to the consultations of the Vatican Council ll outcomes, in the following: 'But although some Protestant churches may offer more in terms of emotional and social experience – the Catholic Church offers something much deeper. There is a degree of spiritual engagement possible in the Catholic Church that is unattainable outside of it, a participation in a threefold unity: unity in truth, unity in Christ, and unity as Church; or to put it another way, unity in doctrine, unity through sacrament, and unity within the community of saints' (p. 139). This statement is ecumenically untrue, disrespectful of reality, and oblivious of our Cosmic Creator, who has not consigned those outside the Catholic Church to nothingness.

Conscience and the issue of Discernment

We need to address the reality of the virtue and value of discernment. If you grew up with parents who taught the theological virtues of faith, hope and love, and who practised on a daily basis the cardinal virtues of prudence, justice, fortitude and temperance, you possibly did not hear the term discernment itself, but home and parish culture showed what discernment is in practice.

It is worth noting immediately that the Rule of St Benedict addresses the concept of discernment (*discretio* in Latin) as 'the mother of the virtues'. And Ignatius extends this concept in the 16th century, broadening the concept of discernment into the whole of life. It seems almost urgent to extend our research about what is to count as discernment into the modern democratic world in both its secular and religious milieux. This is particularly important in addressing the problems emerging in the teaching and monitoring of what is to count as decision making for ordinands. Clericalism and its partnership with narcissism provide a significant urgency; otherwise progress in emotional and spiritual maturity is at risk. To provide some overview in today's climate of extremism and the politics of disruption, we need to examine the role and function of 21st century priest.

There are urgent indications that change processes must start with the re-evaluation of the conception and praxis regarding seminary formation for education of all ordinands. Examination of entry into the ranks of priesthood for male and female candidates of whatever hue must start in secondary school levels where shared experience of general studies include the valuing of what is to count as being good in secular terms as well as religious thinking as per the Genesis creation story. In such a scenario, all subjects and disciplines are taught with precision and creativity in the modes of the Community of Inquiry methodology. (This methodology is based on a series of careful discussion and inquiry, where teacher and class members together become their own research community and share the steps of inquiry, the discussions about values and ethics. This is taken up in detail in a following chapter.) Such a requirement will inform the basis and application of a curriculum and instructional design. An extended example of how this can be, and is done, also appears in a following chapter. In such a way, the ordinand is prepared through lived experience for the rigors of tertiary level thinking skills, decision making processes, and genuine 21st century research scholarship for thorough biblical understanding, without curial demand resorting to the extreme reliance on medieval and scholastic modes of church tradition, presently seen by clericalist and curial leaders as the backbone of seminary formation. This is one way to avoid the blinkered and inefficient recognition of the breadth and depth of skills which underpin the pastoral role of a priest today.

This use of developed discussion, not debate, inquiry not rote learning, medieval not current perspectives, can be used efficiently for the development of study skills of the ordinand. It is of significance in solving or managing problems, dilemmas and paradoxes. So the process of discernment within this milieu is allowing us to deepen our own and our students' relationship with God, with ourselves, with others and within our environment. It is, therefore, a useful addition to the curriculum when guiding the studies and spiritual experience of ordinands. This process of discernment leads directly in a religious sense to reflection in action and reflection on action, to self-correction and to an efficacious approach to examination of conscience. We rely on the Second Vatican Council Declaration

Dignitatis humanae and the work of contemporaries, O'Neill and Black, (2006) to understand conscience. This is important to facilitate *how* to develop a balanced approach to examination of conscience. It does not facilitate or address *what* is examined as this is close to the problem of indoctrination.

In *The Essential Moral Handbook,* O'Neill and Black define conscience as 'a judgment about a specific action', (p. 57) and follow it with a comment: 'conscience is activated when I must make a difficult decision and when I must make a judgment about the rightness or wrongness of a particular choice' (p. 57). They continue: 'Conscience includes both the disposition (or inclination) to do "good" and the practical judgment for this or that action' (p. 57), implying responsible choice.

Acting on conscience is carefully and thoughtfully analysed for us by Frank Brennan (2007) as he explores a responsible mix of law, religion and politics. Portraying the complexity involved in making real and balanced decisions according to a maturing conscience is outlined. This process is echoed in a following chapter as a means of highlighting teaching techniques that do not rely on the old adage of tipping information into the mind of the receiver. The process in simplified form, shown in the figure below, is examination (of the presenting problem), exploration (of the details of the problem, probing for clarity), evaluation (of all the various elements that must be part of any decision making), ethical stance (referencing the norms and regulations we find as necessary to understand the underlying problem and possible predictable actions), ethical action (going ahead with the action that follows the actual decision), followed by re- evaluation (examination again of what we have learned. We evaluate whether the action fixed the problem; whether the problem must be managed or solved) and if necessary, it may be that this process begins again as we learn and develop our ethical behaviour in parallel with our beliefs and for a Catholic in parallel with the message of Jesus.

If successful, the problem is solved; if unsuccessful, it is necessary to take the students if in secondary school, or ordinands if in preparatory studies for priesthood, back to whichever stage of the six steps' process, with added new information from the first time the whole process was used. In the light of new information, re-define the problem, and carefully follow the steps again. It is important to recognise that when the problem is not solved, it is not failure, but a mistake that has the benefit of allowing for new understandings and accurate insights. It is this cyclical pattern that allows the individual, whether ordinand or otherwise, to develop a pattern of thinking and a relevant pattern of approaches to the matter of what action is good, is appropriate and is in the best interests of realistic spiritual development.

The Six Steps of Decision-Making

Define the problem: presenting problem is not always the real problem
List possible options, no matter how unusual: unmasking deeper issues
Investigate each option: canvassing possibilities, predicting consequences, identifying pitfalls
Invite expert opinion, advisement (good counsel) and research internet: rather than rely on advice or counselling
Choose the best likely option, listing other options in order of preference: a mistake is not failure, unless the problem-solver withdraws altogether
Carry out the action, and then evaluate: armed with new knowledge retrace steps for another option if needed.

Source: (Heasly, 2012, p. 161)

It is important to refer to the Second Vatican Council document on Religious Liberty (*Dignitatis humanae*) to be sure that accurate understanding of the whole concept of religious freedom is recognised. The struggle to develop and form conscience is a lifelong journey to promote our a) *response* to God's grace, to find that b) *response-ability* that brings understanding and knowledge, in order to accept our c) *responsibility* consciously to choose the good and just as consciously to avoid evil; to reiterate: response, response-ability, and responsibility.

> 'The Vatican Council declares that the human person has a right to religious freedom. Freedom of this kind means that all (men) should be immune from coercion...' (*Dignitatis humanae*, 2)
>
> 'The search for truth, however, must be carried out in a manner that is appropriate to the dignity of the human person and (his) our social nature, namely, by free enquiry with the help of teaching or instruction, communication and dialogue' (*Dignitatis humanae*, 3)
>
> 'Every family, in that it is a society with its own basic rights, has the right freely to organise its own religious life in the home under the control of the parents.' (*Dignitatis humanae*, 5)
>
> 'God has regard for the dignity of the human person which he himself created; the human person is to be guided by (his own) personal judgment and to enjoy freedom.' (*Dignitatis humanae*, 11)

When as a consequence, we attend to O'Neill and Black, who define and describe Conscience as four 'moments':

First Moment: Conscience as desiring and knowing the good
Second Moment: Conscience as discerning the particular good
Third Moment: Conscience as a judgment for right action
Fourth Moment: Conscience as self-evaluation (2006, pp. 60-84)

O'Neill and Black state that the Catholic tradition recognises conscience as a special moment of contact between our inner selves and our God, therefore:

> Defining the problem becomes a conversation in prayer with our God, communicating all our thoughts, feelings and discomforts.
>
> Listing all possible ways to manage or solve our dilemma becomes a shining of a lens on all four 'moments' to be sure that we are taking account in our responses of what is to the good and what is the best choice for the good.
>
> Inviting expert opinion then includes asking the Holy Spirit for enlightenment, finding the people and sources to teach us what we need to know in order to build the ability to respond accurately. Surely, this is discernment in action.
>
> Investigating each option separately becomes a search for truth and an evaluation of the many ways we might respond. It takes account of the need for response-ability – a central and significant element in the process that brings God into our personal thinking skills. The ability to respond then becomes Grace in action.
>
> Listing all possible actions after responsibly planning and prioritising, means that we have taken the time, reflected on the whole situation, discerned

the best first option, but have not discarded the other considerations. God works in wonderful and unexpected ways, so the first chosen option may not be the one most appropriate.

Carry out the action, and evaluate the results.

Consequences need to be carefully analysed to discern the will of God, to identify the effect on others, ourselves and maybe even on the environment. If the first option when carried out is inappropriate or mistaken, God is surely telling us something important, hence the need to re-evaluate in the light of the new knowledge. Maybe a mistake has occurred, and maybe we have learned something important from this mistake which the Holy Spirit has taught us. This can be addressed in the cyclical arrangement of going back to an appropriate stage of the *Six Step* process, armed with new information and following through. Failure happens only when the person gives up and withdraws from the situation – or deliberately and consciously chooses the wrong or evil instead.

Grasping the various principles of morality laid out for us in Sacred Scripture and in the various documents of Second Vatican Council, provides us with invaluable resources to aid in our journey towards God. Notice that this pattern of thinking is designed to help us in our deliberations of how to examine our conscience, how to discern the significant elements that are deep inside where only God is, how to facilitate our relationship with Father Creator, Son Redeemer-Lifegiver and Spirit Wise Sanctifier. This tool does not impinge on the individual's conscience by trying to make the decisions about what to do, about what is the choice for the good. The moral act is always my own, and each 'I' must follow those 'four moments' to arrive at the point that O'Neill and Black indicate as the best image of conscience – heart.

There are four consequences to the application of this educational tool. This pattern of personal thinking skills is consciously modelling first the value of *prudence*, because it shows methodical planning and measured accounting, by sifting through options, possibilities, likely consequences and possible pitfalls. The second is *justice* which is served equally well by this modelling because there is an implied goal of being fair, authentic and honest with God, with ourselves, with others and within the environment – as we make interim and final choices and judgments.

Additionally, the most noticeable is third, the consistent *fortitude and courage* (together) to continue rather than to withdraw. The moral act becomes, therefore, in itself a channel of Grace gifted by God, drawing us close to the Holy Trinity: Father Creator, Son Redeemer-Lifegiver and Spirit Sanctifier. Lastly, the virtue of *temperance* is the least familiar in today's culture or cults of individualism and extreme risk-taking. Temperance fosters evenness in temperament, care of self and others, reflection: in action and on action. Emerging in these patterns of personal thinking skills is the characteristic of *resilience*, which is a direct consequence of temperance.

To conclude, we find ourselves at times in a complicated place. We need to respond appropriately and we need the personal response-ability translated as necessary knowledge. We analyse and find the best choice and we act in responsibility towards our God, towards others, towards ourselves and where necessary towards the environment. If we are involved in the work of evangelisation, especially in classrooms at primary, secondary and tertiary levels of teaching, we transmit knowledge and model virtues, values and ethics, and this is the disposition and virtue of discernment.

Features that distinguish Indoctrination and Higher-order Thinking

The *Concept of Indoctrination* and the *Concept of Higher Order Thinking* refer to two opposing patterns of thinking skills. Indoctrination refers to the total acceptance of a set of beliefs of political, social or religious origin imposed by some rigid authoritarian structure claiming the right to control the thoughts, the imagination and the daily life of an individual as well as the collective experience of a community or nation. *Higher Order Thinking* as a concept refers to the development from early age for lifelong learning of the various tested patterns of thinking based on careful question-starters, applied questioning, testable options and possible mistakes on the way to attaining an understanding of the various skills sets within the three levels of thinking for learning. The following considerations try to contrast some urgent elements that may cause pitfalls without careful thinking and balanced decision making:

Control of delivered content or *Exploration of Content* refers to the introduction of the individual learner in political, social or religious settings to a completed set of watertight tenets which are the only elements the controllers state are needed in life. The contrast between the *control of delivered content*, with the exploration of that same content, is the respect and patience needed to allow time, practice and exploration of what is to count for understanding of contentious or challenging or mysterious content presented in the student learning experience. This contrast allows the individual to come to a position of understanding, knowledge and possibility in relevant circumstances to faith. If wide and deep learning is promoted at all levels of evangelisation within the church, then it is possible to negotiate the subtle nuances of the message of Jesus, as exegesis and other disciplines provide us with more relevant information to integrate into the deposit of faith so that elements of refreshed church practices are internalised.

Other-centred approach or a *Self-or-independent approach* refers to the perspective and attitude from which the individual views the world. In an *Other-centred approach*, we would emphasise justice, balance, kindliness, understanding and respect to others with different positions or points of view from ourselves about any contentious or complicated topic. The *self-or-independent approach* would focus first on (and sometimes only on) the problems or dilemmas or mysteries from an exclusively personal perspective. Outcomes for each perspective may coincide but often are diametrically opposed to each other. If listening, attending, hearing, as continuing skills are not practised on a long-term basis, there is potential for conflict, as the spectre of prior entitlement often intrudes before the regular communication needed, is able to be effective. It engenders the spectre of clericalism in the tendency towards entitlement and privilege. It is not enough to recognise the two contrasting approaches, because as we grow and internalise the deeper challenges of life, we realise that our own approach will be the outcome of relationship with Jesus and his message, rather than either of these extremes.

Narrow focus of action or a *sifting of options and action* refers to the narrowing down to bedrock of what is to count as content for consideration about planned action, problem solving and predictive leadership. It is a particular problem if it leads to a simplistic approach to the tenets of our faith and a pietistic approach to relationship with Jesus. By contrast, the sifting of all options pertaining to the management or solving of problems, or understanding of apparent mysteries is a slower but more carefully balanced approach to what is to count as a concept, leading a person towards an action. This must not rely exclusively on a blind acceptance of a papal precept, a commandment, an exhortation, an encyclical or a papal edict. It is important here to remember the function of the voices within the *sensus fidelium*, because incomprehension is an accurate signpost indicating that content coming from the hierarchical pyramid without any reference to the daily life of the People in the Pews is misdirected, or worse.

Assumption of power or *Personal autonomy* is the vexed area in religious terms in which we find that discernment of God's will has often been overtaken by papal power and curial control of the People in the Pews. Respect for the primacy of personal conscience is disdained in the claimed priority of creeping papal infallibility. Outcomes lead to conflict, friction, vicious infighting and disruption built on disrespect and ignorance. Careful thinking and reasoning can find the deepening understanding that is needed in the living out of daily life. It must be remembered that 21st century world conditions include the whole digital world, the achievements of artificial intelligence (especially in matters of medical healing as experienced every day), in whichever continent the People in the Pews live their lives. The yawning gap between the enclosed bubble of the Vatican and the daily experience of the People in the Pews must therefore be addressed.

Enforcement rather than *Experimentation and testing and critiquing* refers to the understanding of what is to count as the right action, authentic interpretation, best option, moral decision, best of two or more lesser options, accepted submission, subtle or obvious demand. All of these outcomes pertain to the building of the personal responsibility and growing ethical maturity of the individual in the decisions of life. Enforcement refers to the demand from an apparent authoritative source to follow exactly what is directed without input from the individual. *Experimentation* or *testing or critiquing* refers to that same building of personal responsibility of the individual whereby mistakes are not sinful and can often lead to special and compassionate insights in the decisions of life. Enforcement allows no use of intelligence and creative skills, and a boundary grows between the victim and the use of imagination, where we so often encounter the beginnings of mysticism and the sacred. The intrusiveness of clericalism in its focus on prescription and authoritarian responses from Rome stops the individual, offering diminishment from that personal development of a relationship with Jesus.

Defiance and dismissal of broad evidence and the business of *Response-ability and Responsibility* exists when the authoritarian approach is the familiar approach to governance and moral coding. The phenomenon of *defiance* as a tool of establishing power and control in particular circumstances emerges in partnership with dismissal of broad or noticeable evidence which provides a reason for variation of a given decision. The individual must be able to recognise that a valuable skills set is needed. The ability to respond appropriately is crucial to understanding the place of Higher Order Thinking. Once the ability to respond is in place, mature and effective decisions of a moral and authentic nature can be carried out because the individual accepts the responsibility of attending to any consequences of the particular decision. What is often not addressed is the response-ability and responsibility to attend to the unintended consequences which may result from our decision. A particularly obvious example of this phenomenon seems to emerge in the responses to recent conclaves, and to the haunted history of Vatican Council ll.

Punishment or Re-direction refers to the serious anticipation that decisions and actions not approved by the reigning authority are considered anathema. The threat of punishment of a sufficiently appalling nature is already known by the individual. So the hurt or discomfort accompanying the threat is a punishment in itself, so is the actual punishment when it is carried out. Unfortunately, the threat of continuing punishment is a continuing fear. This blocks the noticeable requirement that the individual needs to learn what is more appropriate, less hurtful, morally desirable, or less sinful. The need for careful re-direction does not accompany the victim of indoctrination, as the choice remains with the authority in charge. Blocking the promotion of generosity and remorse, personal penance is the inevitable outcome of the continued spectre of punishment, and is certainly not what the Jesus message was about. Conversely, the need for both punishment and redirection is needed when clerical sexual abuse is proven, because the predator must serve daily the people who are victims of oppression, cruelty and injustice. It is no punishment to direct a predator to a life of seclusion and prayer, when direct experience of penance must be real, long-lasting and on the same scale as the damage done to his victims.

Attribution of Guilt or *Acceptance of Consequences and the need for recompense* appears when authority is used to attribute guilt to an individual who has offended and the result is that the guilt is worn for the foreseeable future, hence the term 'sinful humanity'. By contrast, when an individual who have given offense, recognises and apologises for the inappropriate or sinful action, mature remorse takes the form of acceptance of all of the consequences which emerge, regardless of the enormity or the inexplicable nature of the consequences. The need for recompense relies on restorative justice. A reality check shows that it is a matter of accepting what is, rather than trying to minimise the effects of the need. The efforts to cover-up the appalling damage of clerical predators contradicts the essential message of Jesus to let the children come to him. Compensation means active means of financial improvement. Justice means restitution and restoration of place in the social milieu, and restorative justice means making appropriate efforts on a life-long basis to bring the victim or survivor fully into acceptance in our social circles. It is not enough to make a verbal apology without serious, immediate and long-term action to right the wrong. If everything that is different, diverse, unexpected, unnecessary, unexplained is considered with disapproval, the consequence is that the essential message of Jesus is being ignored.

Imprisonment or *Empowerment* refers to that concept of restorative justice in which imprisonment may contain the offender so that justice is served. If that restorative justice is not accompanied by various forms of ongoing attention, empowering of the victim is ignored and that offender is imprisoned within a psychological haze that does not allow remorse or forgiveness to flower. Taking a victim out of a familiar personal milieu needs more than the following of the letter of the law. There is a particular need to re-establish that person in the eyes of the world, the church and the law. Indoctrination with one harsh understanding of the world is unjust, inappropriate, harsh, cruel, ignominious and unacceptable to the mission of Jesus. Empowerment, by contrast, is careful, generous, but just and compassionate.

Obligation and *Transformation* can be present if the reigning authority is still bent on imposing the boundaries of acceptable living by means of obligation and edicts. The effect is that no chance is offered to the individual for transformation as a mature, responsive, kindly, and generous model of the Jesus message. The intrusion of the precepts, edicts, exhortations, encyclicals, which have issued from the Roman centre of Christianity in a continuous stream show an almost blind emphasis on obligation. Some documents point to a possibility of transformation, but no modelling of what this means is visible at this time. Another term for transformation is that of 'becoming', where the process of growing ever closer to a deep understanding of the love of our Triune God emerges. The possibility of mercy, compassion and deep understanding is needed. Judgmental responses and attitudes are not needed and are an insulting outcome that stifles transformation, especially when issued towards the People in the Pews.

Rote-learning and *Applied Knowledge* are contrasts, referring to the first-order learning skills that are used in the earliest years of schooling in most countries. The familiar territory of second and third order learning skills is ignored by a reliance on rules of indoctrination. Applied knowledge refers to the critiquing, questioning, testing, prioritising, and trying out whether one optional decision is the best outcome in a given situation. It takes time, patience, modelling, facilitating and leadership skills, especially in Catholic primary, secondary and tertiary levels of learning, to achieve outcomes consonant with the message of Jesus. Reliance on rote-learning alone stops the imagination from developing, and imagination is what leads us into the realm of the mystical and the sacred. As such, it is crucial that indoctrination has no part in the modelling of the message of Jesus.

Required Obedience or *Gathering of Wisdom* in action refers to the system of sanctions and punitive responses that keep the individual in a state of submissiveness, contrasted with no opportunity for asking questions or understanding the normal lessons gained in daily life. The system surfaces particularly in the silencing of theologians who are doing their best to discern deeper understandings of the Scriptures, the tenets of faith and the mystical relationships of human with divine. It causes underlying trauma to the individual who must comply no matter the cost in growing maturity. The emphasis of *Gathering of Wisdom* is very important here. It takes a lifetime to become a functioning follower of Jesus in the transformative way that the Holy Spirit offers us. So the stark reality confronts us of a church requiring us to go back to the reality of a century or more ago. We are confronted by the canonisation of a succession of popes, with the implication that back-then was the golden time. The challenge of realistically adjusting to the diversity that surrounds us in all its colour, the disruption in political worlds, and the dreadful problems of nature's explosions, to add to a menu of quite evil behaviours, require us to be alert, to make decisions of good quality and to take responsibility for the *Gathering of Wisdom* everywhere. We listen, we attend, we hear, but we need courage to develop the maturity for the challenge, both individually and communally.

Ideology versus *World View with a Faith Dimension* refers to the concept of what is to count as a political basis, both individually and communally, for action. Ideology refers to an agreement of some people who lead by developing a theory which corresponds to a political situation and so we have so many 'isms' today. A *World View* is the outlook and chosen perspective of a person who has developed a particular kind of picture of how to read the world. It is usual for such a world view to be consciously or unconsciously in synchronicity with the moral values of that same individual. By following through the process which begins with an understanding first of what we mean by tensegrity, then bio-tensegrity, towards edu-tensegrity and finally into theo-tensegrity, we find ourselves responding to the presence of the Holy Spirit today, when the chaos and ineptitude within the hierarchy is on display. And as an antidote to indoctrination, that world view for a Catholic is to have a *Faith Dimension* that is consonant with that same moral value set. Most importantly, it is the *Faith Dimension* that helps the Catholic to recognise the uncertainty that walks with each person through daily life. This is the Catholic tradition, in all its various diversities of practice. When problem, dilemma, paradox or mystery appears, it is the Faith Dimension that allows us to turn to the Gospels for illumination, to the message of Jesus for the modelling of kindliness and generosity we need, and to the Holy Spirit for enlightenment and discernment to respond as our Creator God would wish us to do.

Rigidity and Discovery – here we pinpoint the underlying difficulty of people who call on the concept of indoctrination to make their place in the world. There is a realisation that rigidity won't allow a person to admit into the normal pattern of thinking any options, any possibilities, and any creative leaps at any time. The demands of an authoritarian source are internalised to such a deep extent that it is possible that the existence of that rigidity is no longer visible. Discovery refers to the humility in action which allows the person to take the dangerous route of examination and exploration of problem-solving, or management of dilemma, paradox or mystery. Having the faith and hope to allow that we may be required to live with uncertainty for an appreciable time is a test of relationship with Jesus, within the Holy Spirit and our loving Creator God. Tiny opportunities, sometimes learning in retrospect, remind us of the presence of the Triune God in our midst, and indoctrination recedes into the mists as it is meant to do. And so we experience ourselves as healed of scrupulosity, addictions, and the unthinking tendencies that may lead us into sinfulness. As long as we distinguish between testing, mistaking, and failure, we can also distinguish when sin is present. One is not synonymous with the other. We can also identify the presence of arrogance, narcissism, authoritarianism, and respond carefully without becoming adversarial in response.

The *Concept of Church Understanding* of what it means to be human versus the concept of 'augmented humans' is evident in the understanding of the contribution of neuroscience as partnered with digital and mechanical aids for disabled People in the Pews and the rest of humankind. The arrogant claims of the past promoted the virtue of the unchangeable Catholic Church. This meant that administration did not need to change internally, but, now, what must be changed must be allowed to happen. Reluctance to face the truth or some undeniable knowledge newly-uncovered from the various disciplines of science and allied application of such new knowledge, now constitutes a serious pressure for most of the world because of the speed with which new knowledge is being uncovered. Much needs to be developed within the Curial offices to address this rather ridiculous situation. Dicasteries need open borders, need members of that disdained group called the laity (People in the Pews) to be on staff, and need distinguished expertise drawn from within their networks. This is urgent to develop enough understanding to provide the process of change by the blending of the secular and the sacred. Much can be learned from the various existing global networks of particular specialists who can remedy this situation in the coming decades. It seems the Holy Spirit is blowing ecologically, environmentally, theologically and experientially and we would do well to listen and hear that Wisdom influence.

We would do well to remember Samuel Terrien's (1985) words:

> Creation as such does not reveal itself. It is Wisdom at play who becomes the mode of revelation. There is no religion without intellectual integrity in scientific research. There is no philosophy of science without a sense of transcendence. There is no humanism without the exacting demands of theism. Human thirst for knowledge is the twin of Wisdom's playfulness in the presence of the Creator. It is in communion with Wisdom, at once transcendent and immanent, that philosophy, science, art, and religion find their ultimate unity. The passion for social justice, the

search for truth, and all the arts, receive their meaning only in the celebration of the God who upholds heaven and earth in their course' (p. 101)

CHAPTER 5

Change Processes already familiar in Education: theory, practice and praxis

It is important for the reader to know that a central emphasis in this project is that the author is promoting three Change Processes meant to replace completely the present system of Seminary Formation. The reader will no doubt find some of this content to be dense, detailed, technical and shrouded in specialist methodology that the Education Specialist will recognise. It is, therefore, easy for the general reader to lightly check the parts that highlight educational methodology, pick out the content and reasons for my substitution and go on to the next section. In this way, both specialists and non-specialists can benefit from the final parts of the project, which concentrate on the possible consequences of this substitution.

As a first channel of change for the formation and development of ordinands, it is recommended that best practice already in so many national curriculums in education, can be offered as a starting point for the needs of those who are dedicating their future to the pastoral and liturgical needs of the People of God. In today's world, the new term is People in the Pews. Sean Winter (2015) sets out the framework from which we can gather our thoughts by connecting the concepts of Journey and Rest; pilgrimage for the Hebrews and pilgrimage for us as a 21st century People in the Pews. He is connecting particularly and precisely with the work of theological education and our consequential challenge.

This is particularly important in the light of Faggioli's feature article in *The Swag* (Autumn 2018), the journal of the National

Council of Priests in Australia. Faggioli examines the polarisation existing in the church and the crisis this polarisation brings to the Catholic mind, both individually and as a community. This means, he says, that our intellectual comprehension faces us as we realise there is theological polarisation, liturgical polarisation, scholarship polarisation, polarised Catholic information service, and alarmingly, 'there is also a problem on the other side of the classroom. In Catholic academia, the polarisation has created ideologically different kinds of Catholic colleges and universities and to some grotesque extremes'. This is extended into the political sphere by the editor of *The Tablet* (10 March 2018) who talks about Pope Francis, the Pope from the Periphery, and in which comment is made of the polarisation existing in appointments to the hierarchy by a succession of popes.

So we must turn to educational figures looking for ways in which we can provide some analysis and possibilities in our search to move forward. Hargreaves and Shirley (2009) in ground-breaking research and a consequent theory of education, introduce us to a historical development of teaching and learning that caters for each individual student (and ordinand) in primary, secondary and tertiary levels of the individual's educational journey. They consciously look to inspire a future of educational change that allows large entities like the Catholic Church to transition towards best practice, without demanding edicts but with careful signposts to support the teaching practice, the learning strategies and the attitudinal expansion so prized in a democratic education system.

We are introduced to what is stated as a revolutionary way to transform educational reform of policy, processes and practice. The needs of the 21st century Catholic tradition are well served if we are able to apply carefully the historical development and swing towards best practice, without forcing belief into straight-jacket formation. It is not good enough for edicts stating that the Catholic tradition is based on reason informed by faith. Poor behaviour and criminal acts contradict this position. It behoves us at this urgent stage of the development of the church in the 21st century, to reply and respond in full measure to the appalling knowledge emerging from the Australian Royal Commission's findings about the extent of clerical child sexual abuse. We need to look for the best ways to avoid the pitfalls which were and are present. It is helpful then to watch how Hargreaves and Shirley have addressed their intention of transformation of education. The authors identify four ways historically in which education has been administered, and we apply these four ways to our present need.

The first way is flagged by Hargreaves and Shirley as innovation and professional freedom but is inclined towards inconsistency of learning outcome, with uneven performance. Classroom practice relies on rote learning, and conformity with little time or interest in creativity. Students can become disengaged and impersonal as a result.

A second way, flagged by Hargreaves and Shirley, is when every part of the curriculum is standardised, taught uniformly, disregarding the need for equity of delivery for students. It reduces and infantilises the learner, as though it were possible to tip knowledge into the learner's brain, which was previously empty. No learner has an empty brain!

A third way, proposed by Hargreaves and Shirley, is when the best and most significant teaching practices are researched, so that professional expertise is supported with accountability. Short-term results are not retained by students whose motivation for real learning disappears.

It is obvious that these three approaches to teaching are used in many different guises in Catholic evangelisation. Intended or hopeful results do not translate into internalisation and deep learning, for classrooms or for passing on the tenets of our faith. Combined with the scandals of 21st century, this experience has resulted in many students turning away from religious considerations, but not necessarily turning away from spiritual matters.

A fourth way has been offered by Hargreaves and Shirley. They talk about an inclusive vision with schools, communities and corporate partnerships working together; learning that is creative, engaging and demanding; shared and ambitious improvement targets; prudent accountability that tests samples of work. They extend into sustainable leadership that is insightful, spreading best practice, sharing research, supporting innovation, and in the case of the ordinand's situation, honing thinking skills and democratic leadership personal tools within entrepreneurship skills needed for the future of the Catholic tradition in the 21st century.

Education specialists will be expertly placed to contribute to the education of ordinands. In the stream of development that has been noted around the world in first world countries, we find many people with similar reasons for trying to transform educational practice so that the needs of our students are met, especially given the pace of new technology, new knowledge and new politics all over the globe. This focus also means that digital expertise must be central to teachers, ordinands and evangelisers.

Philosophy in the Classroom and the Community of Inquiry

The first of three processes is offered as a means of extracting the priesthood from the caste of exclusivity we attach to clericalism. The Philosophy for Children movement began at least six decades ago by Professor Matthew Lipman, and has spread over at least sixty-seventy national education systems, including Australia. Within this movement, the classroom is a truly democratic experience based on what is always called the Community of Inquiry. It is a collaborative system based on an inclusive, shared process in which teacher, researchers and students interact with the topic under consideration, until all question starters (how? when? where? why? what? which? who? what if?) have been used to provide questions pertinent to the topic.

The Community of Inquiry then goes into action as a collaborative means of interactive research and as a way of learning from each other and from the teacher, who functions also as facilitator. There are Philosophy-in-Schools organisations in every State of Australia which include Catholic, Independent and Government school personnel. To make this collaborative system work on a regular basis for student deep learning, all questions on a given topic are prioritised. Some questions will need factual answers; some will need explanation before action; some will need research of different types; and all answers warrant full inclusion of all relevant matters. Nuanced content useful and used for primary, secondary and tertiary levels of students and currently in practice in many schools, will be available to the ordinands.

In Australia, access to the Australasian teacher organisation called DialogueAustralasiaNetwork (DAN) spearheads development of the topics offered in Year 11 and Year 12 studies in philosophy, theology, sociology, religious studies, study of ethics and beyond, in all States of Australia and New Zealand. The DAN teachers' resource magazine uses the Five-Strand approach and is published twice a year. The Five-Strand curriculum includes relevant examination and research: textual strand (Hebrew and Christian Scriptures), theoretical and applied ethics, philosophy of religion, world religions, and the affective strand (Silence and Stillness).

In the United Kingdom, there is another equally impactful organisation called SAPERE, operating out of Abingdon, whose universal influence is in all parts of the United Kingdom. In France, Austria, the USA as well as Spain, the Czech Republic, Turkey, South Africa and Canada and so many other countries, there are regular conferences for teachers and lecturers, meticulously organised to provide curriculum content, to add new and current resources and to demonstrate the skills sets needed for student deep learning. If students finishing their secondary studies are introduced well to these specialist areas, it becomes clear why young people find dull sermons, rather than researched homilies, a reason for retiring from parish liturgical celebrations.

Regenerationism is identified as the obvious need for the skills sets required of today's ordinand, rather than the modelling by garbed figures with little to offer but old answers to new problems. Regenerationism also means expanding our education focus within the Catholic tradition to encompass the awe and wonder that accompanies the dawning realisation of the multiverses (not just the universe), the cosmic infinity (not just the Milky Way); the remarkable inner spectacle of the unique and complex unit called the human person (not just the comfortable geometric equation of what constitutes a human in terms of a moral code and little else). The Community of Inquiry initiates the ordinand into the realm of collaborative and consultative learning.

Virtues, Values and Ethics: from Thinking Skills to Personal decision making

The second of the three processes offered as a means of clearing the priesthood of some of the lax theological sermons, and promoting the art of listening and thinking, is called the HUG/ BUG system, and is built on the same basic principles as Philosophy for Schools, emanating from the same early sources as a particular channel for secondary students. The HUG/BUG system is a methodology useful in classroom discussion because it teaches students about the details of various individual decisions regarding any virtue, any value, and any ethical response. The resultant patterns of responsive behaviours have consequences for which the decision maker must take personal responsibility. This methodology is a way of developing and discerning an authentic personal conscience. The Thinking Skills patterns are the stepping-off point for the general development of logical thinking patterns, which are differentiated from each other: critical thinking, logic and reason; binary thinking; tautologies; dialogue; debate; discussion; narrative; faith and more.

The whole HUG/ BUG system, with its application of four tools for learning, (Heasly, 2015) can be used as an instrument of learning decision making for all major areas of life, and feeds directly into what we will allow to count as conscience. If we are to act on conscience, as Frank Brennan models, we find ourselves looking to the prodigious talent, the people skills, the world inclusiveness, and the ethical stances of Einstein, Bernstein, Dispenza, Prince Harry, de Cardyn, William Barton, Brian Cox *and* Mary McAleese, Genevieve Lacey, Fiona Wood, Jacqueline DuPre, Karen Armstrong, and Christiane Amanpour. This model of teaching-learning makes clear when indoctrination creeps in, when authoritarianism intrudes, when responsibility and maturity begins to dawn in all areas of life rather than compartmentalisation of the moral, emotional, physical, social, intellectual and spiritual elements of a personality.

To aid in the understanding of this whole process, it is useful to understand the connections between these concepts of tensegrity, bio-tensegrity, edu-tensegrity and theo-tensegrity. Explanations of the *Six Steps of Decision Making* which is part of the HUG/ BUG system are set out to show that there are diverse patterns of thinking and reasoning which are the elements of what is to count as conscience in 21st century. In a societal milieu that functions on instant gratification, on prioritised emphases on 'me' at all times, on digital manipulation of the social context in which we live, it is important to lead the students, including the ordinands. We walk with them through the various steps of the process of establishing what it is that will count as individual conscience and what is meant by the term: primacy of conscience.

Regenerationism is the aim of such a large program and it is disrespectful to abbreviate the steps in the process for considerations of organisational convenience, because the presence of the Holy Spirit is central. The steps in the process of developing such a conscience are as follows: examination, exploration, evaluation, ethical stance and ethical action, before the cycle necessarily begins again. We were introduced to this process in an earlier chapter.

Johannes Lindner on Entrepreneurship Education and the choice of skills for priestly ordinands of 21st century

The third of the three processes is offered as a means of clearing the way of some of the ignorance displayed by new ordinands who today know little of normal daily life and the various units of society. In a different way, imported priests from utterly different cultural milieux find themselves in a similar position. The slavish following of papal edicts with simplistic and convenient organisational signposts does not allow the ordinand to function as a co-creator in the third millennium with the wonder and awe by which our loving Triune God wills the future of humankind.

Johannes Lindner provides an overview of entrepreneurship education from which the ordinand of 21st century will learn and choose the skills sets that allow leadership to flourish. The remarkable movement represented by the Baltic and Black Sea Circle Consortium for Change and Sustainability (BBCC) can be a channel to address the sustainability and environmental securitability that fits the moral code of the Catholic Church. This is especially in response to the Genesis emphases that all parts of God's creation, including our planet and the whole extraordinary cosmic creation we are expected to protect, are good. Ignorance presently displayed by many and skills sets including organisational expertise means that education must address the gap, otherwise the practices of transparency, leadership, pastoral insights, accountability for intended and unintended consequences of all decision making, and entrepreneurship education, are not present.

Given the extraordinary leaps in scientific development in psycho-sexual knowledge, in social sciences, in philosophy, in psychology, in psychiatry, and sundry allied sciences, the priest today is not the one-stop problem-solver of the pre-industrial church. If, as an example, leadership skills are to be part of the profile of the 21st century priest, neuroscience too has much to investigate. Daniel Amen and Justin Landy and their research tell us: 'Great leadership begins with managing the weaknesses of others and leveraging their strengths' (in Shields, 2018).

Significantly, the importance of the neuroscientific discussion set out for us by Paul MacLean (2018) alerts us to the new information about the human brain: 'humans have a reptilian brain that is fear-driven and triggers the "fight, flight or freeze" automatic response system'. 'Above this brain', says MacLean, 'sits the mammalian mind, which engages the emotions and needs for communal connection.' Further, says MacLean, 'At a higher level again is the neocortex, which governs the ability to think, reflect and strategise. The neocortex is where leadership begins.' If the candidate responds to the needs of the People in the Pews in 21st century terms, the ordinand must experience enough of the skills, knowledge and foresight to recognise that once ordination happens, adult learning does not stop. Like the disdained world of the secular, in which adult learning continues for the foreseeable future, the new ordinand must also take responsibility for the development of new and improved personal expertise, in the service of the People in the Pews.

Johannes Lindner has provided us with the breadth and depth of what entrepreneurship education is. The particulars of development, the aims of this movement in Baltic and Black Sea Circle Consortium terms, the urgency of education in sustainability for life in 21st century, are encased in Lindner's paper. The priest of the 21st century needs to be a leader and an entrepreneur who maintains the virtues, values and ethics of the Catholic tradition, and the skills sets needed are far different from the feudal, industrial or technological needs of 20th century or before. Much needs to be developed, processes need to be explored, knowledge and skills need to be integrated, and clericalism needs to be understood so that precise planning and curriculum can be developed and promoted. These requirements need to follow particularly the entrepreneurial skills and behaviours outlined by Lindner in order to address the evils of the clericalist cult.

Today, we need the priest and the ordinand to be a central person charged with the responsibility of respectful pastoral care and sacramental evangelisation of a given community, parish or otherwise. It will be many years afterwards that the individual ordinand has been faced with how to run a parish efficiently. It will be necessary at that point, for re-evaluation by taking account of finance, sacramental programs, Masses, particular natural groups within the parish, People in the Pews will choose which geographic parish they join, and the voluntary as well as paid personnel within their responsibility.

The central bureaucracy in Rome is peopled by individuals who have unpredictable gaps in their knowledge of daily life, coupled with a remoteness that allows a gaping hole to emerge and they expect to be able to have exclusive influence in the running of family and communal living in all corners of the world. Entrepreneurship education will identify the skills sets that will be useful and urgent for the ordinand to use. It would be wise to circumvent the evidence of such gaping holes. When a visiting prelate from the Vatican, on what was called a listening tour, recently concelebrated Mass and chose to preach in a central Melbourne parish, the listeners were faced with a person who knew nothing of the various practices of the parish, spoke about matters that had little to do with the culture to be listened to, assumed that the assembled congregation was almost unchurched, and left oblivious of the irritation he left behind.

Regenerationism as a theory means that the central aims of existing experts, in all Papal Dicasteries, are required to understand that they are at the service of the People in the Pews; that collaboration and research needs to be part of the ongoing and continuous democratic conversation between the ordinand and the People in the Pews. All must understand that synodal conclusions and outcomes are the product of that very careful consultation that respects minority opinion. It can *not* be subject to impatient moves from Rome to control the various aspects of the explorations of each topic under investigation. It is important that moves are made to imprint on the personnel in far-away Rome that they are in need of new knowledge, further development of transparency, accountability and personal integrity. This must be far away from the duplicitous pantomime which keeps emerging in so many countries as corruption, criminality and creeping efforts grasping for infallibility and entitlement. And the echoes of such phenomena must be dismissed immediately from the regular daily workings of each national Bishops Conference.

Three well-known learning styles

We need to remember the three orders of learning styles and their implications for ordinands. Stirling (2011) gives clear descriptions of all three orders, and it is imperative that each ordinand understands the relevance of the learning styles, and uses each of those three styles to bring to the experience of responsibly leading a parish. Each of these elements is required by the time the ordinand is appointed to a parish or church organisation. After all, education principals, teachers, lecturers, researchers, nurses, administration leaders in both the secular and the religious spheres, are already equipped with most of these skills when they take leadership positions. The three orders of learning appear here.

First-order learning is provided within accepted boundaries, but learners' basic values about the topic are left unexamined and unchanged. Reading a document from the Vatican Council ll on one of the various topics for discussion over three years is a good example of first-order learning because it is an information-gathering exercise only. Teachers are aware that this is 'step 1' in the introduction of every topic in all disciplines. This is normal and current practice in primary, secondary and tertiary levels of education, but it is necessarily only a beginning for deep learning.

Second-order learning promotes critically reflective learning, alerting students to their personal ethical responses. Gathering together to solve a difficult situation, where contentious possibilities need to be explored and understood, this is a good example of second-order learning because the individuals will favour a choice dependent on what they consider right or wrong, good or bad, helpful or painful. This practice can be inserted in all disciplines in primary, secondary and tertiary levels of studies. In Science disciplines, it is introduced in the application of knowledge to practical problems. In philosophical, sociological, literature, religious studies and theology disciplines, it is an ongoing element of all considerations of learning, as each topic or problem scenario is used to induce student engagement and consequent learning, at primary, secondary and tertiary levels. Deep learning is unfinished at this point.

Third-order learning involves transformational, creative, epistemic learning and possible paradigm change, perhaps seeing a topic or question differently, and possibly leading to influence over personal perceptions. Studies, based on one topic at a time, following the Community of Inquiry approach of the Philosophy in Schools movement, will provide various opportunities to hear various helpful, unhelpful, difficult and hopefully creative possibilities, and these possible channels for action will be prioritised, worked through, reflected upon, and evaluated in different ways, so that opportunities for deep learning take place. It is a continuing surprise for a teacher to be present when sub-primary, primary and special-needs students exhibit the maturity of mind to make remarkable comment and choose the loftiest ways of being, using this mode of learning. Teachers at primary, secondary and tertiary levels of education provide regular opportunities for such third-order learning to take place, no matter which of the disciplines is involved. Such deep learning enhances the retention of knowledge and the reflection on action and in action. Such outcomes are the substance of evangelisation.

It is, therefore, as a particular pathway to such transformational change, that careful analysis of the work of Matthew Lipman and his emphasis on good thinking practices, and his development of the Community of Inquiry, within each discipline and each subject area, is so relevant here. This first recommended process of change, offered for all Catholic educational institutions, takes account of the content that Hargreaves and Shirley have outlined so well. We refer also to the modelling of educational development - to the familiar Community of Inquiry which is the backbone of the system instituted by Matthew Lipman in mid-20th century called Philosophy for Children or Philosophy in the Classroom.

This system uses the term, philosophy, to signal that the basis of children's education respects their intellectual potential from babyhood through primary, secondary and tertiary experience of learning. It is based on a respectful listening for questions, question-starters, collaborative learning, and fearless exploration of dilemma, paradox, mystery and daily experience married to history, diversity and tradition. Included also is the appropriate use of dualistic, that is black-and-white thinking, and trilectic thinking patterns, that is critical analysis accounting for multiple options. This is meant to forge clarity of vision, avoid tautology and circular thinking, and identify flaws in logic. The outcome is the encouragement of reflection, listening, understanding and eventually maturity of vision leading for Catholics to the deepening of faith.

Applying the *Community of Inquiry* to the business of learning in mature decision making takes care, tutelage and continuous practice. Martin (2011) provides a contemporary analysis of many of today's problems (Heasly, 2007, 2015) and the ordinand's progress can incorporate deeper understanding, without resorting only to the adversarialism of dogmatic and authoritarian clerics, in our efforts to learn mature skills in decision making. Applying also the work of the Leuven Network from the Catholic University in Belgium, carefully explored and explained by Paul Sharkey (2015) shows us that the critical thinking required by the authors of the Catholic Identity project is well served by using the Community of Inquiry. The ordinand is therefore required to experience and understand this methodology as part of missiology and evangelisation in the parish, school, and the wider community. Important here is the need to recognise that the methodology itself is concentrating on 'how' not 'what' is to be taught.

Change Processes already familiar in Education: theory, practice and praxis

Following Hugh Mackay (1993), we can trace the suspicion that Australian culture has become more violent than suspected, and ordinand's understanding must accommodate sufficiently the pitfalls of daily living and be capable of walking with the People in the Pews as they negotiate the regular and familiar dilemmas, without individualistic directions based only on dogma without integrating lived experience. Practice and familiarity with the praxis of the Community of Inquiry is a significant channel to make this aim effective.

In the business of Lipman's approach to the content of the Community of Inquiry curricula, we find channels to recognise and understand a variety of concepts of fairness, evidence, proof, controlling thoughts, reciprocity and self-knowledge (Heasly, 2015). Programs of rethinking, responding, reshaping, reconceptualising, reconstructing, and recreating many virtues, many values and much ethical integration of best practice (Davies, 2005), all become significant. Into this mix, it is possible to include the development of deep learning about restorative justice. Movements and associations probing and refining the praxis for teachers, students, administrators, and for our purposes, ordinands, priests, and hierarchical figures provide avenues of learning and leadership.

The ordinand must (not just should) be articulate and communicative about the complexity of what is to count as a balanced process for restorative justice. Such matters as the practice of empathy (not only sympathy) and compassion are the bedrock of such an understanding. It becomes obvious that personal emotional intelligence is central for the ordinand to effect the ethical requirements for such an aim to be realised. If Vatican ll has taught the current church anything of value, then provision for listening and attending to the nuanced development of scriptural analysis is required, and it is obvious that historical-critical analysis is needed urgently. All of this must take account of all that detailed neuroscience can teach us about how the neurons work in the brain. It seems to take about two years for a person – or an ordinand – to identify one's owned paradigm, evaluate its significance in the light of the Jesus message, and to effect the sociological and philosophical changes in that paradigm towards a deeper and more mature personal perspective in line with the Jesus message.

It then becomes a quest to understand what Vatican ll and its teachings can offer the People in the Pews that is distinctive and of more immediate value in what has always before counted as truth. The next step in the process of finding a way to become Christian in the Catholic tradition, is to study how to apply such newer and nuanced understandings of how we understand the message of Jesus, but free of the intrusion of authoritarian influences and indoctrination. The ordinand needs to be aware of such possibilities, and to be ready to support any of the People in the Pews in their personal quest to find a closer relationship with our loving Triune God. Once the way becomes clearer, with the help of the Holy Spirit, it takes around two years to effect, reflect and stabilise the paradigm change which brings us closer to our goal of relationship with Jesus as the most familiar face of our loving Triune God.

The emerging priest-ordinand will gradually develop the needed insights, understandings, and skills just as we the People in the Pews do. Journeying together then becomes a pilgrimage together, supporting each other as Jesus directed us, supported also through the auspices of the Holy Spirit, towards our final resting place in the presence of our Creator and Triune God. Jesus spoke of a wish that we might be 'one', and we find a harmonious aim of travelling together towards the internalisation of the Jesus message in daily life together.

The introduction of the concept of tensegrity, and the application of this concept to God's creation, allows us to recognise the intricate development of humankind, within the world around us, as we come to terms with the new knowledge in so many areas now available to us. 'The thread of continuity that informs bio-tensegrity, edu-tensegrity and theo-tensegrity begins with teachers who teach their students, through the medium of subjects taught, how to apply the broad arc of thinking skills, including knowledge about virtues, values and ethics' (Heasly 2015). We must understand that the myriads of small living entities, us, are the building blocks of the expanding life of created humankind, and this in turn means that each culture as this heaving vital entity becomes one of the building blocks of the expanding creation of the world.

This in turn leads us towards the expanded understanding of the geodesic dome, on which tensegrity is based. Inside that dome, all these living entities, parts of the Catholic tradition though often different from each other, become the web of interactive relationships called the Catholic Church. This is the road less travelled in today's world of instant everything. Patience, integrity, and resilience must (more than should) be the bedrock upon which the priest-ordinand builds the skills sets meant to enable an ability to walk with any of the People in the Pews when life gets painful, problematic and blurred at the edges.

The Community of Inquiry explored

Splitter and Sharp (1995), both pioneers with Matthew Lipman's worldwide movement in education, showed us so long ago in detail how the whole classroom practice is geared towards the promotion of children's gifts of inquiry, curiosity, wonder and eventually awe regarding the world they are discovering in childhood. The ordinand needs to have the benefit of this extensive experience in the early parts of schooling, education and personal development in daily life and in faith. Three separate areas are delineated (pp. 128-129) as central to the whole mode of education: Reasoning and inquiry; concept formation; and meaning-making.

They set out for us a series of strategies for reasoning and inquiry which allow the student or ordinand to progress. Giving reasons and distinguishing good reasons from bad reasons means recognising where clericalism may stifle honest efforts to understand God's complex world. Constructing inferences and evaluating arguments will help to distinguish where false claims can intrude and heresy can be identified and differentiated from exploring necessary and sometimes uncomfortable options. Ability to generalise when needed and using analogies to aid the inquiry is really inductive reasoning and is central to avoiding authoritarian intrusion. Identifying, questioning, and justifying assumptions helps to recognise when new and emerging understandings are addressed. Recognising contradictions and detecting fallacious reasoning brings opportunities to come closer to truth, to mystery, and to God.

Striving for consistency, making distinctions and connections like between part-whole, means-end, cause-effect will also help us to untie the knots and contradictions behind the kind of papal edicts which have banned the People in the Pews from talking about certain taboo subjects like women's ordination. Asking questions and problem seeking, building on mutual interest, and listening to others is central to the community of inquiry and is a parallel to the Jesus message as well – though it is not claimed as such in secular education. Making predictions, formulating and testing hypotheses, offering examples and counter-examples leads to correcting one's own thinking.

This will allow the participants like our ordinands to manage research without being led into side issues that lead to manipulation and disrespect. Formulating and using criteria, detecting vagueness and ambiguity, asking for evidence, and taking all (rather than some) relevant considerations into account brings an opportunity for conscious balance, honesty, and integrity to the interaction of participants. This practice becomes a way of thinking, an attitudinal maturity and a chance to learn from others.

Being open-minded and imaginative, developing intellectual courage, humility, tolerance and perseverance results in being committed to searching for truth. This intention allows us all, including the exalted, to become closer to each other with respect for difference, diversity and personal experience. Significantly, this seems to be the kernel of contradiction between the disengagement of those imbued with clericalism and those who choose the message of Jesus without the intrusion of a myriad of demands that seek to use power and control over the lives of the People in the Pews.

An example of application of the Community of Enquiry: Reasons and Inquiry

Faggioli and Vicini SJ (2015) recently chose the papers of twelve well-known scholars who participated in a conference called to review the legacy of Vatican ll. The voices of the twelve show some diversity, pointing prominently to an approach couched in the terms of the Community of Inquiry. Necessarily, there is a need to untie the knots that deliberate choices of binary thinking and dualistic reasoning have left for us. So often, the use of contrast is confused, vague or blurred. Adversarialism fogs the clarity of thought which accompanies real and deep listening. So often it shows that there is no predisposition to learn from each other: before, during and most particularly after the lengthy event we call Vatican ll. It is necessary to explore these matters in this volume from the twelve because this legacy of Vatican ll is also a legacy of the Holy Spirit, anticipating the reality of the thinking of Joachim of Fiore as we move forward into either the static of the third millennium, or into another dose of Dark Ages or perhaps into the new era of the Holy Spirit. Is that our choice?

Faggioli's introduction (2015) has a historical blend as he tells of the effort to identify the legacy of Vatican ll, highlighting that Pope Francis is the first papal figure who is post-Vatican ll. Not only is this pope from the southern hemisphere, but he played no part in the experience of Vatican ll deliberations. 'It is not enough to read the texts of Vatican ll, and not even to read them well, and it is not enough to read the 'History of Vatican ll' well: we must question those texts in light of these last fifty years of church history' (Faggioli, 2015) because Vatican ll was not a text, it was an event in the history of the church itself. Our 21st century ordinands need the experience of finding the relevant questions in order to incorporate the Community of Inquiry in its various forms in parish life. If we ignore the questions, we run an enormous risk of allowing clericalism to flourish. Faggioli warns us that 'Understanding the Church in the public arena needs a renewed understanding of Vatican ll' (Faggioli, 2015).

So we turn to John W. O'Malley SJ, the first of the twelve referred to above, as he emphasises that Vatican ll gave us an opportunity to become acquainted with the documents of the Council as 'a single, coherent corpus, called for a significant attitude shift and consequently a behaviour shift – on the part of all Catholics and especially on the part of leaders of the Church. It (the Council) wanted to forge a certain personality that radiated benignity, patience, and a limitless abundancy of mercy and goodness' (O'Malley in Faggioli, 2015). We ignore at our peril the changes O'Malley recommends with intensity and integrity.

'From commands to invitations; from threats to persuasion; from coercion to conscience; from monologue to dialogue; from sin obsession to recognition of dignity; from top down to shared; from ruling to serving; from exclusion to inclusion; from hostility to friendship; from rivalry to partnership; from fault-finding to search for common ground; from contempt to appreciation; from behaviour modification to inner appropriation of values; In summary, from *alienation to reconciliation*' (O'Malley in Faggioli).

It becomes obvious that a reason for experiencing the community of inquiry gives a lifelong and rich opportunity of personal focus to attain understanding of the complex legacy of Vatican ll, and allows us to use that opportunity to focus on the message of Jesus. And the ordinand needs the skills set to provide service in any parish or community milieu. O'Malley identifies that Pope Francis is 'asking us to step back, to put behind us the memories of liturgical wars, doctrinal wars, and other wars in which we have been engaged in the past fifty years, and now to turn our gaze outward'.

If we are to put our minds to the exciting prospect that O'Malley signals, we must begin to find the meaning-making that is embedded in the various documents emanating from Vatican ll. Peter Hunermann, the next author, begins the process by trying to pinpoint the actual kernel of a number of the documents which signal a paradigm shift: *Dignitatis Humanae, Nostra Aetate; Gaudium et Spes; Lumen Gentium; Sacrosanctum Concilium; Apostolicam Actuositatem; Christus Dominus; Presbyterorum Ordinis; Ecclesiarum Orientalium; Unitatis redintegratio.* Hunermann gives a profile and a point of focus (Hunermann in Faggioli). If we are to avoid the charge of promoting clericalism that George Wilson, a following author, implies, then the People in the Pews are being challenged to go to work, to gain the knowledge and explore the complex character of the paradigm shift rather than have a papal edict insist that some matters will change and others won't. In 21st century style, the leader of the parish or ecclesial community is expected to take up the challenge too. Leading means promoting and developing such measures, with resilience and perseverance.

In the sad story that Leslie Woodcock Tentler, another of the twelve, tells about the history of the background of *Humanae Vitae*,(Tentler in Faggioli, 2015), we see the dithering of a pope who could not move past the binary thinking embedded in tradition regarding the vexed area of contraception as a moral tenet of Catholicism. He took no account of the waiting, suffering and anguish of the families of People in the Pews. Despite much research, knowledge, life experience and professional approach from the seventy-plus members of the study group that pope Paul VI asked for, the final decision was a disaster. The People in the Pews were devastated by the conclusion, the ruling, the reasoning, and the sometimes appalling future for parents as spouses, and for children whose lives were certainly affected negatively.

Quality of life was not in the mix, and false reasoning which appears to use the slippery slide logic somehow was inserted because it was assumed that parents would include this as the permission for abortion to be a serious consequence of allowing medical means for contraception to be used. These two matters are separate issues, regardless of this connection feared by Ford SJ (Faggioli, 2015), when he insisted that *Humanae Vitae* was infallible teaching (in Faggioli). Richard McCormick SJ, another moral theologian involved in the historic battle for supremacy surrounding this document, did identify that 'questions were raised about the formation of conscience, about the response due to the ordinary magisterium, about the exercise of authority in the Church, about consultative processes and collegiality, about the meaning of the guidance of the Holy Spirit to the pastors of the Church' (Faggioli, 2015).

These six major questions were imperfectly understood by the People in the Pews but we knew that there was room to move as we hesitantly but significantly began to exercise our own maturing consciences in each of these vexed areas. Of course, a variety of final stances emerged, and this became a matter for the long rule of Pope John Paul ll, who wished to bring people *back* to his own reading of such conceptual questions. Theological dissent brought conflict, doubt, impatience, the silencing of good theologians and the groupthink that dogs the clericalist attitude we still find today. Community of Inquiry skills sets are urgently needed as a generally acceptable starting point as we strive to respond to the promptings of the Holy Spirit in our own milieux. This does not mean that existing skills, knowledge, expertise and understanding is deficient or to be discarded. It requires us to respond to the prompting of these leaders to stretch ourselves further towards the living out of the message of Jesus.

Richard Gaillardetz, yet another contributor of the twelve, contributed a remarkable paper as he showed us the value of 'virtue ecclesiology' most attuned to the legacy of Vatican ll – humility. He analyses humility in the church, humility as ecclesial self-assessment, and highlights Pope John XXIII who humbly asks for liturgical reform prior to development of *Sacrosanctum Concilium*: 'The sacred council has set out to impart an ever increasing vigor to the lives of the faithful' (Faggioli, 2015) and good Pope John tries to shift the paradigm of the church from the perfect society to the idea of pilgrimage – not only individual pilgrims as we undoubtedly are, but the 'church on pilgrimage'. For such authentic reform to take place, we need the continual *Community of Inquiry* to help us to attain the deep knowledge to accept the contrast of paradigm, investigate how this aim may be achieved as we negotiate the possible contradictions we may face.

If humility develops, then 'The Church is to be focused not on itself but on Christ, the subject of the Church's proclamation' –

rather than excesses of liturgical celebratory length, medieval dress, pomp and ceremony. Gaillardetz finally tells us that 'This Church rejects the arrogant assumption that divine truth is its exclusive possession. It sloughs off any and all pretensions to triumphalism in favour of patient and open dialogue'. And dialogue is what the familiar experience of the community of inquiry is offering for our use! The 21st century ordinand will develop such skills during preparation for ordination and further develop such skills in partnership with members of the People in the Pews in whichever parish appointment made. It becomes obvious that priests from other cultures would find such requirements a huge challenge. So it is for all of us, but we start from a position of positive cultural knowledge and linguistic skills, whereas the foreign-born priest is starting from a deficient model for evangelisation and pastoral care initiatives.

Lisa Sowle Cahill, a significant female contributor of Faggioli's twelve, takes up the analysis of this legacy from the standpoint of moral theology and social ethics, saying that this legacy is mixed, but that 'enhanced lay responsibility and lay activism are crucial to realising the Council's vision of aggiornamento' (Faggioli, 2015), adding, with reference to *Gaudium et Spes*, that 'The Spirit of the one God sustains all who work for justice in good faith', and we know that the church and the People in the Pews will expect leadership from the appointed ordinand able to collaborate, create and confirm at appropriate levels.

Bradford E. Hinze, another distinguished scholar in this remarkable group, presents a paper on the Vatican ll legacy promoting grassroots democracy. The ordinand and the People in the Pews will need to recognise the urgency of efficient governance, effective and transparent leadership and excellence in accountability within the arrangements of life within the Catholic Church of 21st

century global Catholicism. 'The phenomenon of local forms of synodality or conciliarity in parishes and dioceses is closely related to the Catholic promotion of grassroots democracy' (Faggioli, 2015).

Clericalism with its secrecy, exclusivity, disregard for the daily burdens of the People in the Pews, will not suffice in any form in the newer paradigm. Hinze suggests: 'Local churches can learn from community organisations advancing grassroots democracy, and such community organisations can likewise benefit from practices of local synodality'. Much is therefore dependent on the clear-eyed approaches of the leadership and the faithful in order to rid each ecclesial community of clericalism with the urgent but calm leadership of the ordained minister and the lay leadership team. Hinze concludes: 'Significantly, many of these same practices and skills are needed to advance local forms of synodality in parishes and dioceses, in council development, in pastoral planning, and in other forms of participatory governance'.

Finally, the influence within the legacy of Vatican ll of a number of Jesuit leaders is crucial in four separate conceptual areas to the possibility of a renewed hope for the church. The complexity of addressing in full the biblical and ecumenical conscience of the church; the listening and analysis of what is meant if we describe the whole church as sacrament; the paradigm shift implied and needed when adjusting the whole church-world relationship and finally the understanding and justice of really living the meaning of global religious freedom: all of these became central to the deliberations of Vatican ll. Resistance from different groups like traditionalists, whose comfort and understanding has been challenged, has led to much careful and at times anguished negotiations both then and now.

That renewed hope that bubbled along with the various meetings, clashes of revered and renowned figures of unbounded expertise, led to the realisation that the Holy Spirit was indeed present in the ebb and flow of the Vatican ll deliberations. Regardless of the resistance of the traditionalists who were determined to keep that disengaged clericalism as their tradition, 'Vatican ll inaugurated a season of hope both in the history of the Church and of humankind' says Andrea Vicini SJ (in Faggioli) in his concluding remarks. 'It is not, however, a naïve, generic, superficial and vague hope ... it is biblically inspired, theologically provoking, influenced by the historical context, and in dialogue with contemporary interlocutors' (Faggioli, 2015) at the concluding meeting of this conference.

These authors examined our past, our present and our future from the visionary point of hope. 'Finally, hope animates God's people to envision the future and to contribute in shaping it, with collaborative and reconciling engagement; a hope that is thematic, engaged, and personalist. With renewed hope, and with the commitment that hope inspires, we will contribute to fulfil and even to expand the Council's way of being and of becoming Jesus' disciples in today's world and in history'(Faggioli, 2015). It becomes clearer that we will need to rely on the integrity of the ordinand appointed to each parish and ecclesial community armed with the skills that the *Community of Inquiry* can contribute, so that undemocratic behaviours are minimised, democratic practices are maximised, and clericalism is systematically relegated to the past.

Deductive and Inductive thinking patterns – the technological influence

One of the changes that emerge from the worldwide spread of technology in communications is the reliance on the mobile phone and the computer for increasing influences in lifestyle living. We find that this digital technology is based on a particular form of deductive thinking. This pattern is constrained and constricted by the emphasis on a given process by which we access the various devices and their formats to find and work with material conducive to better quality of life, of business, of economics, of communications, of travel and of research. A series of benefits in collaboration, in consultation, in commercial operations and in technological updates rely on knowing how each device works.

Access is, therefore, the vital tool with which we engage with the world around us in education, in health care, in problem-solving, in recreation and in travel. If technology is impacting the lives of each generation in a more intrusive style than the generation that went before, it becomes obvious why people like Baby Boomers, whose brains were wired towards a mixture of deductive and inductive thinking patterns, might find it difficult to engage in a universal style with the mobile phone. Today's x-generation, y-generation, millennials and z-generations are so familiar with this reliance on one small device in which so much information is stored, that they are not always aware that the brain loses traits and skills if those traits and skills are not used. Advertising slogans like 'use it or lose it' make this clear. However, what is not always a conscious consideration is that this same approach applies to the ability to use inductive reasoning skills where they can produce creative and innovative outcomes for the individual. If all we need to provide us with information of immediate use, like the navigation route to a destination we have not visited before, then we begin also to risk losing the very important brain skill of remembering.

Seemingly, the ordinand, the hierarchy, the People in the Pews and the secular world all need to collaborate and include opportunities to address the possible loss of these faculties before it is too late, and we find ourselves unable to respond to the impulses of the Holy Spirit, whose business it is to prompt us to be possible co-creators in the forward plan, the will of the Creator God, who has embedded these potentialities within humankind. To this end, the experience of the Community of Inquiry needs to be married with the theological arts that are available so that the full potential of each unique human being is allowed to flower. The alternative is to descend into the evil of omission, to the burden of impotence, to the collapse of the extraordinary gifts dimly visible around us. This is not the message of Jesus, who asked that we look towards the love of God and of neighbour, and practice that support, understanding and insight available. If only we can stop the vicious infighting, the claims of privilege and the ignorance of what we as humans are now capable of becoming in 21st century life, we can begin working towards wholeness. That means that we pool our knowledge, our understandings, our new insights and move forward.

We already see examples of this forward movement in the extraordinary ability of medical experts who can provide surgery that separates conjoined twins; brain surgery that relieves all sorts of negative pressures; neurological stimulation that adds important energy to neural highways allowing the existing bodily energy to upgrade the general health of individuals. The extraordinary results of cancer research, aged and degenerative conditions, and the emerging understanding of how the individual can help themselves by alternative processes, provide situations where the human condition does not appear to follow predicted courses. This highlights the need for those inductive thinking patterns quite dramatically. This line of reasoning will be further expanded below when it will be possible to begin the first steps of what is to count as a theology of the human condition, rather than a theology of the body. It must be understood as building on what has already been the tradition of the Catholic faith.

In the tradition of Habakkuk, we see echoes of today's confused scenario:

'O Lord, how long shall I cry for help, and you will not listen? Or cry to you "Violence" and you will not save? Why do you make me see wrongdoing and look at trouble? Destruction and violence are before me; strife and contention arise. So the law becomes slack and justice never prevails. The wicked surround the righteous – therefore judgment comes forth perverted.' (Habakkuk 1:1-4)

Habakkuk's vision is the one we need to be alert about today. 'Then the Lord answered me and said, "Write the vision; make it plain upon tablets ...' (Habakkuk 2:2) and we follow suit...

HUG/BUG
The Heasly Behaviour Uncertainty Grid

OUTCOME							OUTCOME
Behaviour	Consequences	Features	ELEMENTS	Features	Consequences	Behaviour
Aggression	Stultification	Laziness	PHYSICAL RESPONSE	Skills Appetites	Strength	Perseverance Courage
Tyranny Deceit	Unpredictability Hopelessness	Hysteria Moodiness	EMOTIONAL RESPONSE	Wishes Dreams	Response-ability	Honesty
Greed Avarice	Narcissism	Selfishness	SOCIAL RESPONSE	Communication Love	Openness	Patience Justice Forgiveness
Jealousy Envy	Prejudice Inconsistency	Arrogance Presumption	INTELLECTUAL RESPONSE	Inquiry Logic	Critical skills	Discernment
Abuse – self or other	Despair	Nihilism	SPIRITUAL RESPONSE	Quest – satisfaction wholeness	Personal paradigm	Integrity

Begin with the middle column, then contrast the left and right side columns.

CHAPTER 6

The 'how' of developing Conscience

We turn now to a second process of major change which is of value to the ordinand of the 21st century. This whole system is built on the principles of the Community of Inquiry, but takes these principles further into the daily life experience of students at primary, secondary and tertiary levels. Given the development of the patterns of thinking and the application of thinking skills already well-known and practised, but highlighted above, we are led by the various developments of the Philosophy in the Classroom via the Community of Inquiry.

The next step is to apply such principles and practice to the business of what could be detailed and systematised for the teaching of virtues, values and ethics in maturing students at senior secondary level. It is important to understand that each virtue, each value and each ethical concept is separate and can be taught and understood first as an abstract human attitude, easily identifiable in literature, social studies and other milieux. Young and not-so-young People in the Pews find themselves facing a problem, and are uncertain at first of how to proceed. This uncertainty dogs the teenager, and it became the bedrock reasons for the development of this system.

In a democratic tradition and in true educational form, these concepts were taught in abstract as the precursors of how to make quality decisions and lead now quite naturally to recognition that it is possible to teach today's students in the Age of Instant Everything, how to make decisions which can contribute to the development of conscience. It is certainly to be distinguished from what decisions are to be made. So the title of HUG/BUG was devised by the students in the research program as 'Heasly Uncertainty Grid and Behaviour Uncertainty Grid', and they shortened such a term to HUG/BUG for convenience.

In the business of the current problems faced in our church, the People in the Pews will have views about many of the elements of the scandals which are rife today, one of which is the cult of clericalism. To address this situation, we can apply and test whether tensegrity can be the starting point for refreshment and regeneration in the daily life of the People in the Pews today. We would consider that tensegrity is the concept of a whole organism which has many and varied parts, all of which have their own inner life but all of which become known as part of a larger whole entity: in this circumstance of the whole church.

The concept of tensegrity allows us to recognise that the inner life of each part prompts it to cleave to the whole larger entity by push-pull factors that distribute the weight and significance of each in relation to the whole in such a way that the whole remains a single entity. If any part breaks away, the whole is diminished or broken. If we apply this as a parallel to our church today, the vicious adversarialism and infighting in different parts of the world can be addressed. If mercy, compassion and reconciliation are part of the principles of daily church life, then restorative justice demands that this is an urgent and immediate task. The HUG/BUG system allows for the next generations to have opportunities that may not have existed previously. It also does not allow indoctrination and disregard for the primacy of conscience to be inserted into the lived experience of the People in the Pews.

Tensegrity is the basic concept. Bio-tensegrity is the application of that concept to the biological studies that Ingber (1997) discovered last century. Following on from that, it seemed appropriate to apply tensegrity also to the whole entity called education, and so edu-tensegrity was born. It seems appropriate now to recognise another parallel which can be called theo-tensegrity, which is the application of the concept of tensegrity to the whole of the Catholic Church today, with all its many parts, practices and priestly efforts to minister to the People in the Pews today.

In fact, it would not be an anomaly to stretch the concept further and include all of the Christian denominations in an ecumenical sense into the next step as the Holy Spirit directs. Much will need to be developed and patience is needed, but action is needed now and authors like John Maguire (1999), Linda Hogan (2000), and Frank Brennan (2007) have much to contribute, about the idea of decision making in the business of what is to count as conscience, and to offer as they discern the variations, problems of understanding, and building blocks of paradigm change which we face in a democratisation of the Catholic tradition today.

Hogan's careful introduction analysing what she calls the problem of conscience, is a recommended starting point. When she identifies a 'personalist theology of conscience', it is possible to recognise the connection which is part of the background of the Uncertainty Grid (HUG/BUG). It is also possible to explore with her the daily lived experience of living with contradictions. She gives implications regarding the paradigm change towards personalist theology of conscience as 'a greater recognition of the role of history and change in ethics; a focus on the moral significance of intentions and circumstances in addition to the act itself; a greater degree of sophistication in categorising the different kinds of moral norms and the kinds of claims they make; a rethinking of the relationship between the individual and magisterium on the basis of the relocation of moral authority' (Hogan, 2000).

To address the contradictions, disagreements and the possibility of dialogue within the church, resting on cultural diversity and competing theologies that are embedded in binary thinking, it is useful to remember her opening remarks: 'The divisions that exist within the church today can partly be explained by the presence of competing theologies of conscience. Throughout this book I have suggested that it is entirely understandable that such differences have emerged, given the confused and contentious history of conscience in the Catholic tradition. Not only have there been disagreements among theologians about the precise nature and role of conscience in the life of the Christian, but there have also been inconsistencies and contradictions with regard to the practical application of the various theological principles' (Hogan, 2000).

Urgently, we need to recognise the underlying implication in the HUG/BUG system of decision making that sexuality is present in each of the elements of personality set out in the HUG/BUG grid. These elements are listed in the central column of the grid. As such, it is also very important to recognise complexity, diversity and depth within each and all of the People of God, their circumstances, their difficulties, their journeys. The corollary of this recognition is that the one-size-fits-all edicts, which have characterised the moral theology of Christendom up to and past Vatican Council 1, need careful, extensive and expert review.

New research in so many disciplines takes place, takes precedence, and takes account of myriads of relevant details. Application of the details of the HUG/BUG system rests on the underlying understanding that our personalities are unique; that we have a range of possible choices from very positive to very negative; that patterns of behaviour have from time immemorial been called virtues or values or ethics – or their opposite. Each line of the grid can therefore be read as naming certain virtues or their opposites on a spectrum. Students and teachers can substitute other virtues, values or ethics in any line and compose the requisite notes when discussions and learning strategies are being built.

Respect, patience, and understanding must accompany knowledge and relevant skills when engaged in educative evangelisation. Effectiveness in accompanying each of the People of God, especially in matters surrounding individual decision making skills and the development of personal conscience are paramount. Other virtues need to be promoted to bridge the individual-community scenario. HUG/BUG study and analysis will ease the young, the ordinand and the mature towards the compassion, the prudence, the careful acceptance of self, others and the expanding consciousness of the spiritual that we need on life's journey.

Jesus began his ministry with a call to a change of heart and mind – implying that if people are to accept him, they would need to put aside the old ways of seeing (Levo in Claffey et al, 2013). Levo pinpoints that we are 'on holy ground, re-visioning, re-imagining what it means to be human and sexual (Mark 10:42-45) as pinpointed by Richard McCormack: 'hoping, critiquing past and present, regretting, forgiving, inspiring, dialoguing and dreaming' (Faggioli,2015).

Catholic culture influences how we understand sexuality, as the church has considered itself as the authority. Levo identifies the dualism: 'spirit and matter, sacred and profane'. That influence quite deliberately discriminates quite illogically against women, denying women autonomy and independent decision making capacity. It is also significant that a distorted emphasis on women leads to being blamed alone, rather than equating blame to both partners in sexual activity. This is especially significant when the practice is to inspect any incident as a one-off act, without recognising that patterns of behaviour can be virtuous or vicious, especially in the area of sexuality.

Thankfully, Levo, writing in *Broken Faith* (Claffey et al, 2013) draws our attention to the Foucault position on accepted Christian dogma: a tradition which reflects male experience only; recognises sexuality as genital act only; sees sexual action as uncontrollable and a pall on actual spirituality and can only see woman as the eternal Eve of the Hebrew tradition, as a source of evil. Even in reference to Bishop Geoffrey Robinson, Levo highlights Robinson's view that the Catholic Church approach is dangerous because of a presumption that reduced God's creation of woman, in whom new life is engendered. Such contradiction, in presuming to know exclusively the mind of God is a product of the dualism which insists that the sacred is within the church and the secular is somehow not. Yet at the same time, a deeper contradiction is promoted by the stance of being in the world but not of the world (John 17) thereby downgrading God's created world yet further.

This tendency to compartmentalise humankind into disintegrated categories which are separate from each other has led to the cult of clericalism, to the oppression of women, to the adversarial assumption of power and control over the People of God. A false understanding of humility, with its outcome of patient and painful submission, forces that unreality that borders on psychological imbalance, but is called within clericalism by the name of holiness. The concept of holiness, therefore, is one area in the tenets of the Catholic faith needing extensive deep analysis to rescue human sexuality from that imbalance. As Levo recommends: 'Each generation's task is to expand its understanding in light of its experience and what it has come to learn from many disciplines'. This at least will lead to wholesome understanding of human sexuality, and avoid the splintered effects of its claimed tradition.

In examination of ways to be authentic, Levo introduces us to Judith Jordan. Jordan identifies areas of the human prism. The emphasis on elements of the human personality can become focused on empathic knowing and sexual desire – in modes of knowing which connect that knowing with empathy, connectedness and love (Levo in Claffey et al, 2013). It is, therefore, important to examine another consideration that Levo outlines, helping us to understand four ways of being human: to love and be loved; to discover one's gifts and give them in service; to be in relationship with mystery and with God; to meet basic human needs in healthy appropriate ways.

Does that sin of presumption that the Catholic Church has for centuries called tradition, mistake the meaning of what we understand when we refer to what it means to be human and what is to count as recognition of the depth and mystery of divinity? This stance is to be distinguished from the revelation of God's will at precise times, in precise situations and for precise human need. God created humans to be the best that a human can become. We are limited by whatever boundaries of wonderful entities we can become – as humans.

So perhaps we have not reached the zenith of what being human can be. God created humankind to be in relationship with the Godhead, even being co-creators with the Godhead in various ways, otherwise sexuality and fecundity are a contradiction. God did not create humans to acquire the ontological change from human to divine. There is a boundary, no matter the wishful thinking of those who yearn to experience the life of God in its deepest divine sense. After all, being divine is the mystery of Divinity, and the created beings called humanity are distinct, complex and extraordinary in themselves, but not divinity. We, therefore, can become co-creators of much that is new, as yet unimagined, both for good intent which we call the will of God, or for evil intent, which we call sin. Joachim of Fiore had a point when he referred to the three millennial eras of the history of humankind: the first for God as Creator; the Second for God as Redeemer or perhaps Life-giver; and the third for God as the Holy Spirit, who seems lately to be shaping us into co-creators in the future of the Cosmic wonder we call his Creation.

Perhaps we can say: Humans are created, but God IS. So does Perfectionism become the striving for a holiness which implies aspiring to be divine? Co-creation with the Trinity means using our human gifts including our sexuality for God and his purposes, not for becoming God. Similarly, Levo recommends a series of fundamental shifts: biological, psychological, sociological and theological. Levo recognises a centrally urgent stance: 'These changes highlight the fact that our understanding of sexuality has shifted from something we do, to something we are, a central dimension of being human'.

This central dimension can be analysed by using the twelve Categories of Influence applied as a consequence of the HUG/ BUG skills set. These Categories of Influence are listed for consideration (Heasly, 2015): dimensions of daily life; dimensions of thinking; dimensions of education; input from research theorists which in this project will be called theologians but more effectively will be People in the Pews; constructs and existing knowledge which in this instance will include realistically and humbly approaching the problems and dilemmas we face with courage and authenticity. This is augmented by medical-biological and philosophical-theological theory: bio-tensegrity – edu-tensegrity – theo-tensegrity which means including the new knowledge from science in all its various disciplines, especially neuroscience and psychology.

Included also are constructs about meaning, reasoning and choice: dependence, independence and interdependence founded on an understanding of the various patterns of thinking that extend our understanding beyond simplistic binary contrasts. Of course, we must expand our notions about teachers and teaching: professional collaboration, democratic leadership, teaching about the virtues-values-ethics web, with careful inclusion of effective and efficient and ethical teaching-learning practice rather than indoctrination. Then there is integration of the whole process of change.

This is demonstrated in the process of teaching how to develop decision making skills in today's instant culture which expands students' and ordinands' new knowledge, understanding and expanded skills by complex study programs. Of course, the aim is to give them confidence that they can support and give pastoral insights to the People in the Pews. We must include emerging connections of neuroscience to learning, without the false dichotomy of secular and the sacred stopping the development of appreciation and awe of the wonders of our God. We therefore need collaboration between teaching staff at all levels of primary, secondary and tertiary education so that the basic principle of theo-tensegrity can prevail eventually.

By redefining our concept of human sexuality to include the new knowledge and understanding available today, we discover the 'emphasis on relationship, connection, communion, wholeness and presence'. Levo's claim that sexual energy links with 'both personal and communal wholeness' as she connects with Rolheiser's definition: giving myself over to community, friendship, family, service, creativity, humour, delight', so that with God, we can bring that life into the world in physical, emotional, social, intellectual and spiritual ways as shown in the central column of the HUG/BUG grid.

We must persist with the theological exploration that Levo sets out for us as she examines the qualities of underlying wholeness and integration naming our emerging self-awareness, rather than self-focus; responsible freedom, rather than wilfulness; developing creativity by dint of our baptismal responsibility 'to re-new and re-shape creation'. There is an urgent need, rather than use and degrade, dominate and control, towards deepening our capacity for an intimacy which listens to our deepest longings and outreach towards our Creator. This, rather than the current and limited idea that intimacy is equated with genital sex, is the central emphasis. This understanding makes the ludicrous demand on priests of the Latin Rite for a mandated lifelong oath of celibacy quite obvious.

Importantly also, shame and sexuality linked in Catholic current teaching is analysed by Levo and she recognises that personal integration of a maturing personality does not repress, suppress, sublimate or gratify one's sexual longings. Levo examines the Hines work on reframing sexual integration, stating: 'Shame-based stances towards sexuality only lead to unhealthy, non-integrated sexuality'.

We need to expand our understanding of intimacy: with self, with others, with our God, knowing that this expansion impinges significantly on the current formation practices in separated seminary conditions, where aloneness, or maybe loneliness, and the practice of ignoring sexuality leads often to various personal consequences because these consequences 'of not living an intimate life can help us to see perhaps the greatest failure of our time is the failure of intimacy on the part of many – clergy, religious and lay', says Levo. This is central and a very significant outcome.

The question of conscience development becomes central. The quality of decision making impinges directly on life, sexuality, prayer, faith, spirituality, and strength of purpose. We were created to aspire towards the best form of wholeness that humans can become, rather than try to become spiritual automatons with collapsed personal emotional landscapes, intellectual deadness and spiritual infantilism – whether hierarchical or lay person.

Levo points us again to Richard McCormick: 'Moral Theology in the Year'. She examines nine separate issues that we need to pursue regarding our Christian understanding and attitudes to build up a

21st century response: Christocentric and anchored in charity; universalising in its appeal; appropriate subsidiarity; personalistic; modest and tentative; ecumenical; inductive; pluralistic; aspirational.

In response to changes of emphases set out in this list, Levo concludes that tradition must (not just should) be understood as a living entity needing continuous re-contextualisation. Urgently needed is a deliberate recalibration and shift away from equating guilt and shame with sexuality. So is an emphasis which is needed on the relational aspect of human sexuality, central to the message of Jesus to love. Only then, inclusivity and integrative communities must give full attention to the voices and role of women in all aspects of church life, rather than the present tokenism.

The glaring ongoing need for education of both clergy and laity must be addressed allowing knowledge, understanding, skills sets to be honed together to integrate the whole of Christianity today. This is certainly first in the Catholic life of each nation and culture, but must be expanded honestly and respectfully in an ecumenical sense. Seeing spirituality and sexuality as part of the complex character elements of humanity, rather than as in opposition to each other, will aid integration and allow hope to resurface, says Levo. In this way, social symptoms of unease, depression, psychosis, narcissism and arrogance will not mitigate against the existence of hope by increased resignation, aggression, despair and often suicide.

Paradigm change needs a series of well-understood steps as we begin the challenge of change with inevitable demands of personal skills sets that include deep listening, partial or full immersion in the difficulties of the vulnerable in our midst; strongly learned patterns of trilectic complex thinking skills. Space and time to try out options and distinguish mistakes from failures coupled with patience, prudence and tolerance (not toleration) in our interactions with those in all aspects of our lives will enhance personal balance and growth.

Edu-Tensegrity, Theo-Tensegrity and the Geodesic Dome

> 'This theory of edu-tensegrity derives from the architectural concept of tensegrity, using tension and compression as building strategy (e.g. London's millennium dome; Melbourne's soccer stadium); modelling inductive thinking before deductive thinking; employing dialectic, trilectic and quadrilectic logics' (Heasly, 2015).

Categories of Influence model trilectic thinking (the practice of including as many options in our thinking to maximise balance in our logic). They present responses, response-abilities and responsibilities, to inform teachers' planning, execution and facilitation for teaching of thinking skills in primary, secondary and tertiary levels of education. We need to reapply this whole system to the paradigm change needed to rid ourselves of clericalism.

This theory of edu-tensegrity can be expanded to incorporate the architectural concept of tensegrity, to construct an adjacent concept of theo-tensegrity. This new concept would identify the many efforts of theologians and others when probing deeply for clarity, coherence and creativity in understanding more of what Christians, especially Catholics, believe. What faith practice means in 21st century terms, and consequently how the understanding of what is to count as understanding the Triune God, must expand in the face of medical science, neuroscience, 21st century education, cosmology and quantum physics.

What is tensegrity?

Donald E. Ingber (1997, pp. 48-57) indicates tensegrity is a concept founded on rules guiding the design of organic structures, from simple carbon compounds to complex cells and tissues. He highlights a structure using self-assembly as tiers of systems within systems. Ingber (1997, pp. 48-49) realised that 'tensegrity structures are mechanically stable not because of the strength of individual members but because of the way the entire structure distributes and balances mechanical stresses'. Ingber indicates this is used by architects, who model understanding of distribution and balanced weight. The 'push-pull factors' become counteracting forces, equilibrating throughout the structure enabling stabilisation.

Ingber's challenge to our understanding is contained in one awesome statement: 'An astoundingly wide variety of natural systems, including carbon atoms, water molecules, proteins, viruses, cells, tissues, and even humans and other living creatures, are constructed using a common form of architecture known as tensegrity' (1997, p. 48). Ingber tells us about his discovery of Tensegrity: 'The molecules and cells that form our tissues are continually removed and replaced; it is the maintenance of pattern and architecture, I reasoned, that we call life. Tensegrity structures are mechanically stable not because of the strength of individual members but because of the way the entire structure distributes and balances mechanical stresses' (p. 49).

And so was born the geodesic dome in architecture. In analysing the features of this concept in architecture, he realised 'an increase in tension in one of the members results in increased tension in members throughout the structures' – and if we apply this concept of tensegrity as a metaphor for the whole Catholic Church, we recognise that the shame, guilt, distress, anger and serious pain within the People in the Pews, is causing serious stress to all parts of the church. It is not enough to identify the elements of that stress. We must address all parts of the problem area before collapse inevitably destroys the whole.

The geodesic dome becomes a metaphor for overall education, on which are imposed educational Categories of Influence. The concept of the geodesic dome is the underpinning influence in the new paradigm. The twelve coloured triangles below provide a framework integrating the subjects taught. There are twelve separate areas inside the dome, representing each category of influence. Other triangles represented refer to the myriad of topics, subject areas, specialisations and particular learning areas existing today. Included are the meta-concepts of education: philosophy, psychology, sociology of education, administration, curriculum development, provision of relevant resources for students and teachers, professional development for teachers, specialists, theorists, and administrators. In theo-tensegrity terms, these twelve dimensions can be translated by theologians steeped in the Catholic tradition and capable of the discernment beyond that which a student of theology can provide. Herein lies the urgent challenge to provide the content that will wipe out the ills, the illogicality, and the disengagement of clericalism. Theologians have much work to do as they assume rightful leadership in various specialisations within theology today.

Edu-tensegrity and the 12 Categories of Influence

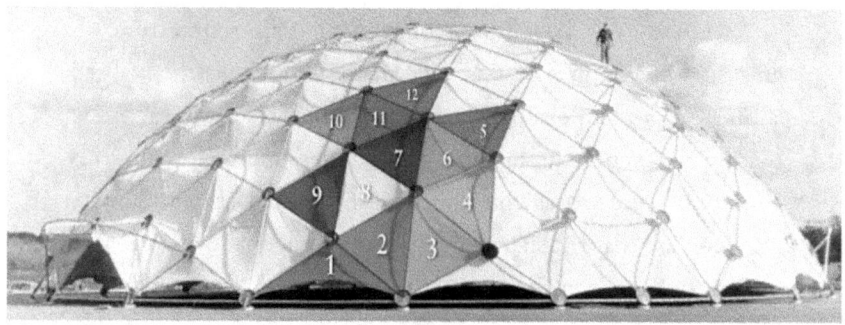

Source: *Scientific American*, January, 1998, p. 48; digitally altered by Scott Larritt-Evans

Each triangle has three sides connecting to produce a complete balanced concept of how future education needs to function. This is trilectic thinking in action. We cannot afford to exclude any Categories of Influence without finding that the whole structure weakens. This whole concept is set out in detail in Heasly (2015).

Mulford (1994, p. 38) says: 'Education should be preparing tomorrow's adults to meet ethical as well as economic imperatives – preparing them not only for a life of work, but also a life of worth. We must not only educate to serve the purposes of others, but also develop their capacity to question the purposes of others. We must bolster students' will to seek wisdom. We must enable them to communicate, to think creatively about complex issues, to act responsibly, and – when necessary – to act selflessly. A skills crisis would indeed be bad enough but a values crisis would be devastating.' If it is pertinent to general education needs, it is also pertinent to the precision with which we educate ourselves and our children in the message of Jesus. It follows then that the ordinand will need to understand all that is inherent in this approach to education within the Catholic tradition.

The concept of edu-tensegrity is an attempt to harness the various Categories of Influence that drift significantly throughout education. These connect by the unifying theme of a geodesic dome and the twelve triangles. These Categories of Influence are equal in significance and priority, and colour-coded to emphasise the following points. They connect by the unifying theme of the geodesic dome and many triangles, many yet to be constructed, especially when applying this theory to the concept of theo-tensegrity. They will be equal in significance and priority and they do not rely on binary thinking patterns for efficiency.

Each category of influence within theology will provide highlights of interdependent elements of theology: Christology,

Philosophy of religion, Psychology of Religion, Sociology of religion, Liberation theology, Feminist theology, Negative theology, Process theology, Fundamental Theology and Practical theology. We now must model what Practical theology can offer us.

Three dimensions for each Category of Influence

The first step in edu-tensegrity and in theo-tensegrity, using trilectic thinking processes, outlines three interconnected components for each category of influence.

'Dimensions of daily life' incorporates ontologically virtues, values and ethics. 'Dimensions of thinking' incorporates ontological, epistemological and pedagogical influences. 'Dimensions of education' incorporates ontologically philosophy, psychology and sociology of education. 'Curriculum theorists' includes ontologically my view about the centrality of three experts – Wilson, Lipman and Vardy for education, but Vatican Council ll indicates much for theo-tensegrity – maybe Congar, Murray and Kung? The choice will vary depending on the cultural milieu.

'Constructs about knowledge and the thinking curriculum' incorporate ontologically Wilson's Moral Components List, Lipman's Community of Inquiry and Vardy's study of Religious and Values Education, so useful for theo-tensegrity as well. Relevance of Vatican ll content is obvious here. 'Three central historical and philosophical figures in education' epistemologically are Aristotle, Dewey and Schwab for education purposes; but the scourge of clericalism must be cleared out by the effort to introduce theo-tensegrity as descriptive of the global Catholic Church, so maybe Paul Collins, Massimo Faggioli and Ian Linden could be the starting point? Each cultural group will insert familiar leading theologians here.

The particular historical and philosophical constructs epistemologically are 'Meaning, Reasoning and Choice' whereby numerous research resources will be needed to include the new knowledge, and to inaugurate the newer paradigm that seems to be surfacing through the Holy Spirit in the third millennium. This new knowledge emerges through an inspired approach to the Gospels; through willingness to pray together; and through the careful use of thinking skills already noted.

'Teachers and teaching' are shaped epistemologically by philosophical, eschatological, and educational goals, and the inclusion of what is to count as respectful evangelising of future generations must be allowed to emerge in God's own time. Using the possibility of paradigm change, acknowledging that this does not mean changing the basic tenets of our faith, is central to this part of the process. 'Instrumental contributions to support thinking and decision making' for life skills beginning epistemologically with personal understanding (using the 'ME' diagram) extending this to decision making (using the Six Steps process) and exploring behavioural concepts and their consequences (using the HUG/BUG) is offered to those whose expertise is sufficient to incorporate these matters universally.

'Outcomes and issues of dependence and rich learning' technologically include student dependence (requiring distinct help to acquire new knowledge), independence (requiring space to access and display new knowledge) and interdependence (requiring scaffolding of collaborative experience for internalisation and application of new knowledge). The ordinand will need to be well-versed in this area of praxis. The instinct of students 'to construct a belief system, make decisions about the good life and a career' allows students to accept technological responsibility for connecting and constructing their personal belief system, their preferred future and their career of choice. Evangelisation emerges as all of this learning becomes the foundation of what is to count as faith, hope and love between the Triune God and humble humankind.

'Integration of student, teacher and curriculum' incorporates technological emphasis placed on collaboration and interdependence of student, teacher and curriculum or instrumental design expert for today's educational needs, and this must be expanded to include the continuous promotion of thinking skills in parallel with the tenets of faith. Ordinands then will have a foundation worthy to become the bedrock we need to address the many complications in our changing world today.

In a similar and parallel fashion, it will be possible to develop the three-dimensional profile of these concepts which will contribute to a deeper exploration of what is to count as faith, and what is to count as knowledge of the Triune God, the Three Persons in the Trinity, and the relationships of each to the other. This exploration would be supported by further analysis of how kenosis of the Triune God, that outpouring of selfless and unlimited love, might be a channel to achieve clarity, coherence and creativity in the vast field of theology for humans to advance and approach deeper personal relationships with that loving, merciful and compassionate Triune God. This would be tasking the budding theologians who are also ordinands with the responsibility of understanding these considerations at a deep enough level to effectively use their knowledge in pastoral care of the People in the Pews, where the voices in the *sensus fidelium* will of course expect address of fundamental questions of faith, hope and love.

It is worth analysing the 'ME' diagram as the visual impact of the six expanding boundaries gives us an appreciation of the daily lived experience of the ordinary person expanding personal knowledge and social mores from babyhood, through the various stages of physical, social, intellectual, emotions and spiritual development which must be integrated gradually as the person matures. The ordinand must be capable of understanding the diversity of such interactive and integrated matters, with the aim of walking with any person as problems, paradoxes, and purposes are identified by the individual, whose need of guidance and support must not include manufactured conclusions and imposed solutions.

Research into what constitutes Conscience: the Issue of Discernment

We now provide the four-part Thinking Skills System (pedagogical tools) developed and noted in the previously chapter, all of which contributes to our understanding of what constitutes Conscience, with particular emphases on what is to count as Discernment. It is important to indicate that discernment was treated and developed in the Rule of St Benedict- 'discernment' (discretio in Latin) says Benedict 'is the mother of the virtues'. It is equally important to record at this point that Ignatius extends this concept in the 16th century. It seems urgent to extend this virtue, as Ignatius did for his era, into the modern world of our current secular and religious milieux.

The reason for this as an educational goal is couched in the prevalence today of the culture or cult of individualism. The tendency towards extreme risk-taking, especially by young people, seems to accompany simplistic and random binary (black-and-white) thinking patterns. These tendencies often don't allow students or others the opportunities they need to build a balanced set of skills to develop a profile which promotes a noticeable and authentic Catholic Identity. It is significant that z-generations, for instance, live more in a digital and virtual community than they inhabit the interactive community understood by Baby Boomers and those who came before them.

Particularly in primary, secondary and tertiary education, those decisions are often unaided and unfocused, unshaped and haphazard in nature. Part of this haphazardness includes a somewhat random student approach to planning, to classroom infrastructure and to personal decision making. To address this apparent societal phenomenon, the Four-part Thinking System is offered. Examination and analysis of each of the four pedagogical tools will uncover meaning, understanding and insights useful to students and teachers alike, as we address the Jesus message of the incoming reign of God.

The use of the System facilitates student thinking skills and allows for independent and responsible progress in maturity, focused particularly on developing further the Catholic Identity of our coming generations. Examination of the meaning of Conscience can be facilitated by the four pedagogical tools: the art and science of questioning, the 'ME' Diagram, the Six Steps of Decision Making, and the HUG/BUG diagram. It will be invaluable in prompting the responses of the ordinand towards mature and balanced evangelisation.

The Art and Science of Questioning

The first of the tools is the Art and Science of Asking Questions. Initially, this may seem simplistic, but in today's world of individualism, ever-present and instant digital technology and extreme risk-taking, the opportunities for reflection, rumination and speculation are reduced often to instant answers, finger on the search engine button.

There is an art in the asking of questions. The creativity, the awe, the wonder of the human mind propels us often to pursue questions about the world around us, about the people within our relationships, about our growing self-understanding and about the striving for insight into 'the Beyond'. It is important to take account of both Socratic and Aristotelian methods of questioning, as the one leads all questions to analyse in minute detail all facets of a topic being addressed, (a wonderful use of deductive reasoning) whereas the other allows similar and opposing questions to include side issues, speculation and synthesis, (an efficient use of inductive reasoning). Importantly, one is not more important than the other, but careful use of each system is recommended.

The science of asking questions is the emergent impetus to learn in all the experiences of daily life. That experience and that impetus both look towards sources and resources within ourselves, from our peers, from education, from technology – further propelling us towards the pursuit of answering authentically the central questions of human existence: Who am I? How do I live my life? Is there a God? What happens after death?

As a consequence, maturity and wisdom develop as we learn; as we experience the vagaries of life; as we discover some answers. Having a pattern of thinking skills based on the Question-starters, is used as an ongoing system, allowing knowledge and insight to grow into further application. The Question-starters we already know, are: How? When? Why? Which? What? Who? Where? What if? This is not a new approach, but by making it the first of the four pedagogical tools, what is initiated for students, ordinands and teachers alike, we allow a familiar strategy to be available with specific focus for any subject area. One of the skills promoted within the Community of Inquiry on a consistent basis is the art of self-correction as the experience of collaboration where students learn together include the confidence to respectfully disagree and manage difference and diversity among their classmates. This is the starting point for conscience and decision making.

Collaboration and coordination within such a system allows for advanced skills in thinking, through analysis, synthesis, making distinctions between binary and trilectic thinking approaches, prediction and speculation, critiquing for flawed logic, and many other elements of thinking for learning purposes. Where the topic is introduced, pre-reading is assumed, and class members provide as many questions as possible in the introductory session, these questions are recorded, prioritised, grouped for ease of action, but no question is dismissed. As the topic progresses in further sessions, all questions are discussed, information shared, notes taken, conclusions reached by individual students, and answered in the preferred form for assessment of learning. It becomes part of the learning curve to apply good decision making then in daily life.

Students become adept at broadening knowledge in both the Socratic and Aristotelian frameworks. Both frameworks are needed as students reach upper levels of education, because the first framework uses questions that are fully focused on and only pertaining to the topic itself as a problem is solved or a file of research and evidence is compiled. The second framework uses questions to connect the elements of the topic to other interlocking topics and the whole is a broadening yet again of the possibilities of learning, of new knowledge. Arrestingly, when applied in all humanities disciplines, we find advanced learning and higher-order thinking skills consistently become apparent in students' work. Ordinands would similarly respond.

The change in student attitudes towards deeper engagement with eschatological questions is sudden, authentic and becomes prayerful, consistent, and increasingly faith-filled. In inter-faith and ecumenical classes, mutual respect dawns, as the variety of questions is recorded. Students become aware of how much they share in curiosity, in cultural similarities, in similar interests, and the texture of the class culture changes accordingly. Virtues, Values and Ethics become familiar territory. Students are engaged by the process. Ordinands will need to be similarly educated.

It becomes central now to expand the way that the question-starters are used to promote understanding and meaning about the Catholic tradition and the Catholic identity. Within each topic in any existing curriculum, there is opportunity to shape the classroom scope and sequence of curriculum content in Religious Studies classes. Introducing the topic, followed by an extended period of finding questions from each of the Question-starters listed above, is important. It means that there are areas for exploration, research, analysis and synthesis and opportunities for introducing students to Scripture, to Second Vatican Council documents, and to relevant authors even from an early age. As the process of finding answers progresses, input from an authentic and inclusive Catholic curriculum can be provided, and students appreciate the discovery of their answers. It is important then to recognise that there is opportunity to demonstrate when questions don't have answers because of mystery. And that is the edge at which the first glimmers of faith understanding reason emerge. In today's digital world, ordinands will need to understand how this process works, before adjusting their other skills sets for evangelisation.

The 'ME' diagram

Starting with the beginning at the centre point in the diagram (Figure 1, p. 201), the teacher emphasises that the 'ME' in the diagram is each individual student. The democratic element is established immediately by teacher comment that what follows applies in the unique experience of each person listening.

	'ME' The maturation influences on the individual	
Stage	1	Babyhood
	2	Kindergarten
	3	Primary/ Secondary schooling
	4	Hobbies, friendship clubs, sporting teams, cultural experience
	5	Learning and living in a suburb, a town, a district or a State
	6	A globalised world with unpredictable impact

Each 'ME' experiences the first influences of the world from the family with its own culture of religious, secular and cultural mores. The tiny baby is situated within its first influences and absorbs and adapts to the small world within which life is lived.

When judged appropriate by parent and carers, the child of 21st century parents experiences secondly new and broader influences in day-care, or with a nanny and eventually in a kindergarten-like setting. Learning about the world becomes a bigger picture, again absorbing and adapting to a second set of influences within which life is lived.

The third set of influences emerges as the young person experiences the broadened and varied world of education. Learning now includes physical, emotional, social, intellectual and particularly for a Catholic classroom spiritual elements of the world in which we live. That absorbing and adapting now operates at a challenging rate as adaptation to school life is learned.

The fourth set of influences that the child discovers sometimes begins to surface as hobbies, friendship clubs, sporting teams and training, school excursions and camps which broaden the child's view of the bigness and the diversity of the world around them. Learning accelerates, and the need for discernment, understanding and real knowledge, as distinct from cultural complexity enters the world of the child's experience.

Integrating those experiences and that burgeoning knowledge allows the child to begin making distinctions about what to believe, what to recognise as truth, what responses make sense in our world, and in particular how to distinguish the moral good by choosing right action consciously and by deliberately identifying and avoiding evil. The student could be beset by confusion and uncertainty, so the teacher must recognise the significance of teaching the person, rather than just the topic or discipline. Of course, the tertiary student, when first introduced to this scenario, can reflect, remember, memorise and categorise early learning experiences. This set of influences is a crucial foundation for the ordinand, in personal life and in the lives of those who will be served.

The fifth set of influences is often forgotten as the student learns how physical, emotional, social, intellectual and spiritual needs are to be identified and developed, so that maturity can begin. Whether the student lives in a suburb, a city, a town, or a shire has a specific impact on how life is lived. The district, the State, and even the National arena will have influences at particular times, during which the maturing student needs to integrate political and other influences, absorbing and adapting to the knowledge within which life is to be lived. This is central to the variations needed for the ordinand because seminary formation is dismissed as limited, in favour of the broadening and balancing of all the influences that must be understood in the responsibilities of evangelisation

There are increasingly the influences of a globalised 21st century world, whose impact at times can be catastrophic. Natural disasters and man-made suffering can impact the life of that young person in an invisible way, including severe Church intrusion. Teachers can help with integration within the various educational disciplines by giving students opportunities in discussion to articulate their concerns, to learn to integrate their responses and to make sense of a very complex world. Ordinands must be familiar with these teaching tools to bring coherence and ethical values to the task of evangelisation. National, international, universal considerations like climate change, while political in nature, have varying impacts on the student, and discernment about what is to be left to the experts, is needed.

The impact is continual, and the learning takes place when the light goes on in students' eyes as they identify different complexities that surround them. This whole concept is familiar to all educationalists, but it is in the conscious use of the elements of the diagram that we help students make sense of this world, to clarify personally other considerations that are still to be absorbed and adapted to the new 21st century knowledge within which life is to be lived. All of this, of course, is delivered in democratic vein, ensuring no indoctrination, undue influence or distorted belief systems, and the ordinand needs to be fully cognisant of these matters. Here, the ordinand is to be tasked with understanding the nuances and the pitfalls of ensuring democratic action, with absolutely no indoctrination or ideological content or undue influence. It is a particular responsibility of the ordinand and the priest to recognise and be wary of distorted belief systems that are present within some Catholic cultural practice.

The sixth set of influences that is often dismissed is that expanded perspective that allows for what Science has taught us about our world, the universe within which we exist, the possibilities of other Universes outside our galaxy, and whatever is 'beyond'. The eyes of faith will provide with awe and wonder the existence of a Creator God, and the Catholic faith will provide us with details of the message of the Son Redeemer and Life-giver, who showed us as

Word what the will of that Creator God is for humankind, and we are spurred on by the promise and the existence of the Spirit Sanctifier whose wisdom we strive to understand and live, in accordance in our Catholic identity.

Figure 1: The 'ME' Diagram

What does not appear in the 'ME' diagram is a series of arrows coming from outside, through each of the rings, coming closer and penetrating the Subjective 'ME'. Those arrows represent the incoming reign of God, as Jesus, the Word, taught his followers, and which has been faithfully handed down over the millennia to us today. Here, the ordinand is given the opportunity to encourage, ensure integrity, and propose elements of the Catholic faith as part of evangelisation techniques.

It is important here to acknowledge that a particularly significant diagram of Paul Sharkey (2015) responding to the question 'What is Catholic Identity?' as another way of visualising the idea of self-reflection that precedes action. Where Sharkey centres his diagram on God, the 'ME' diagram centres on the individual. It is not the comparison that is pointed out here. Both diagrams as tools in curriculum development can partner each other as the teacher begins the critical inquiry and careful thinking that is required, and which, as Sharkey pinpoints, young people today prefer to handle.

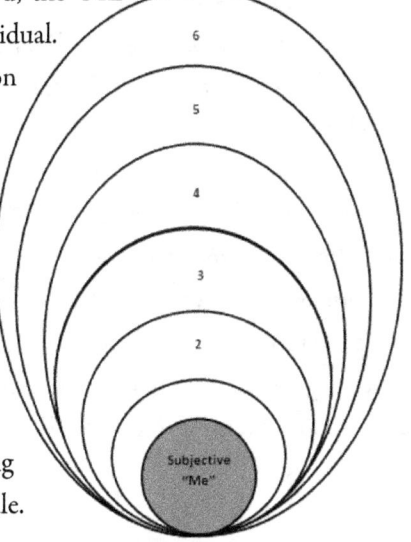

Six Steps of Decision Making

Recognising that there are eschatological aims for the Catholic person to spend a lifetime of challenge to develop a personal relationship with the Holy Trinity: Father Creator, Son Redeemer-Life giver and Spirit Sanctifier, the third pedagogical tool, outlined in chapter 4, is now applied precisely as the third part of the system to be analysed, understood, applied to a particular need, and offered as a theological tool. It is meant to reduce substantially the tendency to stay inside the chains of binary thinking and its practical arm – adversarialism. It is the *Six Steps of Decision Making*.

It is to be applied here as a parallel of aiding the individual person, including all People in the Pews, and all members of the present and future hierarchical arms of the church. It is applied as an evaluation tool to the health and well-being of ecclesial communities by the leaders and by the members of each individual community. It is applied to the evaluation of the health and well-being of the whole Catholic Church, through synodal action regularly and honestly undertaken. In this way, we are addressing the present urgent need for accountability, transparency and an inclusive democratic paradigm based on the message of Jesus: his truth, his way, his life.

It is important to refer to the Second Vatican Council document on Religious Liberty to be sure that accurate understanding of the whole concept of religious freedom is recognised. The struggle to develop and form conscience is a lifelong journey to promote our (a) Response to God's grace, to find that (b) Response-ability that brings understanding and knowledge, in order to accept our (c) Responsibility consciously to choose the good and just as consciously to avoid evil; to reiterate: response, response-ability, and responsibility. We therefore look again at the wording of the Vatican ll documents.

'The Vatican Council declares that the human person has a right to religious freedom. Freedom of this kind means that all (men) should be immune from coercion...' (*Dignitatis humanae*, 2)

'The search for truth, however, must be carried out in a manner that is appropriate to the dignity of the human person and (his) our social nature, namely, by free enquiry with the help of teaching or instruction, communication and dialogue' (*Dignitatis humanae*, 3)

'Every family, in that it is a society with its own basic rights, has the right freely to organise its own religious life in the home under the control of the parents.' (*Dignitatis humanae*, 5)

'God has regard for the dignity of the human person which he himself created; the human person is to be guided by (his own) personal judgment and to enjoy freedom.' (*Dignitatis humanae*, 11)

This tool must now be applied to the parish community, other ecclesial communities, dioceses, national churches, cultural settings, and to the whole global church community – before we are able to add in what we can learn from other Christian communities, equally focused on the message of Jesus. The sins of omission and commission must be avoided as we channel our efforts beyond the clericalist attitude of silence and disdain. Coercion can be present in silence as well as in action.

Table 2: The Six Steps of Decision Making – applied a second time

Define the problem: presenting problem is not always the real problem
List possible options, no matter how unusual: unmasking deeper issues
Investigate each option: canvassing possibilities, predicting consequences, identifying pitfalls

Invite expert opinion, advisement and research internet: rather than rely on advice or counselling
Choose the best likely option, listing other options in order of preference: a mistake is not failure, unless the problem-solver withdraws altogether
Carry out the action, and then evaluate: armed with new knowledge, retrace steps for another option if needed.

Source: (Heasly, 2012, 161)

Remote figures issuing edicts must not intrude into the family unit with idealistic or ideological demands, even if they are made for benign reasons. Dignity of the individual person extends to women as well as men, and the primacy of conscience is taken care of in this set of parameters.

Grasping the various principles of morality, laid out for us in Scripture and in the various documents of the Second Vatican Council, provides us with invaluable resources to aid in our journey towards God. Notice that this pedagogical tool provides a pattern of thinking designed to help us in our deliberations of how to examine our conscience, to discern the significant elements that are deep inside where only God is. This tool does not impinge on the individual's conscience by trying to make the decisions about what to do. The moral act is my own, and we must follow those 'four moments' to arrive at the point that O'Neill and Black (2006) indicate as the best image of conscience - heart.

One of the outcomes is a gradual change in the definition of *authority in action*. Authority becomes a listening, a reflecting, an analysing, an exploring, a deepening, an understanding, a responding, an urgent need to play one's part in contribution to the good of the whole community. This then is the paradigm change that can emerge without the loss of the faith we claim and revere. It is possible then to highlight that the fear of previous papal figures about contamination of the central tenets of the Jesus message can be avoided.

To conclude, we find ourselves at times in a complicated place; we need to *respond* appropriately; we need the *response-ability* translated as necessary knowledge; we analyse and find the best choice; we act in *responsibility* towards our God, towards others, towards ourselves, to our ecclesial community and where necessary towards the environment, both social and spiritual. If we are involved in the work of evangelisation, especially in classrooms at primary, secondary and tertiary levels of teaching, we transmit knowledge and model virtues, values and ethics in God's time.

The HUG/BUG

The Grid is set out in Table 3, below. As the student advances in age, and reaches towards the wisdom of adulthood, it is possible to build further on human understanding of discernment, analysing patterns of behaviour as foundations for recognising virtues, values and ethics in daily life for the ecclesial community in a democratic society. As the ordinand begins the journey of preparation for service as priest in a given ecclesial community, it becomes obvious that the HUG/BUG tool can be of central value. This is the fourth pedagogical tool and is offered specifically to broaden understanding of those patterns, naming and recognising each pattern as a virtue, a value, an ethical standard – or the opposite. This tool is a Grid known as The HUG/BUG: Uncertainty Grid or the Behaviour Uncertainty Grid.

The Uncertainty Grid/ Behaviour Uncertainty Grid (HUG/BUG), is definitely not to be a measuring tool – rather an illustration for students and ordinands to explore. The central column is the starting point, showing elements of personality, so diversity is immediately accommodated. By recognising the first column on the left and right of this central column, it can be seen that contrasts or choices of response are listed. By comparing the middle column on the left and right of the central column, it can be seen that certain consequences of choices emerge and these consequences can, by implication, influence our choices and our experience. By checking the outer columns on the left and the right of the central column, contrasting patterns of behaviours can be identified as suitable or otherwise. Decisions and choices are now significant as moral norms support the quality of the moral action as the individual consciously chooses the good, and just as consciously chooses to avoid the evil.

Students were the first to label this pedagogical tool as the HUG/BUG because they identified the positive (right hand) side of the Grid with a hug, corresponding to the choice for good. Equally, they saw the negative (left hand) side of the Grid as portraying a bug, corresponding to a choice which could be an evil.

One other illustration for students and ordinands is that the behaviours in these columns can be researched, analysed and discussed for deeper meaning and fuller understanding. This will apply to these and many other virtues, values and ethics that might appear in the curriculum under many guises. Teachers and students can vary the entry of differing patterns of behaviour and test the outcome in both negative and positive patterns, using the HUG/BUG system.

Table 3: The Heasly Behaviour Uncertainty Grid

OUTCOME						OUTCOME
Behaviour	Consequences	Features	ELEMENTS	Features	Consequences	Behaviour
Aggression	Stultification	Laziness	PHYSICAL RESPONSE	Skills Appetites	Strength	Perseverance Courage
Tyranny Deceit	Unpredictability Hopelessness	Hysteria Moodiness	EMOTIONAL RESPONSE	Wishes Dreams	Response-ability	Honesty
Greed Avarice	Narcissism	Selfishness	SOCIAL RESPONSE	Communication Love	Openness	Patience Justice Forgiveness
Jealousy Envy	Prejudice Inconsistency	Arrogance Presumption	INTELLECTUAL RESPONSE	Inquiry Logic	Critical skills	Discernment
Abuse – self or other	Despair	Nihilism	SPIRITUAL RESPONSE	Quest – satisfaction wholeness	Personal paradigm	Integrity

In a similar fashion to those patterns of behaviour named in the Grid, it is important that we look to New Testament messaging from Jesus. We find a particularly helpful framework for moral formation in the Beatitudes: the Sermon on the Mount. It is equally important to include the earlier Old Testament narrative where Moses received the Decalogue, as a charter for living the good life for the Israelites.

Rather than imitate the exact thinking of the people of Old Testament or New Testament times, we need to absorb the style of thinking and the habits of mind which help us to apply those values and understandings to the challenges, the dilemmas, the paradoxes of today's world, where so many questions never uncovered till this new century, need our particular attention. This is particularly urgent for the aspiring ordinand. At all times we tend by choice towards those patterns of behaviour which lead to the good, and make the necessary adjustments in our thinking, our reflections, our evaluations, so that we follow Jesus, and resist the possibility of choosing evil rather than the good. This is no idle or trivial approach, as we face the elements of daily life in our century, including the shame we as church must face as a result of the appalling criminal behaviour of both paedophilic priests and the criminally arrogant cover-ups of predatory and corrupt behaviours inherent in clericalism.

As a consequence of this research and these reflections, the ecclesial communities of the church can rely on foundations of understanding, knowledge and insight from an array of sources available. We analyse, develop and synthesise details from the narratives of Scripture, already offered by moral theologians through the tradition of our church. Ordinands would be served well by curricula during pre-ordination studies by inclusion of this content.

Research naturally will include some of the resources, as a major element emerges from the Community of Inquiry. A balance between these sources will be found by referring to the work of moral theologians to effect a careful and rigorous examination of how this Thinking Skills System can become an aid for teachers, lecturers and ordinands to facilitate and promote an approach to resilience and reflection for students in and on daily life. It must be emphasised that these pedagogical tools are not measurement-based or assessment-based, nor do they impinge on the religious freedom of the student by directing the student choice.

Sharkey (2015) has drawn attention to a concept which patterns very successfully with the HUG/BUG educational tool. It is the use of the term 'frontier space' in which people learning and critiquing can meet those whose initial response is very different to each other. They can meet and communicate by recognising the two ends of the spectrum in concepts, and the cultural diversity present in differing schools, parishes and places of Catholic presence. The ordinand will need to be fully conversant with such matters, and these tools are at least being offered as steps in the process.

Every effort has been made during the compilation of this research project to remain 'Open to God and Open to the World' as Cardinal Franz Konig was. His creedal poem written for his friend (Konig, 2005) speaks volumes:

> I believe in God, our Father,
> Creator of Heaven and Earth.
> Many peoples who speak different languages and have
>   different faiths are on their way to you,
> Let all those who seek you find shelter in you!
>
> I believe in Jesus Christ.
> The strong and the weak,
> The old and the young.
> Call them to serve you so that they can learn
> to be brothers and sisters to one another.

I believe in the Holy Ghost,
Who strengthens our good thoughts.
To you I commend all those who question and seek,
But also those who know.
They are all waiting for your word.
Let them seek the truth in love.

On the eve of my life I thank you, dear God,
For my Church which is with you on its journey through time.
Let your messengers protect and lead our children.
Help us, together with your angels and with the children,
To renew the face of the earth and make it more peaceful.

I put my own and all our lives into your hands.

Cardinal Franz Konig, Advent, 2003.

And therein emerges the openness of theo-tensegrity.

CHAPTER 7

Applying *Theo-tensegrity*: the concept of a church of accountability, inclusivity, diversity and transparency

In order to balance out the three change processes that have been offered to theologians as a way forward for ordinands' preparation for priesthood, it is necessary to examine and analyse the theology that Pope John Paul ll promoted. This is not to say that he did also promote some extraordinary work in his home country and contributed to the fall of the Berlin Wall; he was active in interfaith communications especially with Lutheran, Orthodox and other religions. A complex man, his intellect and personal energy kept him very active, and his death on the world stage was his way of modelling a holy death.

He demanded that the church not discuss anything to do with the possibility of the ordination of women. He focused the whole evangelisation impetus on his own personhood by travelling continually and he refused to laicise priests who needed to change their life direction. He focused on a theology of the body which was born out of a childhood of extremes and he wrote insistently on moral matters in a lyrical but unforgiving style. He promoted lay movements which at times have been shown to be dangerous and damaging in many aspects of psychological personal balance. As the decades have passed, we must try to integrate the particular emphases that John Paul ll used to influence the whole universal church towards his strong convictions about how the church must move forward - with adversarialism intruding in this process.

We proceed then to examine how tensegrity is applied to our beloved and battered church. People in the Pews can perhaps note a deeper sense of the various impulses of Rome, of lack of leadership, of moral conflicts, of needing urgent restorative justice for many. We also examine one of those special emphases of John Paul ll that occupied five years of consistent presentations on sex and sexuality and of what he called the theology of 'the' body. It may be that by integrating very carefully the spirit of his thinking and the new knowledge, new understandings and broadened conceptual thinking, we can propose an extension of that theology of the body into a theology of the human person, incorporating the highly idealised legacy of John Paul ll with authenticity and realistic attention to detail.

The focus on tensegrity allows us to understand that any living entity, either individual or communal, is made up of a myriad of tiny intertwined and collaborative lesser entities which are blessed with their own inner impulses and inner energy. This energy, examined with the eyes of faith, signals the ongoing and evolving presence of our Creator. Architecturally, tensegrity allows the building of large structures which can withstand outside pressures and remain an integrated whole. This allows architects and builders to construct buildings able to withstand earthquakes and extreme weather events. It allows also the building of structures which rely on the push and pull of tension which balances each stressed point enough to contain any tendency to part or fracture. An example would be the millennium dome in London, which allows a domed roof to withstand disintegration even though there are no upright beams internally to hold the weight of the outer structure. This concept applied as a metaphor has its parallel in the theology of personhood.

The focus on bio-integrity allows us to understand how more and more of the tiny elements, neurons, atoms, ligaments, nerves, bones, inner organs, blood and other systems, skin and outer growth of hair and nails holds together to function as each human person. Myriads of tiny amoeba, viruses, bacteria and other entities are still being discovered, as medical science develops and uncovers more knowledge about neurological stimulation of the human brain. Surgery using remarkable skills, and the burgeoning surgery performed by robots with robust efficiency allow our experts to enhance, improve and heal when parts of a human body need intervention to continue normal function. Not only is there a whole new world of augmented humans, which may include robotic and technological support for disabled athletes, patients and victims of trauma, but remedial development of replacement skills for people who have survived massive traffic accidents is expanding exponentially as well. So the field of biology is remarkable for the theory of tensegrity and its ability to provide a web of new knowledge for all living animals, birds and humankind. This understanding of human biology has a direct impact on the theology of 'the' body.

The focus on edu-tensegrity, applied as a metaphor for the whole education scenario, allows us to recognise that the business of education is a huge heaving universal scenario which covers the imbibing of individual learning in a myriad of ways; in which teachers, lecturers, administrators and specialists provide an ever-increasing mass of new content for the student learner (and for our purposes, the ordinand) to access. These major sections, which could come apart at the upper end of primary, secondary or tertiary levels of educational organisation, remain integrated even if sometimes loosely. The student learner can negotiate the way to the desired end.

Some difficulties occur when certain forms of education are offered which are too exclusive in focus, and this has the consequence of pushing the whole scenario of education closer to disintegration. This can happen because of a chosen special emphasis like a belief system or an ideological framework meant to shape the student learner beyond what that individual might wish. Intrusion of governmental impetus towards adding ideological concepts as central emphases is a case in point. The presence of indoctrination, or the offering of a deliberately narrow curriculum or instructional design would be an example of pulling the balance of what we call education today towards disintegration, and this is a serious matter. However, we still have the concept of tensegrity applied to the entity we call education in the 21st century, whether here in Australia or in separate other countries or in the whole world of education. The emphasis of the Baltic and Black Sea Circle Consortium for Sustainability and Change, with its *emphasis* on sustainability, is a direct parallel.

The focus on theo-tensegrity allows us to recognise the existence of a major religion like Christianity which relies on a starting point of relaying the message of Jesus. In the Catholic Church, it has been the experience of the People in the Pews for generations: they are to live what they are taught about that message. Various interpretations today of the emphases seemingly important to Catholic leaders and their adherents have pushed the content too close to schism, as they insist that their particular stance is the right one, meaning that all else is wrong therefore sinful.

Power and control has been used to fight this particular war in such a manner that the warring teams are not aware that the myriad of extra trappings that are offered don't need to be in conflict. It is not a matter of one team of humans being right, but that more than one team of humans are trying to wipe out the other. This is not the message of Jesus. If the concept of theo-tensegrity can teach us that those contrary behaviours, deliberate flouting of just laws and decades of clerical cover-ups in so many countries are hurtling our church towards complete annihilation, then we must choose how, or even if, that entity called the Catholic Church is a functioning organisation any more.

Theo-tensegrity allows us to recognise fully the huge almost volcanic but vital and living entity called the Catholic Church with its inherent diversities and differences. Theo-tensegrity allows us to recognise the need for consultation, collaboration, learning from each other, praying with and for each other. Theo-tensegrity does not allow the intrusion of an exclusivist, cultic, entitled strata of priests and hierarchs, promoted beyond their ability or their importance, let alone accept the idolatry of the ontologically-changed, celibate priestly male. Theo-tensegrity does not allow the disdain and sometimes vicious wielding of authority with little or no understanding of the lives of the people for whom edicts and encyclicals are promulgated.

How do we effect a sufficient change of emphasis to allow the elements of liturgical wars, sacramental wars, language wars, morality wars, administrative wars, theology wars and philosophy wars to lapse? It is important to find some impetus which will provide ballast, so that this shamed and heaving schismatic church of the 21st century can stop long enough to choose less warlike stances. After all, Jesus was not on about war. Says Ilia Delio (2018) regarding the massive scandal of the clerical child sexual abuse and the callous cover-ups by hierarchy (and I thank WATAC for this information):

> It is no longer acceptable for a pope simply to issue a public apology, nor is it sufficient for any group merely to reflect on what happened by issuing positive statements. The Church has a deep structural problem which is entirely bound to ancient metaphysical and philosophical principles, not to mention imperial politics that at this point require either a radical

decision towards a new ecclesial structure or accept the possibility of a major schism. The rock-solid Church has crushed human souls and twisted authority into deceit. The male-dominated Christ centre no longer holds and there is simply no solution or comforting words that can placate the extensive damage to fragile human lives that has taken place over the past decades. The evidence of abuse brought to light in the Catholic Church is simply unfathomable.

We can only try to understand the breadth of the problem from the point of view of the People in the Pews. Some people think we should investigate elimination of celibacy as an impossible way of life. Other people think about barring homosexuals from the priesthood, because they can't understand that homosexuality is another state of nature. For me, it's about a lack of maturity and development in seminaries. For many, it is a crying need for the liberalisation of the church since the Second Vatican Council, and the consequent adaptation and change towards the indications that we find in the documents of the conciliar period.

The theology of the body which was part of the legacy of Pope John Paul ll is a useful area to test whether expansion, exploration and change of emphasis can improve the toxic atmosphere that challenges the People in the Pews currently. The compartmentalisation of different areas of living that is evident in the responses of paedophiles (as attested particularly in the findings of the Royal Commission into institutional clerical sexual abuse published in Victoria, 2018) rests on a distorted emphasis on moral behaviours as they strive to defend themselves. Ilia Delio outlines this from a viewpoint of practical theology:

'There is something profoundly intransigent about the structure of the Church. It is not that Church structures have caused the abuse but they have masked predators hiding as priests in a closed caste system of clerical elitism. ... Church culture is based on operative principles of hierarchy, patriarchy, careerism, and the notorious notion of priestly consecration as becoming "ontologically changed". ... clericalism is a type of corporate ladder-climbing and no different from the quest for power in the world of major corporations.'(28 August 2018)

It is essential that we examine the two principles that Ilia Delio (2018) has outlined as underpinning these dissociative behaviours. 'The Ontology of Being, that is, the notion that the priest is on a higher level of being and thus closer to God (and this notion) dates back to the fifth century to Pseudo-Dionysius'. Careful analysis of the deep meaning contained in these few lines is evidence of an exclusivity which makes no sense in todays' world of knowledge, education, personal intellect and practical morality.

It follows in this scenario that priests are superior to the laity and women are inferior to men. Says Delio: 'A second philosophical flaw is the platonic notion of the body as inferior to the life of the spirit giving rise to several different outrageously flawed ideas, including the notion that women are intellectually inferior to men and the source of sin; that sex and sexuality are inferior qualities of human personhood and need to be closely monitored, as these can easily lead to sin; that the corruptible body needs to be disciplined and subjugated to the spirit.' This idea is then extended by John Scotus Eriugena in the 9th century who claimed that at the resurrection sex will be abolished and nature will be made one – only man – as if he had never sinned (28 August 2018). Today, we understand that we surely do not know what heaven and the afterlife will contain, but we manage our life journey towards wholeness and maturity in a loving relationship with God, which was promised through the message of Jesus and which we rely on the Holy Spirit today to help us to discern the direction.

We know that in essence the church has shied away from a full-blooded involvement in the rapid expansion of new knowledge available through scientific research in every discipline, labelling this whole emerging scenario dismissively as secular, therefore inferior to the sacred. The church has implied that such deliberative and responsible education about God's own creation was somehow sinful too. So no real and consistent understanding of modern knowledge in biology, evolution or quantum physics seems to be incorporated into the official teachings of the Catholic Church. Delio's conclusion is that 'the foundations of theology remain out of sync with nature; the understanding of the human person is outmoded in many respects; and the core doctrines of creation, salvation and redemption are based on outdated cosmological principles. Although Pope John Paul II apologised on behalf of Galileo in 1984, by mid-20th century the Church had not accepted Big Bang cosmology or evolution as fundamental to doing theology'.

The ordinand of the 21st century therefore has a massive task ahead of him or her, because the theological task is a gigantic one which will impact on all tenets of faithful daily living for the People in the Pews. So many, who have walked away and so many who still are faithful today, are already applying as best they can the marriage of science and faith in daily life. Our present theologians and educators at primary, secondary and tertiary levels have a responsibility to proceed carefully and with insight. It is a fact that new technology, new knowledge and new insights are gathering speed and the Catholic Church has a mandate from Jesus to care *fully* for all parts of the world community, the People in the Pews. Restorative justice means that this is an urgent and challenging task. Resistance and defiance from hierarchy, loth to disturb their own comfort levels, need to be prompted consistently to take up these responsibilities immediately. Delio has caused us to take account of Ralph Burhoe who has indicated that 'the discoveries of twentieth-century science, born from the creative human spirit in search of understanding, have far out-paced the ancient myths as formulated in their traditional religions'. He wrote that if religions are to be regenerated, they would have to be credible in terms of this age of science, a point highly consonant with the vision of Pierre Teilhard de Chardin.

So the theology embedded in the theory of theo-tensegrity becomes a central feature because it regenerates the model of church beyond that of Mystical Body, or Perfect Society, or Pilgrim Church alone. The tensegrity angle means that all these metaphors for Church are included, inclusively, in differing ways. Each culture within each ecclesial community adjusts to the new vision of the entity we call the Catholic Church in the ongoing future. This, we know from the message of Jesus, is the will of our loving Triune God. One metaphor is not better or inferior in substance to another, and each has its place in the demanding challenge we face to lift ourselves away from the chains of rigid and overplayed binary and black-and-white thinking patterns and begin the important application of the new principles from within theo-tensegrity to every area of the church: prayer, liturgy, 'lectio divina', the Jesuit 'examen', mysticism, beliefs, theological considerations, philosophical considerations, difference and apparent entitlements. There is much work for theologians here, to bring into focus the more complex thinking skills without losing the benefits of some binary thinking that has contributed much theological depth.

Substantial change must be pointed forward towards a position consonant with third millennium living; humankind has reached a time when active co-creation as the hands of the Cosmic Creator is our new task. The promptings of the Holy Spirit are evident; the possibility of major schism is imminent but avoidable. The pain of the victims, survivors of all forms of abuse and their families demand physical, intellectual, social, emotional and spiritual restitution. The task of regeneration is a mammoth one and the People in the Pews expect and demand in the name of their children that a new future be founded. The pain of the death and resurrection of Jesus demands that we all give assent to this as our new future. Otherwise, we are mired in personalist clericalist attitudes, in imitation of the hierarchical scenario which has wrought so much damage.

As Delio concludes:

> 'We fragile, vulnerable humans are "cooperative co-creators" and it does make a difference how we live our lives. Our participation in the mystery of Divine Love, incarnate and hidden in the brokenness of our world, lies at the basis of a healing world. The shocking news of the abuse crisis crushes our hearts, but know too that God's heart is broken; that the body of Christ is crucified over and over again, for when one member is abused the whole Body is abused. But our faith must remain unshaken. Christ *is* risen from the dead; the final word is not death but Life. We will rise from these ashes but we cannot stand still nor can we turn back. Our hands are now put to the plow and we must forge a new path ahead. The Church will be born anew, for God is doing new things'. (28 August 2018)

We know that Delio is interested in the theology that marries science and religion, and she has delved carefully into evolution, physics, neuroscience and artificial intelligence. We can apply the new theory of theo-tensegrity to the methodology that she is using to contribute to the new practical aspects of theology for today. It is the application of such a wide set of scientific disciplines and the remarkable discoveries we can harvest, that makes for an exciting if painful future. This future, for which we sketch the outline of this new paradigm being proffered by the Holy Spirit through the intellect of those who are also following Delio's approach, is a broad palette. Change and challenge are parallel with the emergence in our understanding of the wonders of the Cosmic World unfolding at the will of our Creator God; whose Son taught and gave us so much; that the Holy Spirit can mould through our intellects, our humility, our resilience and our determination to support the regeneration of our faith in our beloved but battered Church.

Regeneration of our beloved and battered Church – but how?

First, we need to explore the effects of history and the demands of church as understood by members of the laity, who struggle with the underlying nature of the clericalist striving-to-control every part of life in every family in all circumstances. Liberation from those chains must be very carefully addressed so that personal agenda does not intrude unconsciously in the whole project. Paul Lakeland has given us a starting point worth pursuing.

Lakeland (2004) has tackled what we might mean, to understand what is to count as liberation of the laity. He is aware of a list of signposts worth noting: a general malaise hanging over the church; outmoded understanding of ministry; failure to harness the apostolic potential of the laity; plain anger at the powerlessness experienced in the church. This is followed by the first glimmers of clerical sex abuse, which has clarified much and motivated the laity. We are stunned by the experience of being confronted by 'the spectacle of episcopal short-sightedness, incompetence, and arrogance of power'. We face the realisation that the laity has a legitimate voice, pinpointing that solutions will never again be accepted solely from ordained ministers.

As a result, Lakeland indicates three pathways that we need. 'A theology of the laity' must be expanded to include the whole church, because their common priesthood, their baptismal rights must be incorporated so that the bishops and the priests must all be servants, not masters. What exactly is the layperson today? And how are we to build a vision of the Catholic Church of tomorrow? Laity is more than not-clergy, and modernism must be addressed fully. Eventually, says Lakeland, we can delve firmly into a post-conciliar Roman orthodoxy distinctly still neo-scholastic. Today, we can pinpoint that both clergy and laity are immersed in the secular. We can also recognise the need for serious efforts at liberation of the laity, from structural oppression which Lakeland names as a consistent struggle against anti-human pressures of global capitalism: 'In my own mind, I have moved from the historical to the theological, from the more didactic to the more speculative, from the theoretical to the practical' (Lakeland, 2004). He models right here and very authentically the steps of paradigm change.

In his last chapter, Lakeland has travelled a rocky road, examining the possible reconfiguring of the church as an accountable church: 'Henceforth, lay people will look upon the clerical culture of an enclosed society of celibate men as irreversibly dysfunctional'. We must take seriously his further comment: 'we rightly continue to insist on the superiority of a free society over authoritarian political systems, including those which masquerade as theocracy'. This scenario is noticeable in all Abrahamic religions, and we can help each other, without war, through prayer and communication, with transparency, honesty and humility.

It seems, therefore, useful to follow Lakeland's lead and examine the 'three stages of religion in the modern world'. 'First, medieval Catholicism, in which religious authority defined the powers and limits of the political community; Second, the denominational understanding of Christianity, identifiable with American Protestantism; Third, is the world of the primacy of personal spirituality'. Following Lakeland's thinking, we need the papacy, but not the 17th century model. We need episcopal leadership, but not the pomp and imperialism of medieval times. We don't need the distinction on the 5th century grounds of a male, celibate clergy; we don't need the opulence, the curia, and the Vatican sovereign status. Democracy must prevail as *we* appoint popes, bishops and priests.

The legacy of Vatican Council ll means that the laity will now never submit to previous conditions. The People of God in Vatican ll are also the People in the Pews. So a new theology, inclusive and more cognitive of the central teachings of Jesus must emerge, rather than a return to an earlier interpretation. Collegiality, accountability, transparency and respect for diversity must accompany the promotion of consistent lay involvement in preparation for, and involvement in, all facets of church life. These are the considerations urgently demanded by an educated, not indoctrinated, but balanced faithful, a believing mass of the People in the Pews, whether fundamentalist or liberal in personal perspective.

All of this happens in the secular world, inhabited by the People in the Pews, but when human rights are trampled, there are democratic processes available. We are not oppressed in that secular world and to the extent that we are hemmed in by demands for repentance, judgmental accusations and unjust callous decisions meant to enhance the profile of church at the expense of the individual. We can see the implicit logic and pain behind Lakeland's perspective.

Lakeland is honest in recognising Vatican Council ll 'as a record of missed opportunities and unfulfilled promise. There *is* a pressing need to address issues untouched by the council fathers. We know that the gospel message will remain but scholarship from theological specialists released from the threat of being silenced for no good reason, will pursue the conditions of our world in which the Jesus message will continue to evolve. Other specialists in education, literary analysis, anthropology, cosmology, and more, will provide us with channels for integrated change in an enhanced model of ministry, more authentic, more responsive and more inclined towards listening to each other, to us, and above all else, listening to the Holy Spirit.

That process of change will affect: *laity* who must be proactive but not domineering; *parish* in which community is the ballast to support the vulnerable; *diocese* where lay and episcopal partnership will provide compassionate and democratic leadership; where the *cardinalate* may well be deleted; a *pope* would be elected by a wide voting coterie from around the world; and *specialised ministries* would be resourced according to gospel values.

Examination of John Paul ll's Theology of the body

Five years of consistent presentations from John Paul ll, in 129 catechetical addresses, is a vast mine of material to condense into sufficient and balanced content for the reader by a student of theology (not a theologian), so we are aided by the work, as a secondary source of understanding, of Edward P. Sri SJ, (19 November 2018). 'Five Key Features of the Theology of the Body' are picked out for us to learn of the breadth of this theology about love, sexuality and marriage.

One early point of interest is that the individual is characterised as body-and-soul, whereas a more Trinitarian approach would be body-and-soul-and-spirit. Fr Sri states that 'those who actually dare to read these addresses quickly find themselves overwhelmed by the depth of John Paul ll's philosophical, theological and indeed mystical thought on this topic', and these sentiments alert us to an almost obsessive emphasis of a celibate man, holy as we might have found him, ruminating about the qualities of love, sexuality and marriage.

The first of the five key features, says Fr Sri, is the Law of the Gift. 'Human persons are made for self-giving love, not a self-getting love, and they will find fulfilment only when they give themselves in service to others.' In today's world, this assertion is simplistic reductionism, showing binary and black-and-white thinking patterns. This allows only a narrow interpretation of what we recognise today as love-in-relationship which changes as the decades go by, and the two people, though one in a metaphor of partnership, mature often in differing styles.

Sri tells us that 'John Paul ll alludes to how it (the gift) is based on man (sexist language in the third millennium?) being made in the image of the Triune God' (Genesis 1:26); that God exists as a communion of three divine Persons giving themselves completely in love to each other. He goes on: 'man and woman – created in the image of the Trinity – are made to live not as isolated individuals, each seeking his or her own pleasure and advantage of the other' (Sri, p. 1). However, it is important to note that there is confusion here in that it is not clear from Sri's text of what John Paul ll said, that each gender is created in the image of the Trinity, neither is there a balanced picture of isolated individuals who do not necessarily use their opposite as a regular feature of humanity today. If 'man and woman are made to live in an intimate personal communion of self-giving love, mirroring the inner life of the Trinity', there is no evidence here of the norms of process as each person journeys from dependence towards independence and finally to interdependence on the road to maturity. There is an uncomfortable question about idealised thinking, not making allowance for outside influences and responsibilities that impact sometimes daily on the two people in a marriage today. If human persons do 'find the happiness they long for' (Sri's comment), they do so even while handling the burdens of responsibility that are often overwhelming. If mental or emotional illness overtakes a spouse or a child, the difficulties, whether temporary or long-term, are crushing and are often lifelong. This outcome is a far cry from the simplistic uncomplicated scenario envisaged by John Paul ll.

The second feature of the theology of the body is Original Solitude. John Paul ll seems to take the Genesis story of Adam and Eve as literally as a child first reading the script. He quotes 'God's statement' regarding Adam in the Garden of Eden: 'It is not good for man to be alone' (Genesis 2:18). It occurs to a reader that the metaphor of the story is being used particularly to emphasise the apparent, though imaginary, lived experience of a man in a garden alone. It also seems to contradict the mandated celibacy of Latin-rite priests which is such a vexed question in the third millennium of the historical Catholic Church. Accordingly, we are told that Adam has become aware that he has a spiritual dimension as 'a body-soul creature'. Now does the Trinitarian metaphor of body-mind-spirit apply here? John Paul ll 'explains that man only finds fulfilment when he lives in a relationship of mutual self-giving, by existing *for* someone'. But today we know that both, man and woman, are bound by the responsibility to maximise various latent talents, traits and attitudes that will allow each to exist *for* that someone as a mature human being.

The third feature of the John Paul ll theology of the body centres on Original Unity. He has God creating another human person, out of the rib-cage of the man, and this person is to be Adam's wife, imagined as a submissive and accommodating complementary figure. John Paul ll imagines that this is the first time that 'man manifests joy and exultation' because 'he finally has someone to give himself to in this unique way'. One wonders about the imaginary picture going on in the mind of the author. That living out of the proposed relationship would be based on an appreciation and conservation of the environment that God gave them in the garden. Becoming one flesh is an extension of this giving-out to each other. In full Trinitarian fashion, the union whereby they become 'one flesh' means three: body-soul-spirit of the woman as well as body-soul-spirit of the man. It must also contain the perichoresis (inner relationship) of the Trinity and it must contain the Trinitarian effect of male-female-God in its essence. Not an easy concept to realise, and certainly a very esoteric approach to the love, sex and marriage of two people today. Unfortunately, a female reader of this text will be struck by the continued reference by Sri to the emphasis on *man* when he refers to the spiritual dimension of 'man' with no reference to the spiritual dimension of woman.

Referring to the significance of the language of a human body, John Paul ll proceeds towards the impact of sexual intercourse as an outcome. It is important here to add that the body of an individual man in sexual intercourse also expresses the language and spiritual dimension of, and to, the woman equally. Their union, therefore, must address normal differences between two human persons as they commit to each other. 'Bodily union is meant to express an even more profound personal intimacy' but we must remember too that the emotions of one or both are also tied up in reasons for physical intimacy when either of the two needs reassurance, empathy, or even ecstasy. There is an idealised pattern of imagination at work here as the thinking seems bereft of adult acknowledgment of burdens, illnesses, seemingly ignorant of the complexities of each human character: in physical, intellectual, social, emotional and spiritual ways. The element of 'nuptial meaning that God has given to the body' is simplistic reductionism in its approach, with no regard or understanding of this good-or-bad dimension of an imagined reality. Referring to woman as providing the man with 'his own sexual satisfaction', we find an unbalanced and sexist view, because previous comment emphasised the underlying love in the expression of intimacy. Given the strictures imposed by a medieval view of sexuality, there are many difficulties that will hamper the successful achievement of this idealised and quite sentimental vision of what mature sexuality is. An unfortunate outcome here is so often experienced when difficulties occur between the two. The assumption is that the couple have not lived up to the high-order demand of the pontiff to couch their relationship in this idealised and probably unattainable goal. This is inevitably labelled failure and guilt intrudes into the relationship with potentially serious consequences, including deterioration of the marital bond.

The fourth feature emerging for Sri, in the theology of the body, is Original Nakedness. When reference is made to Adam and Eve being 'naked and not ashamed' in the garden, the connection is made to the existence of trust between the two. 'We fear being used or being hurt, so we are afraid of being vulnerable in letting others see us as we really are' says John Paul ll but, shame is also the result of the painful consequences that are the reason for fear especially in victims of rape, whether inside marriage or otherwise. Shame also overwhelms the victim and survivor of various forms of sexual abuse, for children and for vulnerable adults. The connection of a purified form of shame to this imaginary scenario of the first man and woman has no equivalence in today's world. It also takes a lifetime of careful but sometimes mistaken behaviours to achieve a secure and consistent acceptance of each other. 'How were they

(Adam and Eve) able to have this ideal relationship?' Adam and Eve are metaphorically the first man and woman in an idealised medieval scenario, so is this scenario beyond human capacity? Sri gives in to sexist language at times as he refers to the Fall. 'Human persons had self-mastery over their passions and appetites.' It seems that passions and appetites of then and now are only referring to sexuality and the interaction of one couple, when we are painfully aware today of the other passions and appetites for power, control, adulation, entitlement and ignorant and arrogant demands to be at the top of the ecclesiastic pole. Translation of sexual passion into entitlement and enticement of power exists, too.

The People in the Pews, as they adjust to life's vicissitudes, have spent their energy and their labour finding their own way forward. We are focused on the message of Jesus in a confronting world within the church and beyond its reach. John Paul ll talks about the interior gaze, likening it to the gaze of the God we hope to reach when we leave this world. That interior gaze does not need to be always the province of two people in an exclusive sexual relationship. Respect, care, friendship and love can be fully present between two people who are not in an exclusive sexual relationship but who are truly present to each other even though intimate expression of sexuality may not be present.

The fifth feature is that of Original Shame. It is uncomfortable today to read Sri's text at this point because of the unbalanced emphasis on 'man', without any matching reference to woman: 'Wounded by original sin, man finds that it is no longer easy for him to control his passions and appetites. No longer does man look easily on his wife '. It is necessary to take issue with the generalisation inherent in this part of the text as there is no evidence of understanding human marital relationship. 'Now his heart's love for her is tainted by selfish desires to use her. He no longer easily sees her value as a person to be loved for her own sake'. This generalisation is more offensive in that it contains only the polar opposites in thinking patterns that are full of medieval assumptions.

Attributing shock to Adam in the face of original sin, the highlight is dramatic: 'Almost like the animals, Adam now finds himself powerfully swayed by his desire to satisfy his sexual desires.' Normal growing stages of maturity – the pilgrim journey towards God as Love –is parallel to the flowering of human love, in all its diversity and all its intensity. Suddenly, Adam and Eve are said to be ashamed of their nakedness and their sexual state: 'the biblical account of the Fall tells us that right after Adam and Eve sinned in the garden, they were naked and ashamed'(Genesis 3:7). This metaphor may have benefit for upper primary or early secondary introduction to theological inquiry, but is certainly not conducive to maturity in the People in the Pews, in John Paul ll's time or now. 'This shame took the place of the absolute trust connected with the previous state of original innocence in the mutual partnership between man and woman.' And this is also true for the child victims of paedophiliac priests who so regularly took away their victims' original innocence. Given John Paul ll was already aware of early cases of clerical child sexual abuse, he seems to see no contradiction, apparently.

This blind spot is a parallel to the mistrust by the People in the Pews of the authoritarianism exhibited by John Paul ll, as he outlawed so many matters without regard to primacy of personal conscience. The final section of wishful thinking is labelled 'Back to the garden?' as though it were possible. Restorationism is a banal and unreal tendency which is humanly impossible either for an individual or for the church. Apparently, John Paul ll saw no positives in today's daily lives of the People in the Pews. He was obviously oblivious to the daily heroism and the consistent kindliness that permeates Catholic marriage today. Neither does he show in these explorations any sign of intelligent understanding of the life of a marriage. In medieval times, medicine and lifestyle accompanied the couple for about twenty years. Today, the span of life, and therefore marriage is more than twice that lifespan towards forty-sixty years of married state. Sometimes that span means unbearable pain, and theology must address the various problems and paradoxes which abound. Theologians of both lay and ordained state need to focus in depth on this new phenomenon because the People in the Pews need further understanding rather than moral mutterings about no change.

George Elsbett LC has also examined the content of John Paul ll's theology of the body. He has isolated ten points as a summary: The body; Solitude; Innocence; Communion; Nakedness; Lust; Shame; Redemption of the heart; The inner gaze (glance/ look); Spousal meaning of the body. Briefer comment is needed here. John Paul ll says 'dig out your heart from underneath all the dirt that is perhaps thrown on top of it'. This is contradictory in that the presumption of dirt, which is insulting in itself, is present even though he is talking about innocence and the heart's deepest longings. Assuming that the body as sacrament highlights love and includes the presence of God, then the idea of anti-sacrament is drawing a long bow. The body is a gift to the individual first, then to the spouse and also to the glory of God, in the daily living out of the message of Jesus. Neither Elsbett nor John Paul ll seemed to be aware of this point.

John Paul ll seems to limit his meanderings to a single act of sexual intercourse only. This idealised view of love, sexuality and marriage does little to recognise that we make a commitment (gift) to another at a more concrete level than a starry-eyed carnal response. Body, as a term, must indicate therefore a deep intimate communication of insight and response to each other at social, physical, emotional, intellectual and especially spiritual level. In the solitude envisioned by John Paul ll, he disregards how commitment to another in love for a span of 50+ years, both people must know themselves in a mature way, to negotiate the various hurdles of daily life as an individual, as partner, and as social contributor.

Flippant references in the section by Elsbeth on Innocence do little to help the reader to appreciate what John Paul ll was trying to communicate. Adversarial attitudes are not welcome in a marriage. It is not so much trying to 'take on responsibility for that person' as it is trying to respect and support one's spouse, not take on or take over the spouse. 'The egotist hates responsibility, as he is not interested in the other'. This statement reeks of sexist considerations and of an understanding built on Hollywood sentiments and the 1960s flower power era. Then extremist binary thinking assumed two end points of a spectrum with nothing in between. The comment about Communion is an ideological view of a submissive woman, placed with the man for his benefit. The sphere of intimacy mentioned is not real today. No-one is likely to be naked at the first meeting, unless it is a one-night stand, and that is not included in the present considerations.

The reader can't escape the imaginative view of a mythical story which was meant to be used as metaphor, not taken literally to build a reality that can't be attained. We read that Eve discovers *herself* as an outcome of the submission to Adam, a subtle form of sexism easily dismissed by a celibate male of mature years, who is drowning in idealised dream and sentiment. The nakedness issue is embedded in binary thinking which shows no appreciation of the breadth and depth of a love relationship beyond the extremes highlighted in this text. The problem here is the lack of subtlety and the absence of recognition of process. It is as though a human is only sexual passion almost untied.

The comments on Shame are also problematic because no evidence of degrees of feeling are present, just jumping to extremes of bad/shame or good/love. It is uncomfortably close to ideology, rather than of theology. Approaching the feature called 'Redemption of the heart', we find sexist language again which highlights the situation for man. Transforming lust into love is attached here to virtue. Not 'mere human effort, but human effort capacitated by God's power' forgets that God's power is channelled through family, through law, through friends, through daily living and for People in the Pews. It comes from education about a moral code, and its application in a balanced and nuanced way in daily life.

There is a distinct need here to recognise the movement from dependency to independency and perhaps to interdependency as expressed in relationship. It highlights here the reason why we need to nurture our young in decision making as a democratic right. The inner gaze again is attributed to the man and his consideration, rather than to each of the pair, showing an underlying view of inferior woman as being of dependent nature only! Finally, in trying to give credence to the meaning of this term 'Spousal meaning of the body', it must be stated clearly here that in a real relationship, it is not *the* body, *the* soul, *the* sexual act! This wording shows a disengaged recognition of sexual response without any connection to mature strong marital bonding and affection. It shows no understanding of the complexity of the human person, as new knowledge from various medical, philosophical and other disciplines have uncovered for us.

We would do well to engage with Ilia Delio whose paper 'Evolution toward Personhood' gives us a firm grounding encompassing the work of De Chardin and others, finding the beginnings of a pathway that can be developed by theologians (2016). Important too is the need to find ways to incorporate the work of the Leuven Network who are presently developing further insights into what is to count as Catholic identity. It will be the work and responsibility of both lay and clerical theologians to develop these matters within the concept of theo-tensegrity.

So history proceeds

As history proceeded, we endured the long papacy of John Paul ll, the extraordinary resignation of Benedict XVl, and now the papacy of Francis. Paul Collins gives us some enlightening remarks to help us accommodate the change in emphasis:

> 'So what are we to make of Pope Francis five years into his papacy? What has he done with papal power and influence? First, he has decisively changed the pattern established by his predecessors. No longer is the emphasis on the dangers of secularism, relativism, and the false distinction between the so-called hermeneutics of continuity and rupture. Francis' emphasis is in tune with the genuine Catholic tradition focusing on God's mercy, the love of Jesus, and Catholicism's pastoral care for the vulnerabilities, sins, and failures embedded in the human condition ... He has also brought to fruition the opening toward environmental ethics ... Whether he will be able to break the stranglehold of the traditionalists on the central government of the church remains to be seen ... He also needs to recruit like-minded cardinals so that his vision will be continued ... he has not even begun to address practically the equality and role of women in leadership, ministry, and decision making ... Francis brings a completely new perspective, although as an Argentinian of Italian extraction, he is the perfect person to bridge Eurocentrism and the developing world.' (Collins, 2018).

CHAPTER 8

Reductionism, Restorationism, Regenerationism, Reform in the Catholic tradition

To look beyond the present confusion, vicious backlash, resistance and narcissism afflicting parts of our church, we are constrained, first, by the Christian response that requires us to respect the people who believe they are our sometimes sworn enemies, not because we title them enemies, but because of the black-and-white thinking that causes faulty logic patterns. This results, too, in the grabbing of entitlements attaching to present and past positions of importance. Careerism in hierarchical circles has been blatant, demanding, narrow-minded and sometimes downright unjust. Second, we are faced with people whose choices may be ungenerous, who believe that the legal requirements of a just or civil society do not apply to them. The sense of being above the law leads to compartmentalisation intellectually because when justice is jettisoned, hypocrisy and deception are often used to keep control of particular situations.

Third, those who see the People in the Pews as inferior, uneducated, simple, incapable of understanding in spiritual matters, may also be unaware of the virtues, values and ethics that pervade the lives of ordinary believers. Fourth, it seems that when hierarchical interests have been shaping the history of the church in each generation, there is a loss of knowledge and experience which affects those living within the vacuum of the Curial and papal circuit in Rome. Realities, like recognition of the existence of the voices in the *sensus fidelium*, and all that this term implies, fade into nothingness.

Disdain in some quarters allows binary/black-and-white thinking, which does not even take full account of the normal processes of an integrated secular and sacred world, in which the People in the Pews live their daily lives successfully. Fifth, infantilisation of the voices within *sensus fidelium*, by a hierarchy chained in clericalism, becomes a phenomenon that bites into the possible channels of communication. So at crucial times when dilemmas, problems, mysteries, injustices, tragedy, and sin crash into the realities of the present, there is confused recognition of the function and role of hierarchy within these moments of personal or national history.

Conclusions must come after we as the Australian Church analyse the full context of the Royal Commission findings into Institutional Clerical Abuse – all 57 findings. The announcement, made somewhat reluctantly, by the Chair of the Australian Catholic Bishops Conference, on 1 September 2018, accepted and promised responses to all but two of the recommendations. As this announcement seemingly was issued after discussions not made public, it follows that the voices of the *sensus fidelium* have not been fully consulted and the two recommendations not acceptable to the Bishops' Conference need to be fully debated, discussed and fully understood by the People in the Pews.

It is no longer enough and is quite dangerously provocative for the Bishops' spokesperson to issue such a statement. Mandated celibacy is one such contentious unjust issue. The breaking of the seal of confession is a second such contentious issue. The blatant dismissal by the Bishops Conference of normal good manners, in courteously replying and acknowledging any communications from many a person prompted by concern about a particular issue, is a third issue, because of the anger at the callous responses ignoring good manners, a feature of the People in the Pews.

Significantly, Dr Gerardine Robinson, whose clinical work with Catholic clergy, and who appeared at the Australian Royal Commission, also presented at the recent National Catholic Council of Priests convention and her feature article in the latest SWAG (Summer 2018) edition for the National Council of Priests, gives much to study and understand. She stressed that she was speaking strictly through the lens of a clinician, when providing relevant factors contributing to child sexual abuse in the Catholic Church. She highlighted four separate areas for comment: the corrosive culture of clericalism that pervades Catholic culture; celibacy and understandings of sexuality; selection, training, and formation of candidates for priesthood; and ongoing personal development of clergy after ordination. She gives a final recommendation of a list of goals for priests today, highlighting ten interactive ways of being a healthy church. We would do well to note the integration of lay and clerical partnership that underlies her whole presentation.

It was with relief that so many of us attended the Health and Integrity in Church and Ministry conference in late August 2018 in Melbourne. The communique that was issued at the conclusion of the consultations was truthful, balanced and looked to the future. 'For the Christian Churches, we are at a tipping point. Recovery will depend on engaging in a thorough going reformation of theology, structures, governance, leadership and culture' (in *Vox* magazine of the University of Divinity, October 2018). The three days of the conference were distinguished by the quality and calibre of the delegates, and the leader figures of many denominations, but was also distinguished by the discovery that there was a dearth of Australian Catholic Bishops and Archbishops at the Conference.

Not one Catholic bishop was present. The communique, which ended the conference, was addressed to 'survivors of child sexual abuse, to members of Australian Christian churches, including

Australian Catholic Bishops Conference, Catholic Religious Australia and the National Council of Churches.' The Health and Integrity conference called on Australia's churches to *exceed* the minimum standards of implementation in the Royal Commission's recommendations, to undertake thoroughgoing reform of theology, ministry, governance and leadership, and in so doing return to the teaching and example of Jesus Christ' (*Vox*, October 2018).

It was instructional to discover that overall there were 14 conference resolutions, five of which were significant as they appeared to be very critical. It is amplified by the following section of the concluding communique, published in the journal of the University of Divinity:

> 'The churches need to take responsibility for the lifelong care and support of all those, whose lives have been harmed irreparably. This goes beyond the notion of redress. Ongoing care should be based on principles of trauma informed practice. The churches should urgently review their processes for responding to ensure that victims are not re-traumatised when they seek support and redress from the Church. Clericalism in all its forms should be rejected. Any restoration of public trust in the churches will be dependent on a commitment to contemporary ethical standards of good governance based on the principles of transparency, accountability and inclusivity. There can be no theological excuse for poor governance structures and practices. It is essential that the laity, and especially women, is/are supported to take their rightful place in all aspects of church life, including governance' (*Vox*, October 2018).

In the matter of governance, it was instructional to discover that a second annual International Festival of Creativity in Church Management was held in June, 2018 at Villanova University in Philadelphia, USA. Distinguished Australian Professor Gabrielle McMullen AM spoke with clarity and significance about lay leadership in the Australian church. 'It is important that the general knowledge of these special functions is communicated to the People in the Pews, so that coordination, collaboration and creativity is available to us all – otherwise the tendency towards transparency is lost, and the work of this peak body is left unappreciated, to say the least.'

She noted in her paper that, since 1994, ten new foundations (previously titled ministerial public juridical persons [PJPs] in Church law) have been established in Australia to take education, health and community service ministries of religious congregations into the future as works of the Catholic Church'. In the period 2012-2016, representatives of these PJPs explored means of fostering collaboration between the respective entities, leading to the establishment of the Association of Ministerial PJPs in May 2016. This is now the peak body for these new lay-led church ministries and provides a vehicle for them to interact formally with one another and, in a corporate sense, with the Australian bishops and with church agencies.

Recommendations, possibilities, processes lead from reductionism and from restorationism towards regenerationism, with signposts to help us open ourselves to the promptings of the Holy Spirit. And what do we need to do about reform? The word 'reform' means to do again what the formation was as before – and as such is another version of Restorationism. Those signposts are trilectic (comprising complex elements and beyond binary) in connectivity, and conceptually based to provide a fluid, fluent and forward-looking channel of change that points us towards the message of Jesus in our lives: *Compassion*, community and collaboration; *Entrepreneurship*, energy and ethics; *Transparency*, truth and trust; *Accountability*, accommodation and action; *Governance*, God and growth. Each of these triads can be developed by theologians, lay and cleric, to educate the People in the Pews.

Reductionism – this is a theory in which formal efforts are used to provide simplistic dogma and formulae which are expected by curial and other evangelisation units to simplify all tenets of faith so that no thinking, reasoning or faith development takes place. One feature of this particular line of thinking emerges in an authoritarianism that pervades writing about any concepts of faith, any exploration of philosophical themes, and any individual forays into unexpected or supposedly dangerous areas regarding the relationship between the people of God and God as our Cosmic Trinity. In contrast, chosen paths of understanding referring to given areas of faith are to be recommended, partnered by preferred philosophical themes, and it becomes our mandate to resist deliberate banning of supposedly dangerous content as it emerges. We then are assured of a choice between black-and white (binary) fundamentalist logic and a reasoned reflective and respectful path towards real understanding and deep faith.

Allied to this simplistic approach of taking away the freedom to reflect is the promotion of a particular behaviour pattern named as holiness, with a strong emphasis on perfectionism. Perfectionism is addressed in such a way that the individual is never able to rise above a state of guilt and distress, in which God is seen as an angry policeman. But the aspiration is towards somehow becoming closer to divine, rather than becoming the best human that each human is meant to be. The Jesus 'way, truth and life' is, therefore, dimmed by all the extra noise of edicts, recommendations, pious practices, and strivings in daily life.

Take the recent (2018) Apostolic Exhortation of Pope Francis as an example: *Gaudete et Exsultate* (Rejoice and be glad). There are many possibilities that Francis suggests, some of which appeared in the May edition of *Melbourne Catholic*, the archdiocesan magazine (Francis, 2018). It is important that we recognise that trying to be a saint is not the aim here, though Francis seems to indicate this is so. His suggestions highlight single, almost trivial, personal actions, but if there is a growing or mature and loving relationship between the individual and our Triune God, the underlying attitude and general kindliness of the daily living of the Jesus 'way, truth and life' changes the individual perspective into a balanced life experience in which each person lives in communion with others, and with the Lord of all.

In a careful *Tablet* review and evaluation of the new apostolic exhortation (14 April 2018), Laurence Freeman ranges over much of what this exhortation was intended by Pope Francis to address. Freeman states that this is not 'a theological treatise about holiness but a faith-filled pitch for promoting the desire for holiness', and herein is the flaw in the logic. Being faced with people officially and ceremoniously named a saint means nothing in today's world of technology, histrionics and hypocrisy. Freeman says that 'Holiness is a practical life-long process grounded in the mysticism of incarnation'; 'a holiness of small gestures'; 'Francis is angry, as prophets should be, at fake holiness'. So are the People in the Pews, whether prophetic or not!

'A person's perfection is measured not by the information or knowledge they possess, but by the depth of their charity. "Gnostics" do not understand this, because they judge others based on their ability to understand the complexity of certain doctrines' says Freeman – and herein is another flaw in the logic. If the People in the Pews are not allowed to think through, but only accept what appears by edict or exhortation, as the present generations have been required to do, then how does each person find a way to develop virtues, values and ethical behaviours relevant to today, not to the notions of three centuries ago?

It is faintly disdainful, therefore, to provide a beautifully crafted wishful scenario like the latest apostolic exhortation with its very simple, child-like suggestions, when a challenging, complicated, sometimes quite evil world is what we face on a daily basis. The Jesus message requires strong and faithful attitudinal foundations as we live in a secular as well as a religious world. We follow Jesus, as Michael Elligate indicates in our Gospel reflection, by being a model of the virtues, values and ethical behaviours that distinguish us as normal, humble, educated, prayerful People in the Pews.

Reductionism as a theory

Reductionism also contains the sin of presumption: that caste of mind that allows a person to presume that it is an easy or logical matter to know exactly what God wants, what God wills and what is therefore required of the humble sinner. The spray of assumptions here is obvious.

The assumption is that one person of humankind can actually know with certainty exactly what the Divinity called God actually wills, and the breathtaking certainty with which that simplicity of dogma and formulae is produced for all to follow – without further ado. The choice is made by those in power, who somehow read with certainty the events of history from the supposed perspective of the Triune God, needs adjustment to unpack the ambiguities presumed. The promotion of an ideology that shows that authority, power and control are focused on the ever-increasing infallibility of the pope shows as well as on papal pronouncements and on members of the papal retinue.

There is no recourse here for the People in the Pews to develop a personal relationship with the Triune God, through the understanding of the life of Jesus, and with the strength and power of the Holy Spirit hovering within. The practice of promoting the preferred communal activities of the faithful, who are attaching significance to certain sweeps of history, seen as somehow parallel to the preferred ideological thinking pattern, are linked to historical areas of controversy, which have been dubbed as heresy, and terrible punishments have followed. Paul Collins highlights these phenomena in his latest book on *Absolute Power* (2018). John Paul ll used encyclicals to hammer home his understanding of such matters.

Restorationism as a theory

Restorationism demands that the People in the Pews must become a disciplined set of followers who accept that which the pope, with creeping infallibility, requires them to accept. They must be brought back within the confines of the authoritarian conceptual approach to the faith laid down in ceaseless world travel by Pope John Paul ll. This measure is almost impossible for a number of reasons. The possibility of brain-washing and the psychological damage to vulnerable individuals in a vain attempt to blot out questions is present. The spiritual abuse that confuses and compresses the flowering of faith and the likelihood that young people in particular, who have not been anywhere else to be brought back from, is a challenge.

The preferred alternative lifestyle is stated as 'living in the world but not of the world' (John 17), which is a contradiction of immense proportions. This leads to scruples, or rebellion, to secret sin and to a yearning for personal power. It leads also to the downplaying of the development of individual conscience, with no respect for the processes that are present, as the maturing understanding of how decision making becomes more accurate, and mature conscience emerges. The dualistic approach of understanding the world as full of unmanageable contrasts: right and wrong; arrogance or ignorance; an angry God but a loving God; sin and purgatory in some form, brings condemnation rather than the development of a living and loving relationship with the Triune God.

The obsessive emphases emanating from hierarchical sources on individual acts of whichever kind without any attention to underlying attitudes, any reference to intentions, any understanding of what follows when unintended consequences appear; and the apparent belief that individuals are the sum of their sexual desires alone, is unbalanced, unhealthy, and does not allow maturity to develop. Neither does it allow integration of all elements of personality and daily lived experiences to be attained and honed in maturity. Neither does it allow for the inspiration of the Holy Spirit and the guidance of trusted expertise to be followed.

Regenerationism as a theory

Regenerationism is a concept still in its infancy. The enormity of the task that awaits us, equates to the enormity of the problem. Using elements of the three processes of change mentioned earlier, we can plot the beginnings of hope and with some relief allow for the promptings of the Holy Spirit. No one process of change will be acceptable alone because that is reductionism. No simplistic retirement from the world into a pious enclave will be possible because that is Restorationism. No particular channel will be better than another because that is the way of arrogance and superiority.

Possibilities can be shaped through careful reflection to bring about the questions needed for the process of Regenerationism to gain a foothold in the imagination of the People in the Pews. Question starters – how? when? where? why? what? which? who? what if? – all lead us to some of the eminent figures addressing the dilemmas we face along with our present Pope Francis. To address the whole, we need to analyse and plan particularly for the Regeneration of the hierarchy, starting here in Australia in whichever parish and whatever diocese is our designated home.

A careful understanding of the various and many ecclesial movements – especially since Vatican ll – needs to be done in an open, trusting, rigorous, transparent way, in line with the message of Jesus – not in line with the latest preferences of whichever curial figure has the upper hand in the digital dissemination of concepts, edicts and communications. This will include the Regeneration of the priesthood as it exists in the 21st century. Seminary training is a strange name for the development of individuals who will specialise in the liturgical, theological, pastoral, philosophical, social, intellectual and emotional arenas of life within communities of believers we are here calling the People in the Pews.

Training as a concept is related to instinctive physical response, like learning to coordinate hand, arm and eye in a sport like tennis, where a serve at the beginning of a game must be exact to the centimetre. Formation as a concept is related to an approach whereby individuals learn the one-size-fits-all response to problems, dilemmas, paradoxes and mysteries. Each is limited. If Discipleship and Ministry is to be relevant, accurate, respectful, creative, and connected to the responsibility of assisting in the pastoral life of a Christian community, (whether a parish or other entity), much needs to be developed.

There is no place for power and entitlement, and therefore, processes of change are urgently needed. The social pendulum will swing of course, and perhaps excesses will emerge as the adjustments are made for 21st century living. That is the result of the impact of theo-tensegrity. We now are more comfortable with the application of this concept as a democratic but theological path leading us to the message of Jesus: his way, his truth, his life.

It is in the interests of all educators within the tradition of our battered and beloved church, to recognise these matters, and if this means that synods must be held regularly every couple of years, then responsible leadership and academic research into all matters will be approached without resort to relativism, reductionism, restorationism or simplistic reform. Instead, response-ability will provide avenues for careful and honest debate and discussion. Preparation of papers by lay and ordained theologians as well as wide consultation and inclusive collaboration will be a regular feature. As transparency and accountability are increasingly achieved in a global catholicity, we strive to be worthy in our efforts to respond to the message of Jesus. Connection with the reasoning of Constant Mews in his outline of the connections between catholicity and clericalism is relevant here.

Three educational processes have been offered in this project. The first process is aimed at the balancing of the distorted view of authoritarian thought-control, evidenced by the papal edict that insisted that the ordination of women was not to be discussed. The use of the philosophy in the classroom approach (with its rigorous use of the community of inquiry practice) requires much of each student and ordinand. The development of the skills to ask as many questions about a given topic and also to listen to each other's questions, propositions and objections before beginning the process of decision making is central. Candidates for priesthood today do not exhibit enough of these skills. This practice is well embedded in the Australian educational scenario led by the well-established DialogueAustralasiaNetwork (DAN). With over 300 members in Independent and Catholic Schools and Educational Organisations across Australia and New Zealand, their now-famous Five-Strand Approach to Religion and Philosophy Curriculum is beyond reproach.

In the latest edition of their august journal, Michael Parker sets out for teachers and students a careful exploration: 'Critical Thinking in an Age of Social Media'. Using the Community of Inquiry approach inaugurated by Matthew Lipman over six decades ago, it is possible for information-based discussion to give class members authentic experience of what is to count as authenticity in the development of knowledge, evaluative response, and decision making of each individual member. As he opines: 'it is so easy to miss the stop of "critically analyse" and end up at "oh, well, everything is relative". Concepts and vocabulary he uses includes weaponisation, authoritarianism, postmodernism, tabloid sensationalism, logical or bad ethical argument, opinion, reciprocity, and process (Parker, 2018).

The second of the three educational processes offered builds on the first process and aims at allowing for the identification of the relevant virtues, values and ethics normally in operation today. The development of conscience does not take place until the maturing individual, priest or laity, without broad knowledge, balanced understanding and courageous decision making taking place. Integration of the message of Jesus, requiring modelling of compassion, mercy, restorative justice and respect for difference and diversity, emerge as the individual embeds the use of those virtues, values and ethical standards into daily life, whatever the consequences, intended and unintended. Restriction of power-and-control by a secretive cultic caste must be replaced by the resilient and strong pathway to integration of priest and people.

The third of the three educational processes offered here allows for the requirement of 21st century priests to be capable of leadership, entrepreneurship, humility, collaboration, honesty and care for the environment: physical and geographic environment, intellectual environment, social environment, emotional environment and spiritual environment. There is no place for duplicitous, bogus or authoritarian pronouncements which do not respect the various cultural milieux in First World, Second World and Third World countries. Political concerns must not be uppermost in the decision making of priests alone. Collaboration, consultation and careful process provide the channels for the profile of the priest of the future if we are to be co-creators with our loving Triune God in the cosmic emergence of response to the will of our Creator, Redeemer and Inspirational God.

Joan Chittister (2004) has given us food for thought in a thoughtful and transparent exploration of the many delicate elements that complicate our urgent need for action especially as we face the monumental task of reassessing the concept of, the nature and meaning of, priesthood for 21st century People in the Pews. 'What do the people really need in a period when the sacraments are being lost in a sacramental church?' (Chittister, 2004). She asks why this is 'being blocked, obstructed, denied, and suppressed'. So why is there a problem in expanding the ministry suitably so that deacons, married priests, women ministers and every shade of various needs are addressed? Change for change' sake is no recipe for the future planning of a pilgrim people and the old claim that the church never changes is not logical or suitable. 'It is a far cry from the dynamism of the early church in which Prisca and Lydia and Thecla and hundreds of women like them opened house churches, walked as disciples of Paul.'

Today, as in those early times, the People in the Pews need Christian community, not patriarchal clericalism, says Chittister, the sacred not the sexist, more prophets rather than priests even. The answer in her terms is discipleship. She challenges us: 'the following of Christ was not an excursion into the intellectual, the philosophical, and the airy-fairy. It was not an arm-wrestling match with a tradition that was more history warped by culture than it was the spirit free of the system. It was real and immediate and cosmic.'

Today, we must heed her words: 'Flag and fatherland, profit and power, chauvinism and sexism, clericalism and authoritarianism done in the name of Christ are not Christian virtues', Chittister tells us. Today, in the footsteps of disciples over the ages, the People in the Pews must call out the clericalists, whether ordained priests, those in Orders, those in ecclesial movements, or even parishioners to the understanding that the system is not what Jesus was modelling. Today, we must address the tautologies and contradictions that parade as dogma, the rash of canonisations, and the resistance to deep reflection in favour of instant everything! Honest analysis rather than roadblocks to the establishment of the community of believers, who live within the world, influencing those in our cultural milieux, must model the message of Jesus – his way, his truth, his life.

In First World countries, this means a life of educated and ethical decision making, being able to respond, being equipped to model appropriate response-ability and being courageous enough to take the necessary actions in our own areas of familial, personal and communal matters. It is important therefore to recognise here that there are no one-size-fits-all answers. Neither is there acceptance of silence and the obstructionist tactics when processes begin, as they already have, to try and address localised dilemmas. The poaching of foreign-born, newly ordained priests for First World countries like Australia is a tragedy already, and the Third World countries of origin are expected to accede to this distressing choice.

So *discipleship*, says Chittister, as a concept itself is in need of analysis, understanding and adjustment. It cannot allow for the 'pauperisation of women in the name of the sanctity and essentialism of motherhood' as though this is somehow holy. Distant, perhaps damaged, elderly men have no understanding of daily life and confuse the holy with wholeness – the ultimate in spiritual growth. Chittister comments that discipleship is 'not membership in a clerical social club called a church, is not an intellectual exercise of assent to a body of doctrine, is an attitude of mind, a quality of soul, a way of living that is not political but which has serious political implications. Why? Because the church of Jesus Christ is not called to priesthood, the church of Christ is called to discipleship'.

In the regeneration of the church we love, Chittister asks us to ponder on the theology of discipleship. This includes the shapeless mess that has occurred as the clericalism of our time has treated women with no respect, no understanding, no knowledge, and no compassion. Her question is challenging: 'Where is the presence of Jesus to the homeless woman, to the beggar woman, to the abandoned woman, to the woman alone, to the woman whose questions, cries, and life experience have no place in the systems of the world and no place in the church either?' She goes on, 'What does it mean for the women themselves who are faced with rejection, devaluation, and a debatable theology based on the remnants of a bad biology theologised?'

When 'tradition' is used to block any likelihood of communication or listening by the powerful to the powerless, it is important to question what that term now means. Does it mean, to use an old Australian saying: Do as I say, not as I do? Is it possible to aim for the careful construction of a theology of equality? Real equality would mean we must respect those different to ourselves. It would entail acceptance of heterosexual, homosexual and transsexual people without judgmental negative responses. It would mean women and men of all colours, of all cultures, of all diverse life experiences being treated with meticulous respect. It would mean a serious development of resilience as a human skill rather than a retreat into the 'cave' of entitlement and privilege.

To counter clericalism, we have no choice but to address this whole area of present pain and reluctant acknowledgment. As Chittister says 'Men who do not take the women's issue seriously may be priests but they cannot possibly be disciples. They cannot possibly be other Christs, not a Christ born of a woman'. The incoherence and contradiction, the resistance and callousness of clericalism must be replaced by a listening People in the Pews, who allow the Holy Spirit space, time and voice at the beginning of the third millennium of faith, hope and love that Jesus preached, modelled and left as legacy to both women and men. After all, it seems likely that Jesus communicated first his resurrection to Mary of Magdala, apostles to the apostles.

In place of the creeping papal infallibility inherited today and the primacy of the papacy that partners this creeping form of clericalism, we need a regeneration of our understanding of the evolving profile of the priest. Chittister says: 'If, as Vatican ll says, priesthood requires preaching, sacrifice, and community building, then the preaching, shaping, and vision of a new notion of priest and deacon – whatever the cost to ourselves – may be the greatest priestly service of them all right now. So we must keep turning, turning, turning in the direction of discipleship, as women always have'.

Empowering Hope

Faith, hope and love are the familiar virtues we have inherited in the message of Jesus. What follows is an effort to distil elements of these virtues into action-based aims and objectives. It would be part of the journey of Christian maturity for a person to explore in a sustained way the kernel of faith contained in each statement. Translation of each statement would be part of the growing learning of the People in the Pews, empowering balance by the voices within the *sensus fidelium*, and certainly must be understood fully by the ordinand, the priest, all bishops and the hierarchy in general. We must be coherent and sensitive to the message conveyed in our Gospel reflection by Michael Elligate as we proceed.

A believer will be aware of a forward emphasis towards a future built on faith, hope and love in line with the will of the Creator God. A believer will perhaps have experienced present or previous suffering and will look towards the stated love of the Saviour and Life-Giver Son, who has promised his presence with us till the end of time. A believer will be aware of an initial cultural narrative, and is able to explore scriptural and liturgical sources to engender the beginnings of hope. A believer will develop eventual ideals that mirror the Jewish scriptures, the New Testament and the figures of Christian faith so that a foundation for faith, hope and love is able to grow. A believer will follow those ideals with chosen purposes through which personal life experience will not only mirror, but echo and respond to the *kenosis* of God, that emptying out of love from our Creator God to and for humankind.

A believer will experience growing personal attributes that respond, despite difficulties, to a growing understanding and faith in our Triune God. A believer will become conscious of evolving personal attitudes that show independent yearning and groping towards a deepening relationship with our Triune God. A believer will begin to expand a personal resilience, in the face of trial and disappointment, towards a growing strength of faith and love in our Triune God. A believer will know an evolving experiential knowledge that strengthens faith, engenders hope and musters a deep, subtle and ongoing love of our Triune God. A believer will need to shape personal humble and realistic wishes for the well-being of self, for the generation of love in community and for the transformation of the cosmic reality of God's multiverse. A believer will begin to understand the experience of a new and dawning faith that enervates and refreshes the relationship with our Triune God despite disaster, paradox and oppression.

A believer will experience at times those wishes and religious dreams that focus on a better world, a clearer understanding of who we are as humankind, and the vast future that is encompassed in the mind of our Creator God focused on becoming the best our humankind can be. A believer will investigate the growing cosmological expansion of knowledge provided by science and imaged in a myriad ways, deepening our recognition of the vastness of the Cosmos, created by a God whom we will never fully understand.

A believer will begin to recognise the connections within this vast creation, and the transcendence of the immanent God of us all through the process of evolution, becoming so vivid in the life of 21st century humankind, without trying to intrude into the divineness of our loving Creator. A believer will be fully aware of the evolving consciousness of the deepened understanding of the relationship of Creator and creature, and the ecology of this world, responding as co-creators in the development of the future of the cosmos. A believer will focus as a personal response to the *kenosis* of God, that self-emptying of divine love for humankind which evokes a corresponding self-emptying of ourselves in relationship with the Triune God.

Conclusions and Hopes and Fears

We try now to bring together the salient points that permeate this whole project and evaluate aims and objectives, propose and pinpoint curriculum topics and use instructional design to develop a far-seeing, efficient, effective process. Of course, if the changes that were such a central part of Vatican ll agenda are to be developed, we must be true to the message of Jesus for 21st century believers.

Kenosis must be the kernel of the relationship between the individual and God.

Reductionism dismisses the intellect and intelligence of the People in the Pews, so that it is necessary to distinguish where we might mistakenly rely on such simplistic jargon. The conceptual development of the individual tenets of faith which are contained conveniently in both the Apostles Creed statement and the Nicene Creed statement will instead become the starting point for theologians, teachers, pastors, ordinands and administrators to develop understanding within the new paradigm of theo-tensegrity, that marrying of theology, liturgy, philosophy, democracy, justice and compassion.

This will involve the stepping up of ordinands to show that their lived experience is, and will be, portraying the faith they profess, and we would do well to follow this same path as the People in the Pews. The future then in the Catholic tradition will be more communal, more slanted towards wholeness and more focused on responding to the promptings of the Holy Spirit. It will be the responsibility of the People in the Pews, as voices within the *sensus fidelium*, to ensure that accountability, transparency, balance and accurate theology are pursued as this new emerging paradigm is developed.

Restorationism disallows the advent of the many scientific developments to provide their full appreciation as the opportunities given us to begin to recognise what is to count as global Catholicism, with all its diversity and excitement. If we identify the ways in which existing authoritarian tendencies can be shaped to recognise the tenets of faith and moral behaviours in democratic theory, practice and praxis, we may find ourselves reaching for the same end points, but through the use of thinking skills, deeper understanding of the expanding universe and multiverses waiting to be discovered. This also would include the deepening of the relationships between our communal pilgrimages and our relationship with the love, mercy and compassion of our Triune God.

At least, clericalism will begin to be seen as a contradiction of the message of Jesus, more in the flavour of the Roman Senate, and certainly not oriented towards the option for the poor. It will also be seen that the silencing of around five hundred theologians, doing their legitimate work of theology, is completely out of order and smacks of a small-mindedness which is quite the opposite of the essence of the message of Jesus. The alternative way would be to institute a series of negotiations, as we do with ecumenism and interfaith dialogue, in order to strengthen our understanding of new theories of theology, and to use transparency and accountability at all times coupled with respect and resilience in the matters surrounding unusual or uncomfortable new efforts at theology. Of course, stonewalling and weaponising of silence would be identified as blatant clericalism at its boldest.

Regenerationism, then, is a form of looking forward into the future of humankind, in conjunction with all things secular and all things sacred. It will mean identifying where evil exists. It will mean upgrading our understanding of the virtues needed for life in global catholic circles where synodality is free, positive and fully operational, because the alternative is anathema. It will mean sustained, ecologically-sound, care and control of our environment. It will include the theology of humankind, a theology of personhood expanding exponentially on the theology of the body offered last century.

Theologians of all backgrounds will find ways to pray together, work together with and lead the People in the Pews in an appropriate and accountable style. They and we will journey through the various complexities that accompany problems, paradox, paradigm change, mystery and the responsibility of discernment of new questions and their subsequent answers. This will happen under the auspices of the Holy Spirit in a transparent manner, with due process as the norm, and with non-adversarial behaviours allowing reflection, prayer and sacrament to hold us close to the essence of our God. We must heed the comments laid out in our Gospel reflection by Michael Elligate.

A concluding consideration is well mirrored by Paul Sharkey (2015) in his last chapter of a sensitive and insightful setting out of what we need to do. His term of 'doing theology' is an authentic representation of what is set out in this whole project of Countering Clericalism in the Catholic tradition. Instead of listening to the intrusion of vicious infighting and heretical noises hitting the media headlines, we can focus our attention on the service of Catholic schools, run almost exclusively in Australia by dedicated lay people whose leadership is a model of the important impetus points we need for 21st century mission.

This is the challenge for the People in the Pews, and more importantly, the challenge of the ordinand today. It is to translate faithfully in current sociological and spiritual terms the message that permeated the whole of the life of Jesus: his way, his truth, his life. Sharkey (2015) has given clear indications of the steps of 'doing theology' and the ordinand must be aware and focused on these steps of naming the experience, analysing the context, dialoguing with the tradition of faith, developing a vision for action and including reflection on action. If all this is being put into action in our Catholic schools today, it is incumbent on the ordinand to do the same.

Paradigm change takes time, and it is accompanied by steps forward and steps backward as we discern the 'how' to accompany the Holy Spirit on our journey as co-creators in the third millennium. It is a challenge; it is exciting; it becomes our process towards that relationship begun here in daily life but which fits us for the transition into the presence of our loving Triune God. We will have bypassed that pitfall of allowing others to intrude, claiming the title of father, in favour of the presence and response of our loving Father-Creator, our Triune God. This challenge encompasses the use and valuing of binary thinking systems wherever we meet them, but augments that content with more complicated trilectic thinking skills sets. We will then have accomplished in our own lives the message of Jesus: his way, his truth, his life.

For The Church's Flourishing And Renewal

A prayer written by Archbishop William Laud, in around 1643:

> Most gracious Father, we pray to you for your holy Catholic Church.
> Fill it with all truth;
> In all truth with all peace.
> Where it is corrupt, purge it.
> Where it is in error, direct it.
> Where anything is amiss, reform it.
> Where it is right, strengthen it and defend it.
> Where it is in want, provide for it.
> Where it is divided, heal it and reunite it in your love.
> For the sake of your Son, our Saviour Jesus Christ.   Amen.

Reference List

Alison, James (2018) 'Caught in a trap of dishonesty – the McCarrick affair' –feature in *The Tablet*, 4 August 2018.

Alison, James (2018) -The lying game' - feature paper in *The Tablet*, 11 /8August 2018.

Allen, John L. Jnr (2013) 'Between Reform and Realism: How the Sexual Abuse Crisis Is (and Isn't) Changing the Church' in *Broken Faith* Claffey et al. Peter Lang, Bern

Amen, Damien and Justin Landy (2018) –research indicated by Peter Shields, *The Weekend Australian*, 20-21 October 208, p. 48.

Australian Episcopal Conference (1970) *The Renewal of the Education of Faith* published by the Australian Episcopal Conference / E.J. Dwyer, Sydney, Australia

Baird, Julia (2018) Graduation address: https://www.divinity.edu.au/news-events/2018/03/16/congratulations-to-our-graduates-s/ accessed: 30 July 2018

Bausch, William J (2001) *Brave New Church – From Turmoil to Trust* Twenty-third Publications, CT, USA

Beare, Hedley (2010) *Six Decades of Continuous School Restructuring* ACEL Monograph series

Berger, Teresa (2011) *Gender Differences and the Making of Liturgical History* Ashgate Publishing, Surrey, UK

Berry, Jason (1994) *Lead Us Not Into Temptation* Doubleday, NY, USA

Blaskow, Nicholas (2018) 'Human, all too human' - editorial in *Dialogue Australasia*, July 2018

Boff, Leonardo (1985) *Church: Charism and Power– Liberation Theology and the Institutional Church*   SCN Press Ltd., London UK

Bossy, John (1991)   *Giordano Bruno and the Embassy Affair*   Yale University Press, USA

Bourgeault, Cynthia (2003) *The Wisdom Way of Knowing: reclaiming an ancient tradition to awaken the heart*   John Wiley, San Francisco, USA

Bourgeault, Cynthia (2008)   *The Wisdom Jesus*   Shambhala Publications Inc., Boulder, Col. USA.

Brennan, Frank (2007) *Acting on Conscience*   University of Queensland Press, St Lucia, Australia.

Brennan, Frank SJ (2015) *Amplifying that still, small voice*   ATF Theology, Adelaide, Australia.

Brown, Peter (2012) *Through the Eye of a Needle*   Princeton University Press, Princeton, NJ, USA.

Carr, John (2018) *Faith in Focus* article   'He worked with Law, McCarrick and Vigano' in *America* dated 15 October 2018.

CCEAM International Studies in Educational Administration (2011) Vol. 39, No. 2.

Catechism of the Catholic Church – St Paul's Publications, 1994, Homebush, Australia.

Chan, Mark LY, and Chia, Roland (eds) (2003) *Beyond Determinism and Reductionism*   ATK Science and Theology series.

Reference List

Chittister, Joan (2004) In *the Heart of the Temple* BlueBridge NY, USA.

Chittister, Joan (2010) *God's tender mercy: Reflections on Forgiveness* John Garratt Publishing, Mulgrave, Victoria, Australia.

Claffey, Patrick, Joe Egan and Marie Keenan (eds.) (2013) *Broken Faith –why Hope matters* Peter Lang, Bern, Switzerland.

Collins, John N (2016) *Gateway to Renewal* WIPF & STOCK Oregon, USA.

Collins, Paul (1986) *Mixed Blessings* Penguin Books Australia, Melbourne, Australia.

Collins, Paul (1997) *Papal Power* HarperCollins Religious, Blackburn, Vic, Australia.

Collins, Paul (2001) *From Inquisition to Freedom* Simon and Schuster (Australia) NSW, Australia.

Collins, Paul (2004) Between *the Rock and a Hard Place* ABC Books, Sydney, Australia.

Collins, Paul (2005) *God's New Man* Melbourne University Press, Australia.

Collins, Paul (2008) *Believers* University of New South Wales, Sydney, Australia.

Collins, Paul (2018) 'God and Caesar in Australia' in *Australian Book Review Inc.*, March 2018. Published under the auspices of the Australian Government, State Governments and other Creative Arts bodies, Southbank, Melbourne, Australia (pp. 40- 50).

Collins, Paul (2018) 'Sniffing the Ecclesiastical Wind' http://www.johnmenadue.com/paul-collins-sniffing-the-ecclesiastical-wind/ accessed: 7 January 2018.

Collins, Paul (2018) *Absolute Power – How the Pope became the most influential man in the world* PublicAffairs, NY, USA.

Coloe, Mary (2018) 'Act justly; Love faithfully; Live humbly: The Prophetic Challenge to the Contemporary Church' Address given in Brisbane, 2018.

Congar, Yves (2012) *My Journey of the Council* translation published by ATF, Adelaide, Australia.

Coolman, Holly Taylor (2018) 'We Have Not Made Ourselves – *Humanae Vitae* at 50' in 'America' 23/7/2018, pp. 26-31; and 'From the archives' editorial statement 17 August 1968.

Cornwell, John (1989) *A Thief in the Night* Penguin Books, Middlesex, UK.

Cornwell, John (2001) *Breaking Faith* Penguin Books Ltd, Middlesex, UK.

Crowther, Frank (2010) *Building and Sustaining Capacity in Your School – The COSMIC C_B model* in monograph series by ACEL, Australia.

Davies, A. C. (2005) 'A new democracy for professional development and learning' – unpublished thesis Victoria University, Melbourne, Australia.

Davies, Paul (1992) *The Mind of God; Science and the search for Ultimate Meaning* Penguin Books, London, UK.

Delio, Ilia (2018) 'Death in the Church: Is New Life Ahead?' – https://www.omegacenter.info/death-in-the-church-new-life-ahead. Accessed with thanks to WATAC October 2018.

Dispenza, Joe (2007) *Evolve Your Brain: The Science of Changing Your Mind* Health Communications, Inc. Florida, USA.

Doherty, Tony (2013) *So you're seeking to renew your faith: a friendly guide to the Catholic tradition* Garratt Publishing, Melbourne, Australia.

Downey, Jack (2018) 'A history of evil' - book review (pp. 56-57) in *America*, 19 March 2018, NY, USA.

Doyle, Brian (2013) in *So You're seeking to renew your faith – a Friendly Guide to the Catholic Tradition* by Tony Doherty (2013) Garratt Publishing, Mulgrave, Australia, p. 3.

Editorial of *The Tablet* – accessed: 10 March 2018 (editor: Brendan Walsh) www.thetablet.co.uk – 'Pope from the Periphery'.

Editorial of *The Tablet* – accessed: 25 August 2018 (editor: Brendan Walsh) www.thetablet.co.uk – 'Clerical Child Sexual Abuse – Saying Sorry is not enough'.

Editorial –'Our Take' 'The Pattern of Sin Is Clear' – a paper analysing the Pennsylvania grand jury report on sexual abuse – in 'America' pp. 8- 9.

Editorial of *The Tablet* (2018) 'Vigano and the Political Agenda' - (p. 2, 27 October 2018).

Editorial of *The Tablet* (2018) – 'From the Archives' (p. 29) from the Editors 17 August 1968.

Egan, Joe (2013) 'Renewing a Faith that Is Broken: Trajectories towards Healing and Wholeness, Truth and Reconciliation' in *Broken Faith*. Claffey et al, Peter Lang, Bern.

Elsbett, P. George (2018) 'A Theology of the Body- Ten Point Summary' – accessed: http://www.zentrum-johannes-paul-ll.at/2014/04/22/a-theology-of-the-body-10-point-summary/.

Faggioli, Massimo (2008) *Sorting Out Catholicism – a brief History of the New Ecclesial Movements* Liturgical Press, Minnesota, USA.

Faggioli, Massimo (2012) *Vatican ll – the Battle for Meaning* Paulist Press, Mahwah, NJ., USA.

Faggioli, Massimo (2014) *Sorting Out Catholicism* Liturgical Press, Minn. USA.

Faggioli, Massimo (2015) *A Council for the Global Church* Fortress Press, Minneapolis, USA.

Faggioli, Massimo and Vicini, Andrea (eds) (2015) *The Legacy of Vatican II* Paulist Press, NJ, USA.

Faggioli, Massimo (2016) *The Rising Laity – Ecclesial Movements since Vatican ll* Paulist Press, Mahwah, NJ, USA.

Faggioli, Massimo (2018) 'The Catholic Church's Biggest Crisis since the Reformation' - https//johnmenadue.com/massimop-faggioli-the-catholic-churchs-biggest-crisis-since-the-reformation/ accessed: 3 November 2018.

Faggioli, Massimo (2018) 'Polarization in the Church and the crisis of the Catholic mind' – feature paper in *The Swag* of Autumn, 2018.

Fawkner, Patty SGS (2018) 'Calls for change within the Church will be its salvation' – in 'The Swag', Winter edition, 2018.

Fergusson, Maggie (2018) *The last taboo* feature article in *The Tablet*, 6.10.18.

Filochowski, Julian with Peter Stanford (eds) (2005) *Opening Up: Speaking out in the Church* Darton, Longman and Todd, London, UK.

Filochowski, Julian (2018) 'A martyr for our time' feature article in *The Tablet*, 13/10/18.

Fisher, Archbishop Anthony (2018) 'Speaking the truth in love Eph. 4:15' Letter regarding the Plenary Council 2020-21 published: archbishop@sydneycatholic.org.

Fisher, Robert (1990) *Teaching children to think* -reprint by Nelson Thornes, Cheltenham, UK.

Flannery, Austin OP (1975) (Gen Ed) *Vatican Council ll –The Conciliar and Post Conciliar Documents* Costello Publishing Company, New York, USA.

Freeman, Laurence (2018) 'Rejoice and be glad' –feature article in *The Tablet* - p. 4, 14/4/18.

From The Archives – An Editorial Statement on 'Human Life' on 17/8/1968 reprinted in *America* 23/7/2018, p. 29.

Gaillardetz, Richard (2018) 'Francis under Fire' - in *The Tablet*, 22nd Sept., 2018, pp. 4- 5.

Geraghty, Chris (2018) *Jesus: the forgotten feminist* Garratt Publishing. Mulgrave, Australia.

Goldburg, Peta (2012) *Religious Education: a Foundation for Freedom of Religion and Belief* Peter Lang AG, Bern, Switzerland.

Gray, John (2018) *Seven types of Atheism* Allen Lane of Penguin Books, UK.

Gula, Richard M. SS (1989) *Reason Informed By Faith* Paulist Press Mahwah, NJ, USA.

Halik, Tomas (2009) *Patience with God: the story of Zacchaeus continuing in us* Random House, NY, USA.

Halliday, David (2018) 'The Third Place ' in *Melbourne Catholic* magazine published by Catholic Archdiocese of Melbourne.

Halliday, David (2018) 'Talking about child safety' - (p. 11, June, 2018) published by Catholic Archdiocese of Melbourne.

Hamilton, Andrew (2018) 'Clerical culture produces poor fruit' in *Eureka Street Journal* (online) 10 April 2018.

Hargreaves, Andy and Dennis Shirley (2009) *The Fourth Way* Corwin, CA, USA.

Hargreaves, Andy (2009) *The Fourth Way of Educational Reform* monograph series No 45 by ACEL, Australia.

Harris, Robert (2016) *Conclave*, Hutchinson, London, UK.

Harries, M. et al (2018) 'Communique from the Health and Integrity in Church and Ministry conference' accessed: 8/9/2018 from healthandintegrity.org.au

Hazelwood, Tim (2018) Review of 'A Priesthood Imprisoned' by John E. Ryan – in *The Swag*, Spring edition, 2018.

Heasly, Berise Therese (2007) 'A Reflection on the Moral Bases for Teachers' Planning and Practice' – seminar paper for Education week at ACU, Melbourne 22 March 2007.

Heasly, Berise Therese (2015*)* *Towards an Architecture for the Teaching of Virtues, Values and Ethics* Peter Lang Ltd., Oxford UK.

Hebblethwaite, Margaret (2018) 'Theologian warns against the inevitability of abuse' in *The Tablet* 15 September 2018.

Hill Fletcher, Jeannine (2018) *The Sin of White Supremacy* Orbis Books, USA.

Hodgens, Eric (2008) 'New Evangelisation in the 21st Century' in Voices, vol. 1, no 3, Quarterly Essays on Religion in Australia. Johngarrattpublishing, Melbourne, Australia .

Hodgens, Eric (2018) 'Storms and Synods' http://www.johnmenadue.com/eric-hodgens-storms-and-synods/ accessed: 1/7/2018.

Hodgens, Eric (2018) 'Spare a thought for the New Archbishop' https://johnmenadue.com/eric-hodgenspare-a-thought-for-the-new-archbishop/ accessed: 27.7.2018.

Hodgens, Eric (2018) *'Humanae Vitae* – a 50 Year Odyssey' reproduced in Parish Newsletter, St Carthage's Parish, Parkville, p. 5- 6; from Catholica Commentary (3/11/18) and https:www.catholica.com.au/gc3/eh/025_eh_070818.php

Hodgens, Eric (2018) 'Revisiting the Theology of Clericalism' accessed: https://www.catholica.com.au/gc3/eh/026_eh_101018.php

Hoffner, Anne-Benedicte (2018) 'Woman appointed to head battle against sexual abuse in Chilean Church' in *La Croix* 13/8/2018.

Hogan, Linda (2000) *Confronting the Truth: Conscience in the Catholic tradition* Paulist Press, Mahwah, NJ, USA.

Holy See (1994) *Catechism of the Catholic Church* St Paul's Publishing, Homebush, NSW, Australia.

Holloway, Richard (2018) 'Count thou my unbeliefs' – a review of Gray's *Seven Types of Atheism* in *The Tablet* (p 17, 28/4/18).

Hogan, Anthony (2018) 'Law and the seal of Catholic confessional' – https://johnmenadue.com/anthony-hogan-law-and-the-seal-of-catholic-confessional -accessed: 22/7/2018.

Ingber, Donald E (1997) 'The Architecture of Life' in *Scientific American*, January 1998.

Investigative Staff of Boston Globe (2002) *Betrayal* - Updated Edition from Profile Books London UK, 2015.

Johnson, Elizabeth A (2015) *Abounding in Kindness: writings for the People of God* Orbis Books, Maryknoll, NY, USA.

Johnson, Kevin (2018) 'Clericalism and psychopathy' - in *The Swag*, (pp. 34- 35) autumn edition, 2018 – a quarterly magazine of National Council of Priests of Australia.

Johnston, Peter (2018) 'Should Australian Catholic bishops be Trusted?' https://johnmenadue.com/peter-johnstone-should-australian-catholic-bishops-be-trusted- in *Pearls and Irritations*. Accessed: 12/7/2018.

Johnston, Peter (2018) 'An Open Letter to the Catholic Bishops of Australia' https:/johnmenadue.com/peter-johnstone-an-open-letter-to-the-catholic-bishops-of-australia/ accessed: 12/7/2018.

Johnston, Peter (2018) 'Breaking the seal for the common good' https://johnmenadue.com/peter-johnstone-breaking-the-seal-for-the-common-good/ accessed: 30.7.18.

Kavanaugh, James (2018) 'Searching for identity – James Kavanaugh Live in concert' – https://www.youtube.com/watch?v-D8Xshxgnaw. Accessed: 5/11/18.

Kelly, Michael SJ (2018) 'As Holy Mother Church has always taught' http://www.johnmenadue.com/michael-kelly-as-holy=mother-church-has-always-taught/ accessed: 1/7/2018.

Kelly, Michael SJ (2018) 'Six archbishops examined by Australian judge' https://johnmenadue.com/michael-kelly-sj-six-archbishops-examined-by-australian-judge accessed: 21/7/2018.

Kelly, Michael (2018) 'Change of era in Australia' -published in English editions of *La Croix International* and *La Civilta Cattolica* and appearing in weekly newsletter of St Carthage's Parish, Parkville, Australia.

Keneally, Kristina (2018) Speech by Keneally given to the Catholic Secondary School Principals Conference, Cairns in June, 2018.

Kennedy, Philip (2006) *A Modern Introduction to Theology* I.B.Tauris, London, UK.

Kennedy, Philip (2010) *Twentieth-Century Theologians – a new introduction to modern Christian thought* I.B. Tauris, London, UK.

Konig, Cardinal Franz (ed. C Pongrats-Lippitt, 2005) *Open to God, Open to the World* published by Burns & Oates, London, UK.

Laidler, Terry (2018) 'Catholic Clericalism' https://johnmenadue.com/terry-laidler-catholic-clericalism/ accessed: 21/7/2018.

Lakeland, Paul (2002) *The Liberation of the Laity* Continuum/Bloomsbury NY, USA – London UK.

Lamb, Christopher (2018) 'Restless Knights' – feature paper in *The Tablet*, 21/4/18.

Lamb, Christopher (2018) Report from Rome (12/05/18) "Lay Voices 'indispensable' to the Church" published in *The Tablet* (p 24).

Lamb, Christopher (2018) 'Culture Wars' in *The Tablet*, p. 4, 8/9/2018.

Lamb, Christopher (2018) 'On the Road to Emmaus' in *The Tablet*, 20/10/2018.

Lamb, Christopher, (2018) 'Vigano adjusts testimony in third letter' (p. 25 *The Tablet*, 27/10/18)

Lee, Michael (2018) 'From inquisitor to saint' – feature article in *The Tablet*, 13/10/18.

Levo, Lynn M. (2013) 'Revising Our Understanding of Being Sexual' in *'Broken Faith'*, Claffey et al. Peter Lang, Bern.

Lewins, Frank W. (1978) *The Myth of the Universal Church* Universal Printing, Canberra, Australia.

Lewis, Hedwig SJ (2013) 'The Blessed Virgin Mary – Untier of Knots' in *Thinking Faith* Jesuit online magazine pp. 1-2, 21/5/2013.

Linden, Ian (2009) *Global Catholicism* Hurst and Company, London, UK.

Lindner, Johannes (2018) 'Entrepreneurship Education for a sustainable future' in BBCC journal: "Discourse and Communication for Sustainable Education" vol. 9, no. 1, pp. 115- 127, 2018.

Lipman, Matthew (1993) *Thinking Children and Education* Kendall/Hunt Publishing, Iowa, USA.

Little, John (2000) 'Mindfulness at work: A Five Rooms Model for thinking about thinking' in *Mount Eliza Business Review* 3:1 (Winter/Spring edition, 19 – 29. p.3 2000).

Lodge, David (2011) *How Far Can You Go?* - Vintage Books, London, UK.

Mackay, Hugh (1993) *Reinventing Australia* - Angus & Robertson, Sydney, Australia.

Mackay, Hugh (1997) *Generations, Baby Boomers, their parents & their children* McMillan Australia.

Maguire, John (1999) *What is Conscience?* Church Archivists' Press, Virginia, Queensland, Australia.

Malik, Kenan (2014) *The Quest for a Moral Compass: a global history of ethics* Atlantic Books, London, UK.

Malone, Matt SJ (2018) 'Of Many Things' - Editorial in *America*, 2/4/18.

Malone, Matt, SJ (2018) 'Why Stay?' Editorial in *America*, 17/9/2018.

Markey, Eileen (2018) 'The Reckoning' - in *America*, 25.6.2018.

Martin, D (2011) *The future of Christianity* Farnham, Surrey, UK, Ashgate Publishing.

Martin, James SJ (2017) *Building a Bridge* HarperOne, NY, USA.

Massam, Katharine and Fotini Toso (eds) (2016) *The Greening of Hope – Hildegard for Australia* Morning Star Publishing, Northcote, Australia.

Matheson, Peter (2018) 'Confession after the Royal Commission' – published in *The Swag* (pp. 35- 37 Autumn edition, 2018) – a quarterly magazine of National Council of Priests of Australia.

McCarthy, Joanne (2018) 'Church, Confession and Power' https://www.theherald.com.au/story/4861234/joanne-mccarthy-on-the-church-confession-and power/ accessed: 3/7/2018.

McCarthy, Joanne (2018) 'Woman groomed for sex by church leader says it's time to speak' in *The Age*, p. 18, Sat. Sept., 2018.

McCormick, Richard SJ (2018) '*Humanae Vitae* – 25 years later' reprinted from the Archives of *America* from 17/7/1993. In *America*, p. 31, 23/7/2018.

MacDonald, Sarah (2018) 'Priest says celibacy should no longer be compulsory' – in *The Tablet*, 29/9/2018.

MacDonald, Sarah (2018) 'Martin condemns polarisation and bitterness dividing the Church' - in *The Tablet*, 6.10.18.

McElwee, Joshua J. (2018) https://www.ncronline.org/news/vatican/vaticans-doctrinal-prefect-reaffirms-ban-women-priests-calls-teaching-definitive accessed: 30.5.18.

McFague, Sallie (1987) *Models of God* Fortress Press, Philadelphia, USA.

McLaughlin, Vincent (1998) *A Priestless People?* Canterbury Press, Norwich, UK.

McMullen, Gabrielle AM (2018) 'Creativity in Church Management' published in *Vox*, Issue 8, October, 2018 – University of Divinity, Australia.

McPhillips, Kathleen (2018) 'Royal Commission hearings show the Catholic Church faces a massive reform task' –accessed: 9/4/18. http://johnmenadue.com/kathleen-mcphillips-royal-commission-hearings-show-catholic-church-faces-a-massive-reform-task

May, John D'Arcy (ed.) (2014) *Social Justice and the Churches: Challenges and Responsibilities* ATF Theology, Adelaide, Australia.

May, John D'Arcy (2000) *After Pluralism: Towards an Interreligious Ethic* Transaction Publishers, Piscataway, NJ, USA.

Menadue, John (2018) 'Royal Commission into Institutional Responses to child sexual abuse' accessed: 9/4/18. http://johnmenadue.com/royal-commission-into-institutional-responses-to-child-sexual-abuse-john-menadue/

Michael, David J (2018) 'A Christian Intellectual for the Internet Age' in *America*, p. 8, Spring edition, 2018.

Michael, David J (2018) 'Alan Jacobs confronts our "failure to think"' in *America*, pp. 9- 15, Spring edition, 2018.

Moloney, Francis J (1990) third edition: *Body Broken for a Broken People: divorce, remarriage and the Eucharist* Garratt publishing, Mulgrave, Victoria, Australia.

Moloney, Francis J. (2018) *Broken For You: Jesus Christ, The Catholic Priesthood and the Word of God* Coventry Press, Bayswater, Australia.

Moore, Basil (1986) '5 Strategies for Teaching' – papers prepared for 11th conference of the Australian Association for Religious Education, Brisbane, 31/8/1986 – 5/9/1986.

Morris, William Martin (2014) *Benedict, Me and the Cardinals Three* ATF Press, Hindmarsh, Australia.

Morwood, Michael (1997) *Tomorrow's Catholic* Spectrum Publications, Richmond, Victoria, Australia.

Morwood, Michael (2007) From *Sand to Solid Ground* Spectrum Publications, Richmond, Vic, Australia.

Mowe, Aloysius SJ (2018) 'Walking through the valley of the shadow of death: Exile and Solidarity as a Foundation for Values in Education' in *Dialogue Australasia*, pp. 13- 21, issue 39, July 2018.

Nelson, Matt (2018*) Just Whatever – how to help the spiritually indifferent find beliefs that really matter* Catholic Answers Inc. Press, Cal. USA

Nowell, Jennifer (2018) Book Review of *Just Whatever* by Matt Nelson.

O'Callaghan, Vic (2018) 'The Third Wave' – published in *The Swag* (pp. 41- 42) autumn edition, 2018 – a quarterly magazine of National Council of Priests of Australia.

O'Collins, Gerald SJ (2018) 'Still open to doubt' - a feature article on Ordination of Women p. 11, *The Tablet,* June, 2018.

O'Dea, Frank (2018) 'What is clericalism?' – published in *The Swag* (pp. 37- 39) –autumn edition, 2018 – a quarterly magazine of National Council of Priests of Australia.

Oelich, Anthony (2011) *A Church Fully Engaged* Liturgical Press, Minnesota, USA.

O'Loughlin, Frank (2012) *This Time of the Church* Garratt publishing, Mulgrave, Victoria, Australia.

O'Neill, Kevin, C.Ss.R and Peter Black C.Ss.R (2006) *The Essential Moral Handbook* (Revised edition) - Liguori, Missouri USA.

Parker, Michael (2018) 'Critical Thinking in an Age of Social Media' in *Dialogue Australasia,* No 39, July, 2018.

Parker, Stephen et al (eds) (2012) *Religious Education and Freedom of Religion and Belief* vol. 2 in *Religion, Education and Values* series, Peter Lang AG., Bern, Switzerland.

Pell, Cardinal George (2007) *God and Caesar* Connor Court, Australia and the Catholic University of America Press, Washington, USA.

Pepinster, Catherine (2018) 'A gross betrayal of trust' in *The Tablet,* pp. 5- 8, 18/8/2018 .

Plekon, Michael and Sarah Hinlicky (2001) *Discerning the Signs of the Times –the Vision of Elizabeth Behr-Sigel* St Vladimir's Seminary Press, NY, USA.

Pongratz-Lippitt, Christa and Christopher Lamb (2018) 'Schonborn at odds with CDF statement on women priests' in *The Tablet*, on 1 June 2018.

Pope Francis (2015) *Laudato Si'* St Pauls Publications, Strathfield, Australia.

Pope Francis (2015) *Misericordiae Vultus - a Bull of Indiction of the Extraordinary Jubilee of Mercy* St Pauls Strathfield, Australia.

Pope Francis (2016) *Amoris Laetitia- post-synodal apostolic exhortation on love in the family* St Pauls Publications, Strathfield, Australia.

Pope Francis (2018) *Gaudete et Exsultate* St Pauls Publications, Strathfield, Australia.

Pope Francis (2018) 'Go against the flow' – extracts picked out by Laurence Freeman from the apostolic exhortation 'Gaudete et Exsultate' –listed in *The Tablet*, 14/4/2018, p. 5.

Pope Francis' Apostolic Exhortation (2018) 'On the call to holiness in today's world' - Extract from Gaudete et Exsultate published in *Melbourne Catholic* May, 2018 presumably by The Editor, who is not named.

Pope John Paul II (1994) *Crossing the Threshold of Hope* Random House Australia (Pty) Limited, Sydney, Australia.

Quinn, John R (1999) *The Reform of the Papacy* Crossroad Publishing, NY, USA.

Robertson, Geoffrey (2010) *The Case of the Pope* Penguin Books (Australia), Camberwell, Australia.

Robinson, Bishop Geoffrey (2007) Confronting *Power and Sex in the Catholic Church: Reclaiming the Spirit of Jesus* johngarrattpublishing Mulgrave, Australia.

Robinson, Bishop Geoffrey (2010) *Love's Urgent Longings* John Garratt Publishing, Mulgrave, Australia.

Robinson, Bishop Geoffrey (2013) For *Christ's Sake* Garratt Publishing, Melbourne, Australia.

Robinson, Bishop Geoffrey James (2015) *The 2015 Synod, The Crucial Questions: Divorce and Homosexuality* ATP Press, Hindmarsh South Australia and Catalysts for Renewal Inc., Swansea, NSW, Australia.

Robinson, Gerardine Taylor (2018) 'A church in crisis needing attention' in *The Swag,* Summer, 2018.

Rozier, Michael, SJ. (2018) 'Treating "Diseases of Despair" ' in *America* published by America Press Inc. p. 54, May 28, Vol 218, No 12.

Saines, Don (2015) 'Learning to be church. The value of learning theory for discipleship and mission' in *Pacifica*, vol. 28, Issue 3, (pp. 290- 307) October 2015 - Sage Publications, Melbourne, Australia.

Schneider, Nathan (2018) 'Don't blame the sex abuse crisis on queer Catholics' in *America,* p. 10, 17/9/2018.

Schneiders, Sandra M. (2000) *Finding the Treasure: Locating Catholic Religious Life in a new Ecclesial and Cultural Context* Paulist Press, Mahwah, NJ, USA.

Schneiders, Sandra (2014) revised edition: *Beyond Patching: faith and feminism in the Catholic Church* Paulist Press, Mahwah, NJ, USA.

Scorer, Richard (2018) 'Wheels of change still grind too slow' – feature article on Clerical Sexual abuse in *The Tablet*, 16/6/1.8.

Sharkey, Paul (2015) *Educator's Guide to Catholic Identity* Vaughan Publishing, Mulgrave, Victoria, Australia.

Shields, Peter (2018) 'Leaders who judge others would do well to examine themselves' - in *The Weekend Australian*, (p. 48), October 20-21, 2018.

Smeed, Judy and Anita Jetnikoff (2016) 'Lessons to be Learnt from Two Professional Development Programs' in Leading and Managing, ACEL journal Vol 22, No , 2016).

Smyth, Geraldine OP (2013) 'What Lies Beneath: From Purity and Power to Crisis and *Kairos*' in '*Broken Faith*'. Claffey et al. Peter Lang, Bern.

Snook, I. A. (1972) (ed.) *Concepts of Indoctrination* Routledge & Kegan Paul, London, UK.

Splitter, Laurance J & Ann M Sharp (1995) *Teaching for Better Thinking: the classroom community of inquiry* -ACER, Melbourne, Australia.

Sri, Edward P (2018) 'Five key Features of the Theology of the Body' https://www.catholiceducation.org/en/marriage-and-family/sexuality/five-key-features-of-the-theology-of-the-body. Accessed: 19/11/2018.

Strynkowski, John J (2018) 'A Ministry of Listening' in *America*, 29/10/18.

Tacey, David (2015) *Beyond literal Belief: religion as metaphor* Garratt Publishing, Mulgrave, Australia.

Tanner, Kathryn (2005) *God and Creation in Christian Theology* Fortress Press, USA.

Tanner, Kathryn (2010) *Christ the Key* Cambridge University Press, Cambridge, UK

Tapsell, Kieran (2014) *Potiphar's Wife* ATF Press, Hindmarsh, Australia.

Tapsell, Kieran (2018) 'A Response to Francis Sullivan' accessed: 9/4/18 http://johnmenadue.com/kieran-tapsell-a-response-to-Francis-Sullivan/

Tapsell, Kieran (2018) 'Accountability, Clericalism and Culture in the Catholic Church' accessed: 9/4/18 http://johnmenadue.com/kieran-tapsell-accountability-clericalism-and-culture-in-the-catholic-church/

Taylor, Charles (2007) *A Secular Age* Belnap Press of Harvard University Press, Cambridge, USA.

Terrien, Samuel (1985) *Till the Heart Sings – a biblical theology of Manhood and Womanhood* Fortress Press, Philadelphia, USA.

Tishman, Shari, et al (1995) *The Thinking Classroom: Learning and teaching in a culture of thinking* Allyn and Bacon, Needham Heights, MA, USA.

Tobin, Greg (2012) *The Good Pope* Harper One publishing, NY., USA.

Tracy, D. with Hans Kung and Johann Metz (1978) *Towards Vatican III* Dove Communications, East Malvern, Australia.

Urquhart, Gordon (1994) *The Pope's Armada* Corgi Books, London, UK

Vardy, Peter (2010) *Good & Bad Religion* SCM Press, London, UK

Vox magazine, Issue 8, 9/4/18, October 2018, of the University of Divinity report on Health and Integrity Conference in Melbourne, 2018

Warhurst, John, (2018) https://johnmenadue.com/john-warhurst-major-catholic-church-consultation-ambitious-but-will-it-succeed-canberra-times-5-7-2018/ accessed: 5/7/18.

Warhurst, John (2018) – https://johnmenadue.com/john-warhurst-lets-talk-about-the-catholic-bishops/ accessed: 30/7/18.

Warhurst, John – 'Major Catholic Church consultation ambitious – but will it succeed?' – *Canberra Times*, (5/7/18).

Williams, Rowan (2000) *On Christian Theology* Blackwell Publishing, Oxford, UK.

Wills, Garry (2000) *Papal Sin* Doubleday, NY USA.

Wills, Garry (2013) *Why Priests?* Viking Penguin, NY USA.

Wilson, George SJ (2008) *Clericalism: the death of Priesthood* Liturgical Press, Minn. USA

Winters, Michael Sean (2018) 'Cardinal McCarrick faces fresh claim of sexual abuse', p. 25, *The Tablet*, 28/7/18.

Winters, Michael Sean (2018) 'Cardinal suspended from ministry over abuse allegation' in *The Tablet*, 30.6.18

Winter, Sean (2015) 'Journey and rest: Hebrews, pilgrimage, and the work of theological education' – article in *Pacifica*, vol. 28, no 2, June 2015 Sage Publications, Melbourne, Australia.

WWITCh – an Action group (Women's Wisdom in the Church (2018) 'Catholic Leadership Must Apologize' issued on July 22nd, 2018- as a letter to the Australian Catholic Bishops' Conference – the feast-day of Mary Magdalene, Apostle to the Apostles. Featured in the St Carthage's Parkville parish newsletter on 30/9/2018.

Zubik, David A (2018) 'Nine Rules to Promote Civility –Timely wisdom from the Catholic tradition' in *America* – Jesuit review of faith and culture, 9/7/2018.

www.ingramcontent.com/pod-product-compliance
Lightning Source LLC
Chambersburg PA
CBHW051938290426
44110CB00015B/2024